What Wondrous Love!

by
David H. Thiele

TEACH Services, Inc.
PUBLISHING
www.TEACHServices.com • (800) 367-1844

Copyright © 2014 David H. Thiele
Copyright © 2014 TEACH Services, Inc.
ISBN-13: 978-1-4796-0269-8 (Paperback)
ISBN-13: 978-1-4796-0270-4 (ePub)
ISBN-13: 978-1-4796-0271-1 (Mobi)
Library of Congress Control Number: 2014933145

All scripture quotations, unless otherwise indicated, are taken from the King James Version. Public domain.

Scripture quotations marked (NASB) are taken from the New American Standard Bible®,
Copyright © 1960, 1962, 1968, 1971, 1972, 1973, 1975, 1977, 1995 by The Lockman Foundation.
Used by permission.

Scripture quotations marked (NIV) are taken from the Holy Bible, New International Version®, NIV®.
Copyright © 1973, 1978, 1984, 2011 by Biblica, Inc.™
Used by permission of Zondervan.
All rights reserved worldwide.

Published by

TEACH Services, Inc.
P U B L I S H I N G
www.TEACHServices.com • (800) 367-1844

Table of Contents

Introduction

In the history of the conflict between Christ and Satan, the devil has done all he can to deceive God's people into departing from the truth as it is in Jesus. The Bible is full of stories regarding these deceptions, from the ventriloquism act at the tree of knowledge of good and evil to the coming impersonation of Christ's impending return. As we read the apostle John's vision in Revelation, it is revealed that Satan is intent on tricking as many people as possible into following the whore, which represents "that great city which reigns over the kings of the earth," and holds "in her hand a golden cup filled with abominations and ... fornications," symbolizing the false teachings and doctrines that depart from the truth as it is in Jesus.[1]

We have reason to believe ourselves in greater danger from deception than ever before. From the time that Lucifer first tempted the angels of heaven until now, he has artfully increased his powers of deception and trickery. Those under his influence are even more prone to bitterness against others who—motivated by love—attempt to correct their error.

> Satan has the same power and the same control over minds now, only it has increased a hundred-fold by exercise and experience. Men and women today are deceived, blinded by his insinuations and devices, and know it not. By giving place to doubts and unbelief in regard to the work of God, and by cherishing feelings of distrust and cruel jealousies, they are preparing themselves for complete deception. They rise up with bitter feelings against the ones who dare to speak of their errors and reprove their sins.[2]

But God would not have us be deceived, or remain deceived. He calls reformers to reveal truth and expose error for what it is so that God's people may remain in the paths of righteousness for His name's sake. Consider Gideon's call to lead God's people in warfare against their enemies the Midianites. The children of Midian were descendants of Abraham and, therefore, related to the Israelites. Yet they eventually became the avowed enemies of God's people because they departed from the faith handed down to them by Abraham. Interestingly, God used the Midianites to punish Israel for their own departure from His commandments.

Gideon's first job commenced under the cover of night. Obeying God explicitly, Gideon destroyed the

---

1   Revelation 17:18; Revelation 17:4
2   Ellen G. White, *Gospel Workers* (Battle Creek, MI: Review and Herald Publishing Co., 1892), 86.

grove dedicated to Baal and made an offering to the Lord with the wood from that grove.[3] The people were deceived by the gods of the nations around them and were worshipping a lie. Gideon's work began with the overthrow of that lie, trusting in God to protect his life in the face of the resulting threats leveled at him.

When Lucifer rebelled against God's government, a new awareness of the existence of moral law and God's character were brought to the forefront as Lucifer leveled allegations against God's divinity and authority. Lucifer worked hard to plant questions in the minds of the angels. Questions such as, Is God arbitrary? Can He be trusted? Is He wise enough to love enough? Can He love more? What is the relationship of justice to mercy in the context of rebellion from the time of its origin to the moment of its complete destruction? Even as the chief rebel was working against the principles of love and law, the angels were awakening to a consciousness of something they had never before contemplated.

> The will of God is expressed in the precepts of His holy law, and the principles of this law are the principles of heaven. The angels of heaven attain unto no higher knowledge than to know the will of God, and to do His will is the highest service that can engage their powers.
>
> But in heaven, service is not rendered in the spirit of legality. When Satan rebelled against the law of Jehovah, the thought that there was a law came to the angels almost as an awakening to something unthought of. In their ministry the angels are not as servants, but as sons. There is perfect unity between them and their Creator. Obedience is to them no drudgery. Love for God makes their service a joy.[4]

The angel's joyful response to God's law of love should be ours as well. We should rejoice to have God's law written upon our hearts so we can give the same unselfish, loving service Christ gave us. Paul wrote to the Romans, and consequently to us, "But God commendeth his love toward us, in that, while we were yet sinners, Christ died for us."[5] While God reveals His love to us and then advises us to accept it, we who receive His love are called to be His ambassadors. We are to recommend God's love to those who have yet to heed God's commendation. What kind of love is it that we are recommending? A love that is founded upon the Word of God—by the pen of inspiration—or one that is rooted in the soil of human philosophy?

Truth is far too valuable a commodity to neglect or allow to be transformed into something it isn't.

In the following chapters, I hope to share the answers I have discovered through many years of personal study. As we grapple with the concepts inherent with scrutinizing the nature of God's love—mercy and justice combined—we need to prayerfully remember that Satan is seeking to do all he can to misrepresent God's character and destroy His reputation. Our only hope is

---

3   Judges 6:25–32
4   Ellen G. White, *Thoughts from the Mount of Blessing* (Mountain View, CA: Pacific Press Publishing Association, 1896), 109.
5   Romans 5:8

to rely upon the Word of God, which is revealed to us through Scripture and the Spirit of Prophecy—"to the law and the testimony: if they speak not according to this word, it is because there is no light in them."[6]

In this book, I will expose false teaching surrounding the concept of unconditional love by reviewing the historical basis for the idea and examining how it is used in the world today. We will examine the history of the Seventh-day Adventist denomination in order to determine how this concept made theological inroads, as well as how it impacts our beliefs and perceptions of our spiritual condition. Those promoting the teaching of unconditional love are most likely sincere people who truly desire to lead godly lives and lead others to know and understand God's love for all who are born to Adam's race. Yet they present these teachings in ignorance of the point of origin. They do not see their conclusions in their true light.

I hadn't thought much about the concepts of unconditional love, unconditional acceptance, or unconditional grace for my own self until I read two quotes on posters sold in a Christian bookstore. When I laid eyes on these posters, I was strongly impressed to search out the truth regarding the sentiments expressed. The first poster read, "Unconditional love is love without preconditions, or judgments, or discriminations." The other poster only partially quoted from Philip Yancy, a well-known Christian author. It said, "Grace means there is nothing we can do to make God love us more ... and there is nothing we can do to make God love us less ..." The whole quote says:

> Grace means there is nothing we can do to make God love us more—no amount of spiritual calisthenics and renunciations, no amount of knowledge gained from seminaries and divinity schools, no amount of crusading on behalf of righteous causes. And grace means there is nothing we can do to make God love us less—no amount of racism or pride or pornography or adultery or even murder. Grace means that God already loves us as much as an infinite God can possibly love.[7]

The messages conveyed by these two posters motivated me to prayerfully study the Scriptures and Spirit of Prophecy in a search for the truth about the nature of God's love—a balance between justice and mercy, which is finally demonstrated as grace. In sharing with you the things I have learned from years of private study and public discussion, I hope you will embark upon a spiritual journey that can stand the test of close scrutiny. Truth is far too valuable a commodity to neglect or allow to be transformed into something it isn't. In searching for it perseveringly, you will find strength and assurance that what you believe is grounded in bedrock—that firm foundation which is the Lord Jesus Christ.

Some questions, however, cannot be answered without asking other questions, which may cause discomfort and defensiveness, especially when those questions expose the weaknesses of concepts long held dear. It is not good enough to say, as do proponents of evolution with their circular logic, "We know how old the fossils are by which layer of rock they were found. We know how old the rock is by the age of the fossils found in them." Reasoning powers are so important to the vital process of scrutinizing logic, facts, and data when

---

6   Isaiah 8:20
7   Philip Yancy, *What's So Amazing About Grace?* (Grand Rapids, MI: Zondervan, 1997), 70.

comparing and contrasting them to the standard of the Bible and Spirit of Prophecy, which were given to us under the inspiration of the Holy Spirit. However, no fault ought to be declared against the formation of linear questions and answers where one shows logical conclusion grounded in cause and effect. Some may cry out against a perceived creation of straw-man issues to make a point, but when compared to the law and to the testimony, the importance of the topic, and its related issues, there is nothing to the accusation of holding up a mere scarecrow figure while making loud noises solely for the purpose of generating panic amongst the birds that would otherwise snatch up the seed of truth.

Considering the case then, based upon the premise of unconditional love as a love that has no conditions, what would be the effect? If God's love were unconditional, if it had no restriction imposed by a condition, then there would be no such thing as hate, because there would be no condition by which hate could exist (whether it be for sin or sinners). Unconditional love has no power of choice because there are no options other than love.

In other words, God would not even have the power to hate sin if His love were unconditional because there is no condition by which sin could be defined. If God's love were unconditional, if it had no restriction imposed by a condition, then there would be no such thing as forgiveness, because there would be no condition by which injury to love could occur, thereby necessitating the possibility for forgiveness. Therefore, unconditional love removes even the possibility to choose forgiveness upon being injured. Unconditional love needs no justice because there is no condition by which justice is required to exist. Unconditional love needs no mercy because there is no condition by which mercy would need to be exercised. If God's love were unconditional, if it had no restriction imposed by a condition, then there would be no such thing as salvation, because there would be no condition by which one could be lost. If God's love were unconditional, there would never be a need for second chances. If God's love were unconditional, then there could be no conditional immortality, no potential for death—for only by transgression of the law can the wages of sin be death.

It is of greatest importance as we study this topic to make a distinction between the true and the false. It is possible that we are confused by a love that has conditions that promote the welfare of others rather than those conditions that focus on our own self-serving conveniences, desires, or interests.

As we study God's love, prayerful submission and attentiveness to our heavenly Father and His desires must undergird our efforts to arrive at the truth as it is in Jesus. We ought not to study His revelations to us so that we can better explain Him to others, but with the objective of serving Him more perfectly. How can we explain God when we do not understand ourselves well enough to accurately explain our own existence or substance?

> God's word and His works contain the knowledge of Himself that He has seen fit to reveal to us. We may understand the revelation that He has thus given of Himself. But it is with fear and trembling, and with a sense of our own sinfulness, that we are to take up this study, not with a desire to try to explain God, but with a desire to gain that knowledge which will enable us to serve Him more acceptably.
>
> Let no one venture to explain God. Human beings cannot explain themselves, and

how, then, dare they venture to explain the Omniscient One? Satan stands ready to give such ones false conceptions of God.[8]

Jesus warned His disciples, "Beware ye of the leaven of the Pharisees, which is hypocrisy."[9] The disciples were led to understand that Christ's warning was aimed against "the doctrine of the Pharisees and of the Sadducees."[10]

> The scribes and Pharisees were insinuating deceptive principles. They concealed the real tendency of their doctrines, and improved every occasion to instill them artfully into the minds of their hearers. These false principles, when once accepted, worked like leaven in the meal, permeating and transforming the character. It was this deceptive teaching that made it so hard for the people to receive the words of Christ.
>
> The same influences are working today through those who try to explain the law of God in such a way as to make it conform to their practices. This class do not attack the law openly, but put forward speculative theories that undermine its principles. They explain it so as to destroy its force.[11]

Just as in past times, people have distorted and misapplied Scripture in teaching about God's law, so today their teachings about love are perverted to conform to their own standard of living. In the process of teaching about God's love, they "explain it so as to destroy its force"—they emasculate the power of love to strengthen us for meeting the high standard of righteousness, the obedience of which love demands.

> In Christ's day, as in our day, the people were looking to the educated men, to the scribes and Pharisees, to explain to them the meaning of that which the God of heaven had revealed. These teachers had departed from God, and were following their own understanding, and did not follow the ways of the Lord. They thought they must interpret the Scriptures in a way that would harmonize with their course of action. They were seeking the praise of men, and departing more and more from the plainly revealed way of the Lord, following the traditions of men's devising. Of them Christ declared, "In vain do they worship me, teaching for doctrines the commandments of men."
>
> The Pharisees and the religious teachers so misrepresented the character of God that it was necessary for Christ to come to the world to represent the Father. Through the subtlety of Satan, men were led to charge upon God Satanic attributes; but the Saviour swept back the thick darkness which Satan had rolled before the throne of God in order

---

8   Ellen G. White, *Medical Ministry* (Mountain View, CA: Pacific Press Publishing Association, 1932), 91, 92.
9   Luke 12:1
10   Matthew 16:12
11   Ellen G. White, *The Desire of Ages* (Mountain View, CA: Pacific Press Publishing Association, 1898), 408, 409.

that he might intercept the bright rays of mercy and love which came from God to man. Jesus Christ revealed the Father in his true character to the world, representing him as full of mercy, love, and light.[12]

The greatest danger we face today is that, in misrepresenting God's love, souls will be led to an erroneous belief so powerful in its deception that no correction will be made before Jesus comes again. Too late they will realize that God's love is uncompromising with any who have forsaken justice and trampled grace to such an extent that in thinking and doing sin they have irreversibly become what they had unrepentantly cherished—sin. Too late they will comprehend that permissiveness is not love, and presumption is not faith. Only by obtaining the gold tried in the fire—genuine faith and love—will we be able to stand in the great day of the Lord. Then we will be motivated to seek the praise of God and not the praise of wicked men who wish to have God conform to their low estimation of what is good and holy. There can be no middle ground created by a compromise in which truth is in conformity with and united to error. "An unjust man *is* an abomination to the just: and *he that is* upright in the way *is* abomination to the wicked."[13]

It is my prayer that, as we journey through this study together, we will be united in the truth as it is in Jesus. It is my hope that we will truly begin to comprehend just what wondrous love God has for those who seek Him with all their hearts—having been drawn to Him by His loving-kindness.[14]

---

12   Ellen G. White, "The Bible to be Understood by All," *The Signs of the Times*, August 20, 1894.
13   Proverbs 29:27
14   Jeremiah 31:3

Chapter 1

My Kingdom for a Superlative!

The English language is absolutely amazing in its evolution and versatility. Granted, communication can be made easier or more difficult depending on one's level of comfort and varied ability in using a language. Yet by the use of modifying words—adjectives—the very meaning of words can alter significantly the message they otherwise would convey. Of course, with the passage of time, the meanings of many words can change, whether modified or not. More often than not, however, they take a downward trend to the level of slang. Go to any unabridged English dictionary, and one can see the etymology of any word, as well as the definitions—including obsolete and archaic ones. Consideration of how the meaning of a word changes by the usage of adjectives is important to determine how we communicate. For example, we would be foolish to openly use the term "evangelistic crusade" in a Muslim country because of the historical nature of military crusades commenced in the name of Christ all those centuries ago. Public relations would never forget or forgive such a mistake.

Having said all this, it is possible to abuse adjectives. Use of the wrong modifier results in abusing the word modified. The newly coined blurb, with its faulty descriptive, may become widely accepted because of the appeal to our emotions. But will the newly created concept withstand the scrutiny of close examination using reasonable logic?

Have you ever considered the term "unconditional death"? Uriah Smith did—once. I would like to ask him what makes death conditional or unconditional in that those who die are dead. One is either dead or not. Taken in context with the concept of "conditional immortality," all free moral agents have the possibility of being subject to death simply by disobeying. Yet Uriah Smith wrote:

> We have seen that the death that threatened Adam has passed upon all his posterity; it is unconditional; the righteous suffer it as well as the wicked; all, irrespective of age, character or condition, bow before it; "In Adam," says the Apostle, "all die." But we find that the penalty for personal transgression is death also; simply death, just as was threatened to Adam. "The soul that sinneth, it shall die." But inasmuch as all die for original sin, or on account of the sin of Adam, no one can die for his own personal sins, without first being raised to life again; and thus we find expressly declared, as we should unavoidably conclude

from the facts now before us, "that there shall be a resurrection of the dead, both of the just and unjust." The life to which they are thus raised will be a second life; and the death the wicked are then doomed to suffer, will be in reference to the first, a second death. But why will not the wicked when they are raised, live forever; since they have died once, and death is the penalty of the law? Because the death which they die in Adam is unconditional; over it men have no control; we suffer it without any reference to our moral character. But as we have before said, the Bible every where represents man as exposed to death also for his own personal sins.[1]

However, God has never seen fit to retrieve a wicked person from this sinful planet to live forever with Him—as He did righteous Enoch and Elijah, both of which never experienced death. It seems kind of ridiculous to call death unconditional, since only God can give life and is well able to preserve it as He chooses. It appears that Uriah Smith is trying to make a distinction between the temporary death and the finality of an eternally irrevocable death that will occur after judgment is completed—a judgment that distinguishes between those who accept God's grace and the conditions by which certain benefits are extended and those who reject God's free gift. Certainly death is not unconditional, or there could never be immortality—even for God, because He would never be able to give to others what He does not have in Himself. The unfallen angels of heaven and sentient beings on other worlds have the promise of life so long as they obey. They would be subject to death if they disobeyed—the force of the penalty being universally applied to all free moral agents. Yet a time will come when voluntary obedience will be established as irrevocable and the status of immortality will be granted by God to those who perfectly reflect His character.

Another example of modifier abuse that comes to mind is "nearly perfect." Now, who wants to be described as anything less than perfect? Would you buy a gift for your most significant other if near perfection was satisfactory but the occasion called for absolute perfection? Even the postmodern mind struggles to grasp how it is possible to improve upon perfection. We may even foster doubt that Adam and Eve—or even Lucifer for that matter—were created perfect. Yet the Bible tells us about God's work: "*He is* the Rock, his work *is* perfect: for all his ways *are* judgment: a God of truth and without iniquity, just and right *is* he."[2] So, when God says, "Thou *wast* perfect in thy ways from the day that thou wast created, till iniquity was found in thee," He is speaking truth, and without iniquity.[3] Therefore, any attempt to declare something "nearly perfect" when indeed it is perfect can be nothing less than a misrepresentation of the truth.

Another abuse of modifiers is found in the term "partially unique." It isn't often used. In fact, the only possible usage would be as an example of how a modifier so changes the meaning of the word modified as to establish a contrary idea. Perhaps it lacks emotional appeal because no one desires partial uniqueness. Each one of us is looking to establish our uniqueness—mostly in competitive ways that ultimately are destructive because of our individual quests for superiority. What is definitely obvious about this abuse is the change of meaning

---

1   Uriah Smith, "What Is the Penalty of the Law?" *Advent Review and Sabbath Herald*, April 9, 1857.
2   Deuteronomy 32:4
3   Ezekiel 28:15

exerted by the modifier when associated with such a concrete noun. After all, something is either unique or it is not—just like something is either perfect or imperfect.

I have personally experienced modifier abuse in referring to my wife and children as my favorite family members. Let me explain. Before we had our second child, my wife and I went to a Marriage Encounter Seminar. Early in the weekend, each couple was asked to introduce their spouses. When my turn came, I decided to be clever with my words, so I proudly said, "This is Kaoru. She is my favorite wife." Those who knew us were quite comfortable with the introduction since they knew she is my first and only wife. But the message conveyed by this combination of words could be quite harmful to relationships, as in the case of Elkanah, Hannah, and Peninnah. Or, for that matter, the relationships Jacob and Rachel had with Leah, Bilhah, and Zilpah.

After the birth of our second child—another son—I had to give up the idea of having a favorite son and a favorite daughter. As the boys grew up—despite our attempts to be impartial in our discipline and affections—they tried to discover which one was the favorite. They were never satisfied with my response of: "You are my favorite first-born son" or "You are my favorite second-born son." Even as children, they easily recognized that the meaning of favorite was somehow diminished by the way I was using the term.

> *We had better not follow Humpty Dumpty in making words mean whatever we please.*

Conversely, the lack of modifiers can lead to embarrassing situations. While teaching English as a second language in Japan, I once introduced a very attractive female student to my supervisor. When he asked her where she lived, she replied, "I live in the same apartment as David." My supervisor looked at me with raised eyebrows and said, "Oh really?" Of course, he well understood the reality of the situation. She had made a common mistake of attempting to convey an idea by translating from her Japanese thoughts into what spoken English she knew. But while it was appropriate to refer to the whole complex as an apartment within the Japanese grammatical structure, the intended meaning in English was not complete without using the noun "building," and making "apartment" the modifier.

It appears that I agree with C. S. Lewis's perspective on language, as something which is clearly flawed and has many defects. Therefore, we cannot rely upon it as an "infallible guide" to the perfect communication of ideas about God, although it contains "a good deal of stored insight and experience. If you begin by flouting it, it has a way of avenging itself later on. We had better not follow Humpty Dumpty in making words mean whatever we please."[4]

So as we study the nature of God's love, we must determine to learn about it just as the Bible teaches, with additional light from the Spirit of Prophecy as it is consistent with Scripture. Then as we see God's love demonstrated, revealed, and expressed within the parameters of the conflict between Christ and Satan, we will also begin to see how Satan has worked to represent God and His love in a completely different light, and for

---

4   C. S. Lewis, *The Four Loves* (New York: Harcourt, Brace, 1960), 2.

completely different purposes than would otherwise please God. In his attempt to become as the Most High, Satan needs to portray a quality that he can pass off to us as genuine when it is indeed a counterfeit.

"'God is love.' 1 John 4:16. His nature, His law, is love. It ever has been; it ever will be."[5] In order to attack God's law—which is love—Satan needed to prove his allegation that God is arbitrary and selfish in requiring obedience to that law. Consider this statement regarding Satan's plan: "Satan declared that it was impossible for the sons and daughters of Adam to keep the law of God, and thus charged upon God a lack of wisdom and love. If they could not keep the law, then there was fault with the Lawgiver. Men who are under the control of Satan repeat these accusations against God, in asserting that men can not keep the law of God."[6]

Satan's purpose is best served by reworking the definition of love by attaching just the "right" modifier. In essence, he needed the perfect superlative or else his kingdom could not grow. Only then could he have even the slightest success by charging God with "a lack of wisdom and love."

We are certainly at a disadvantage if left to deal with Satan's deceptions and delusions in our own strength. The carnal nature is enmity with God's law. Paul reminds us of just how helpless we are: "Because the carnal mind *is* enmity against God: for it is not subject to the law of God, neither indeed can be."[7] The natural inclination of fallen humanity is best summed up by the term "erroneous sentiments." Having departed from God's law, we no longer are capable of having right feelings or thoughts by which genuine love can be expressed. Knowing he can claim those he successfully deceives as legal trophies, "Satan is ever on the alert to deceive and mislead. He is using every enchantment to allure men into the broad road of disobedience. He is working to confuse the senses with erroneous sentiments, and remove the landmarks God has placed in the pathway."[8] We have gained knowledge of good and evil because of Adam and Eve's transgressions, but we are powerless to do good without the intervention of the One who is more powerful than Satan.

Satan knows that as long as we cherish a wrong concept of God's love we will continue to disobey God's law. Therefore, it is paramount that he should encourage us to separate God's mercy from His justice. He can keep us right where he wants us as long as we view God's love as permissive and God's justice as harsh or abusive. So, it is no wonder that he so successfully perverts our understanding by causing us to believe in a preferential love based upon erroneous conditions. Instead of developing loving relationships with others based upon the principles established by God's immutable law, we love our family and friends based upon their abilities to satisfy our selfish interests. If they don't obey us in the proper time and manner that suits us, we harshly punish beyond what constitutes genuine justice. Why else would God remind the children of Israel that they should not exceed justice in their exacted punishments?

In the laws of Moses, God instructed the Israelites that they should take an "eye for eye, tooth for tooth, hand for hand, foot for foot, burning for burning, wound for wound, stripe for stripe,"[9] And "beast for beast. And if a man cause a blemish in his neighbour; as he hath done, so shall it be done to him; Breach for breach,

---

5   Ellen G. White, *Patriarchs and Prophets* (Washington, D.C.: Review and Herald Publishing Association, 1890), 33.

6   Ellen G. White, "Sin Condemned in the Flesh," *The Signs of the Times*, January 16, 1896.

7   Romans 8:7.

8   Ellen G. White, "Ministering Spirits," *Bible Echo*, December 10, 1900.

9   Exodus 21:24, 25

eye for eye, tooth for tooth: as he hath caused a blemish in a man, so shall it be done to him *again*."[10] "And thine eye shall not pity; *but* life *shall go* for life, eye for eye, tooth for tooth, hand for hand, foot for foot."[11]

By these precepts God did not intend for mercy to be extinct. Jesus reminded His hearers to love mercy and forgiveness as He taught about God's law:

> Ye have heard that it hath been said, An eye for an eye, and a tooth for a tooth: But I say unto you, That ye resist not evil: but whosoever shall smite thee on thy right cheek, turn to him the other also. And if any man will sue thee at the law, and take away thy coat, let him have *thy* cloak also. And whosoever shall compel thee to go a mile, go with him twain. Give to him that asketh thee, and from him that would borrow of thee turn not thou away. Ye have heard that it hath been said, Thou shalt love thy neighbour, and hate thine enemy. But I say unto you, Love your enemies, bless them that curse you, do good to them that hate you, and pray for them which despitefully use you, and persecute you; That ye may be the children of your Father which is in heaven: for he maketh his sun to rise on the evil and on the good, and sendeth rain on the just and on the unjust. For if ye love them which love you, what reward have ye? do not even the publicans the same? And if ye salute your brethren only, what do ye more *than others*? do not even the publicans so? Be ye therefore perfect, even as your Father which is in heaven is perfect.[12]

This teaching did not contradict God's law, nor does it establish God's love as unconditional. It is consistent with Micah's exhortation, "He hath shewed thee, O man, what *is* good; and what doth the Lord require of thee, but to do justly, and to love mercy, and to walk humbly with thy God?"[13]

We are to provide justice for those victims who demand justice—and no further than the commandment allows. We are to extend mercy to others who have wronged us—to the extent that the commandment allows. How can we live otherwise before God and still walk humbly with Him? God declares, "The Lord, The Lord God, merciful and gracious, longsuffering, and abundant in goodness and truth, keeping mercy for thousands, forgiving iniquity and transgression and sin, and that will by no means clear *the guilty*; visiting the iniquity of the fathers upon the children, and upon the children's children, unto the third and to the fourth *generation*."[14] Since the "Lord *is* longsuffering, and of great mercy, forgiving iniquity and transgression, and by no means clearing *the guilty*, visiting the iniquity of the fathers upon the children unto the third and fourth *generation*,"[15] we must understand that God's mercy and justice can never be separated without misrepresenting His love. "God is a God of truth. Justice and mercy are the attributes of His throne."[16] "Justice is as much an expression

---

10   Leviticus 24:18–20
11   Deuteronomy 19:21
12   Matthew 5:38–48
13   Micah 6:8
14   Exodus 34:6, 7
15   Numbers 14:18
16   Ellen G. White, *Testimonies for the Church*, vol. 5 (Mountain View, CA: Pacific Press Publishing Association, 1889), 174.

of love as mercy."[17]

Many have heard, and believed, the refrain "God is love" written by the apostle John while overlooking the fact that God is "just and right" as written by Moses. Having erroneous sentiments as the basis for their understanding of God's love, they make John appear to contradict Moses when in truth the apostle agrees with him. "For this is the love of God, that we keep his commandments: and his commandments are not grievous."[18] "But whoso keepeth his word, in him verily is the love of God perfected: hereby know we that we are in him."[19] "As the Father hath loved me, so have I loved you: continue ye in my love. If ye keep my commandments, ye shall abide in my love; even as I have kept my Father's commandments, and abide in his love."[20] By introducing and teaching a concept of "unconditional love," Satan has deceived sinners into believing that one may continue in God's love or abide in God's love while unrepentantly transgressing God's law with impunity.

Many Seventh-day Adventists recognize that God's word is being perverted in this way. So they modify the teaching while maintaining the erroneous sentiment by proposing that God's love is unconditional, but that salvation, His acceptance, and His promises are conditional.[21]

Pastor Richard O'Ffill goes so far as to state in one of his sermons titled "Broken Cisterns" that "God's unconditional love is not expressed to us unconditionally, or else He would not have had to send His Son to die for us."[22] But that statement begs the question of how it is possible for unconditional love to be expressed in any way other than unconditionally without becoming something it inherently could not otherwise be?

When we say that the refrain "God is love" means that God's love is unconditional, then why not teach that God's justice is unconditional since God is just and right? It is only fair to ask, how can unconditional love establish conditional salvation, pardon, acceptance, and promises, or, for that matter, provide expression of itself to us conditionally without fundamentally changing from unconditional love? After all, just as one is either pregnant or not, one is either dead or not. So, one is either unconditional or conditional. It cannot be both ways at the same time or else it is a lie!

> *Satan has deceived sinners into believing that one may continue in God's love or abide in God's love while unrepentantly transgressing God's law with impunity.*

If God's love is unconditional, then how can He hate sin? Unconditional love means love without conditions. Without a condition, by which sin might be identified, the sin problem just dissipates away. It would be like telling someone, "Moderation in all things—but especially moderation." The need for intolerance vanishes. (I discovered that even

17   Ellen G. White, "Christ or Barabbas?" *The Review and Herald*, January 30, 1900.
18   1 John 5:3
19   1 John 2:5
20   John 15:9, 10
21   Examples of this confusing blend of unconditional love with conditional salvation/promises/warnings will be provided in chapter 3, "From the Seeds of the Alpha to the Fruit of the Omega: The Dangerous Deception."
22   Richard O'Ffill, "Broken Cisterns," RevivalSermons.org, http://1ref.us/9 (accessed October 1, 2013).

proponents of unconditional love are intolerant of those who oppose them and are very capable of being quite conditional with their love by the manner in which their intolerance is expressed.) But God hates sin. He finds it intolerable because of the relationship that His justice has with His mercy. He says, "Howbeit I sent unto you all my servants the prophets, rising early and sending *them*, saying, Oh, do not this abominable thing that I hate."[23] The Bible also states, "The foolish shall not stand in thy sight: thou hatest all workers of iniquity."[24]

Clearly, then, the concept of unconditional love robs God of the power of choice. The logic inescapably means that one who has unconditional love cannot choose to refrain from loving anything. Unconditional love must love everything. Therefore, if God's love is unconditional, He would have no power of choice in the matter. This begs the question of how God can give humans the power of choice if He doesn't have that ability Himself. He cannot give what He doesn't already have in His possession. So we see the train of reasoning lead us to the place where we may be excused for sin because we have no choice but to sin—and its connection to the allegation that something must be wrong with the Lawgiver for making a law we cannot keep.

Again, if God's love is unconditional, then why would we need salvation? After all, without conditions of any kind there could be no injury to God (or to love) stemming from betrayal or treachery. Without conditions whereby these injuries could be properly identified, there would be no need for forgiveness, mercy, or salvation! We could lead any kind of lifestyle without worrying about needing to repent of it. Even the act of believing would be unnecessary. There would be no consequences to our choices. All could live unto themselves eternally in a state of unconditional utopia. There would be no need of death! Of course, if we believe this, we are believing the same lie that the serpent told Eve: "Ye shall not surely die: For God doth know that in the day ye eat thereof, then your eyes shall be opened, and ye shall be as gods, knowing good and evil."[25]

Many proponents of unconditional love repeat one of the best known verses of the Bible with erroneous sentiments in the back of their minds: "For God so loved the world, that he gave his only begotten Son, that whosoever believeth in him should not perish, but have everlasting life."[26] Once again, a simple word—so—is either overlooked or made to mean something it doesn't. Those who acknowledge it want this word to amplify the greatness of extent or degree of God's love by applying only one of many definitions related to the word "so." Therefore, they overlook that love has a definite extent or degree—a boundary much like the mouth and banks of the mighty Amazon River that channels an enormous, if not infinite, amount of water.

God so loved that He gave His Son to die as a substitute for the already condemned sinner who believes and repents. The gift would suffice to save the whole world if the whole world believed on Jesus as the perfect Lamb of God who takes away the sins of the world. God so loved that He gave an already condemned world another opportunity to meet conditions of obedience within the limitations of a second probationary period of time. However, He didn't "so love" the world so as to abolish His law or abdicate His throne. He "so loved" as to magnify His law and establish His throne!

---

23   Jeremiah 44:4
24   Psalm 5:5
25   Genesis 3:4, 5
26   John 3:16

God's love for the fallen race is a peculiar manifestation of love,—a love born of mercy; for human beings are all undeserving. Mercy implies the imperfection of the object toward which it is shown. It was because of sin that mercy was brought into active exercise.

Sin is not the object of God's love, but of His hatred. But He loves and pities the sinner. The erring sons and daughters of Adam are the children of His redemption. Through the gift of His Son He has revealed toward them His infinite love and mercy. He "so loved the world, that He gave His only-begotten Son, that whosoever believeth in Him should not perish, but have everlasting life."[27]

The true believer recognizes an already established condemnation because of disobedience to God's law of love and believes that Jesus fulfilled the conditions of perfect obedience to the law within the probationary time allotted to Him—He did this on our behalf not only as our Savior, but as our Example.

God loves sinners to the extent that He gave His Son to pay our penalty and recreate us into His image that He may continue to love those who repent, but He hates sin. "Christ took human nature that men might be one with him as he is one with the Father, that God may love man as he loves his only begotten Son, that men may be partakers of the divine nature, and be complete in him."[28]

We must understand that "God sees every heart and knows the excuses suggested by Satan by which he seeks to ensnare every soul. He fully appreciates our danger, while we do not. He is not willing that any should perish in sin; but that all should repent and live. Hence, the oft repeated plea that we should not be deceived and lost. God is love; and infinite love will devise infinite plans and plead with infinitely long-suffering to save the lost. There is one thing, however, which infinite love cannot do; it cannot requite the unrepentant wicked."[29] Infinite love will never unconditionally allow evil and unrepentant evildoers to exist forever! This is why Satan is engaged in the war of rebellion against God:

> Satan is engaged in leading men to pervert the plain meaning of God's word. He desires that the world should have no clear idea in regard to the plan of salvation. He well knows that the object of Christ's life of obedience, the object of his suffering, trial, and death upon the cross, was to magnify the divine law, to become a substitute for guilty man, that he might have remission for sins that are past, and grace for future obedience; that the righteousness of the law might be fulfilled in him—and he be transformed and fitted for the heavenly courts. Satan knows that no transgressor of the divine law will ever enter the kingdom of Heaven, and to rob God of the devotion and service of man, to thwart the plan of salvation, and work the ruin of those for whom Christ died, is the motive that actuates his warfare against the law of Heaven. He caused the fall of the holy pair in Eden by leading them to lightly esteem the commandment of God, to think his requirements unjust, and

---

27   Ellen G. White, "Mercy," *The Signs of the Times*, May 21, 1902.
28   Ellen G. White, "The Word Made Flesh," *The Review and Herald*, April 5, 1906.
29   Ellen G. White, "Shall We Awake?" *Bible Training School*, November 1, 1911.

unreasonable, that they were not binding, and that their transgression would not be visited, as God had said, with death.

The law of God is the foundation of his Government in Heaven and in earth, and as long as the follower of Jesus imitates his Lord by exalting the divine precepts in word and life, Satan has no power to deceive or mislead his soul.[30]

But it is not by abolishing one jot or tittle of the law of God that salvation is brought to the fallen race. If God were a changeable being, no confidence could be placed in His government. If He retracted what He said, we could not then take His Word as the foundation of our faith. Had He changed His law to meet fallen men, Satan's claim that man could not keep the law would have been proved true. But God did not alter His law. The death of Christ testifies to the heavenly universe, to the worlds unfallen, and to all the sons and daughters of Adam, that the law of God is immutable, and that in the judgment it will condemn every one who has persisted in transgression. The God who rules the world in love and wisdom testifies in the death of His Son to His changeless character. He could not change His character as expressed in His law, but He could give His Son, one with Himself, possessing His attributes, to a fallen world. By so doing, He magnified His name and glory as a God above all gods.[31]

In other words, the God who rules all His creation in love and wisdom cannot change His character of love as expressed in His law of love to save those who rebel against His love. Truly, if there were "no justice, no penalty, there would be no stability to the government of God."[32] Yet, Satan seeks to deceive people into believing that God's love is unconditional and will, therefore, overlook and excuse sin:

Satan deceives many with the plausible theory that God's love for His people is so great that He will excuse sin in them; he represents that while the threatenings of God's word are to serve a certain purpose in His moral government, they are never to be literally fulfilled. But in all His dealings with his creatures God has maintained the principles of righteousness by revealing sin in its true character—by demonstrating that its sure result is misery and death. The unconditional pardon of sin never has been, and never will be. Such pardon would show the abandonment of the principles of righteousness, which are the very foundation of the government of God. It would fill the unfallen universe with consternation. God has faithfully pointed out the results of sin, and if these warnings were not true, how could we be sure that His promises would be fulfilled? That so-called benevolence which would set aside justice is not benevolence but weakness.

30   Ellen G. White, "Faith and Works," *The Signs of the Times*, March 30, 1888.
31   Ellen G. White, "The Sabbath of the Lord—No. 2," *The Signs of the Times*, April 7, 1898.
32   Ellen G. White, "Let the Trumpet Give a Certain Sound," *The Review and Herald*, December 13, 1892.

God is the life-giver. From the beginning all His laws were ordained to life. But sin broke in upon the order that God had established, and discord followed. So long as sin exists, suffering and death are inevitable. It is only because the Redeemer has borne the curse of sin in our behalf that man can hope to escape, in his own person, its dire results.[33]

Before Lucifer was banished from heaven, he sought to abolish the law of God. He claimed that the unfallen intelligencies of holy heaven had no need of law, but were capable of governing themselves and of preserving unspotted integrity. Lucifer was the covering cherub, the most exalted of the heavenly created beings; he stood nearest the throne of God, and was most closely connected and identified with the administration of God's government, most richly endowed with the glory of his majesty and power.[34]

In every manner of deception and falsehood, Satan attacks the love and wisdom of God as deficient in one form or another. This is how Eve and then Adam were tempted, and how before them angels were tempted and led to follow Lucifer in rebellion. By their yielding to temptation, he managed to instill doubt into their minds that, when entertained, led them to separate themselves from God. "Satan exulted in his success. He had tempted the woman to distrust God's love, to doubt His wisdom, and to transgress His law, and through her he had caused the overthrow of Adam."[35] So Satan works to keep us apart from God today. "But your iniquities have separated between you and your God, and your sins have hid *his* face from you, that he will not hear."[36]

> *Are we to dress up truth to make it more palatable to the carnal heart?*

Since sin separates us from God, and God is love, then we are separated from love by our sins. Satan knew this from his personal experience, and it is his single desire to cause God pain by separating Him from those He created in love.

Satan realized that separating people from the God in whose image they were created was the only way he could increase his kingdom, so he propagated the idea of a counterfeit love that separates mercy from justice. He had to destroy a relationship between mercy and justice so as to remove the possibility of judgment resulting in rejection and condemnation. What better way than to lead sinners to mistakenly understand that God ought to love what He rejects? How else could he achieve that objective than by establishing in the minds of postmodern thinkers that a love which does not have prerequisites, preconditions, judgment, and condemnation is an unconditional love? Only by this delusion could Satan manufacture a love that appeared to fulfill a lack of which he alleged God's "arbitrary" love to have.

Many verses in the Bible teach truth that is difficult for us to accept. Are we to dress up truth to make it

---

33   White, *Patriarchs and Prophets*, 522.
34   Ellen G. White, "The Words and Works of Satan Repeated in the World," *The Signs of the Times*, April 28, 1890.
35   White, *Patriarchs and Prophets*, 57.
36   Isaiah 59:2

more palatable to the carnal heart? "The truth is the truth. It is not to be wrapped up in beautiful adornings, that the outside appearance may be admired. The teacher is to make the truth clear and forcible to the understanding and to the conscience. The word is a two-edged sword, that cuts both ways. It does not tread as with soft, slippered feet."[37]

> The Lord would have his people trust in him and abide in his love, but that does not mean that we shall have no fear or misgivings. Some seem to think that if a man has a wholesome fear of the judgments of God, it is proof that he is destitute of faith; but this is not so. A proper fear of God, in believing his threatenings, works the peaceable fruits of righteousness, by causing the trembling soul to flee to Jesus. Many ought to have this spirit today, and turn to the Lord with humble contrition, for the Lord has not given so many terrible threatenings, pronounced so severe judgments in his word, simply to have them recorded, but he means what he says. One says, "Horror hath taken hold upon me because of the wicked that forsake thy law." Paul says, "Knowing therefore the terror of the Lord, we persuade men."[38]

We are not called upon to smooth the way other than God would have us present the truth. We must rightly divide "the word of truth."[39]

God must remain true to Himself. He is love. He is just and right. He has established an immutable, absolute relationship between mercy and justice. He offered His love to the world to the extent that He gave His only begotten Son to pay for breaking the law of love so that those who believe on the righteousness of Christ—and chose to receive the power of grace by faith to demonstrate that righteousness in their own lives by overcoming as Jesus overcame—might continue in His love forever.

Consistent with His character, God—through the pen of inspiration—expresses and demonstrates His love with different superlatives: "merciful love," "forgiving love," "benevolent love," "measureless love," "boundless love," "infinite love," "unselfish love," and, "self-disinterested love," to name a few. But one must still understand the context in which such modifiers are used. There are conditions by which mercy and forgiveness are doled out. There is a condition by which infinite love continues eternally and immeasurably for some while ceasing for others. There is a condition that would require the perfectly innocent Son of God to be separated from His Father's love if we were to be redeemed by His perfect obedience.[40] It is not because some are arbitrarily considered favorites while others are wantonly condemned, rejected, and destroyed. We may begin to comprehend the situation only as we obtain a true understanding of the history of the conflict between Satan and Christ. So then, let us take some time to examine the history of the conceptualization of unconditional love.

---

37   Ellen G. White, "Words to Ministers," *The Review and Herald*, April 20, 1897.
38   Ellen G. White, "Danger in Rejecting Light," *The Review and Herald*, October 21, 1890.
39   2 Timothy 2:15
40   Ellen G. White wrote the following in *The Desire of Ages*, "He must endure separation from His Father's love" (129).

Chapter 2

History Is Fraud Agreed Upon

History can be a fickle, if not outright treacherous, witness. Yet one must call upon this witness to testify to the facts of the matter. Like opposing attorneys arguing an important case before the Supreme Court, historians conduct research, discuss matters, and even spin history to suit their ideology and agenda. So, when dealing with the history of the term unconditional love, I risk potentially portraying this matter in a manner that may not be as true as it could be stated—one way or the other. Let me illustrate it this way.

I recently acquired an audio book of a biography written by John Mosier about General Grant. As I listened to this account of Grant's prowess as a general, I recalled having a rather cynical and somewhat disrespectful attitude toward Grant—largely because of the alleged alcoholism. I remembered one of my American history professors giving us an assignment to present arguments supporting our opinions of who was the best general during the Civil War. I took the position that Robert E. Lee was the best general, arguing that the only reason why he lost the war was because of key information Grant obtained from Confederate deserters and because Grant had so many more resources. But as I listened to Mosier's rendition, I began to see things in a different light, and I better understood the less-than-superior grade I had received for my paper.

I decided to lend the book to my professor and share with him how it had influenced a change in my opinion of Grant as a general. He not only listened to it, but, because he had so much more knowledge about General Grant than I, he sent me this review via e-mail: "I've very much enjoyed it though Mosier is so uncritical that it borders on hagiography." (I confess: I had to look up the definition of that last word!)

Hagiography is the first step in the process of canonizing and extolling, or venerating, saints. It's a part of the process of beatification. Usually hagiography deserves a great deal of skepticism because of the tendency to gloss over the grosser flaws of character and personality. While they may be considered biographies, they should be worthy of more critical scrutiny when determining or establishing eternal legacies—hagiographies are often presented as reliable history!

Napoleon Bonaparte has been alleged to have made some statements about history: "History is a set of lies agreed upon"; "History is the version of past events that people have decided to agree upon"; "History is fraud agreed upon"; and "What is history but a fable agreed upon?"

The Scottish historian, Thomas Carlyle, apparently concurred with Napoleon, saying succinctly, "History is a distillation of rumor." However, my personal favorite attributed to Napoleon is "skepticism is a virtue in history as well as in philosophy." The virtue of skepticism is warranted, considering the stark warning George Orwell raises: "Who controls the past controls the future. Who controls the present controls the past." Perhaps Orwell's concern was derived from his personal observation: "Early in life I had noticed that no event is ever correctly reported in a newspaper.... This kind of thing is frightening to me, because it often gives me the feeling that the very concept of objective truth is fading out of the world. After all, the chances are that those lies, or at any rate similar lies, will pass into history."[1]

So many perspectives of truth are omitted from history because it is written by conquerors determined to glorify their own exploits and demonize the enemy. History becomes the story of the victor, not the vanquished. After many generations, someone may come across a small portion of fact about a defeated, subjected, or possibly even exterminated culture that is stretched until finally it is accepted, and taught, as though it were not only a minor instance of truth but a significant tendency or an inherently traditional part of the culture.

Skepticism is truly a virtuous commodity when researching and pondering the past. Very little remains today of ancient history as given by the participants. Most of what we know has been passed on to us by nonparticipants who have imperfect knowledge and understanding of the actual event; yet they write as though they were unbiased, agenda-free experts. Unfortunately, with skepticism comes another propensity—revisionism. Historical revisionists abound. Yet, more often than not, what they wish to convey as genuine learning and culture is nothing more than delusional fantasy extrapolated from fragments of the whole, which they in turn call pre-historical history—or science—as it suits their fancy. Yet, in some cases, revisionism is needed because error needs to be corrected and, if not corrected, exposed.

One example of unnecessary revision involves America's smallest state—which happens to have the longest official name—the "State of Rhode Island and Providence Plantations." Because the word "plantations" could be associated with the atrocities perpetrated against slaves on plantations in the South, proponents of the name change believe it is time to acknowledge that slavery occurred on Rhode Island plantations and remove the portion of the state name that reminds them of that historical fact.

On the flip side, Brown University in Providence was built by slaves, and half the cost of its first library was underwritten by a prominent slave trader—an uncle of the man for whom the university is named! But no one is advocating a name change for the university because the word "Brown" reminds some that slaves built the school and were there because of the Brown family. (Of course, the college is named for the Nicholas Brown Jr. who was a fervent abolitionist, but we ought not to let the influence of one family member outweigh the contribution of others!)

Never mind that a "plantation" is another word for a farm—"a usually large group of plants and especially trees under cultivation"[2]—and was used long before slaves were purchased to work the land, invoking the new terminology that we associate with the word today. Never mind the history of how Isle of Rhodes and Providence Plantations were two separate communities united by royal charter when King Charles II gave the resulting colony its formal name.

---

1   Keith Gessen, "Introduction," in *All Art Is Propaganda: Critical Essays* (First Mariner Books, 2008), xxvi.
2   "Plantation," Merriam-Webster.com, http://1ref.us/a (accessed October 15, 2013).

These revisionists are closer to achieving their goal than ever before. "It's high time for us to recognize that slavery happened on plantations in Rhode Island and decide that we don't want that chapter of our history to be a proud part of our name," said Rep. Joseph Almeida, an African-American lawmaker who sponsored a bill to that effect that passed the State's House 70-3.[3] However, when the citizens of Rhode Island voted on the proposed name change in the 2010 general election, 77 percent rejected the proposal. Proponents for not changing the name recognize that the name contains history of the state, which includes slavery that occurred after the colony was given its name.

Having said this much, one must always keep in mind that it is dangerous to be skeptical about earth's history as it is revealed by God in His Word. What history He has revealed is truth with a spiritual purpose.

> The Bible has little to say in praise of men. Little space is given to recounting the virtues of even the best men who have ever lived. This silence is not without purpose; it is not without a lesson. All the good qualities that men possess are the gift of God; their good deeds are performed by the grace of God through Christ. Since they owe all to God the glory of whatever they are or do belongs to Him alone; they are but instruments in His hands. More than this—as all the lessons of Bible history teach—it is a perilous thing to praise or exalt men; for if one comes to lose sight of his entire dependence on God, and to trust to his own strength, he is sure to fall. Man is contending with foes who are stronger than he.... It is impossible for us in our own strength to maintain the conflict; and whatever diverts the mind from God, whatever leads to self-exaltation or to self-dependence, is surely preparing the way for our overthrow. The tenor of the Bible is to inculcate distrust of human power and to encourage trust in divine power.[4]

The tenor of secular history perpetuates the concept of people being able to pull themselves up by their bootstraps—accomplishing great things individually as well as through the power of synergy. However, the Bible does not gloss over the defects of believers who yield to temptation—as in the case of King David and Bathsheba.

> Very many, reading the history of David's fall, have inquired, "Why has this record been made public? Why did God see fit to throw open to the world this dark passage in the life of one so highly honored of Heaven?" The prophet, in his reproof to David, had declared concerning his sin, "By this deed thou hast given great occasion to the enemies of the Lord to blaspheme." Through successive generations infidels have pointed to the character of David, bearing this dark stain, and have exclaimed in triumph and derision, "This is the man after God's own heart!" Thus a reproach has been brought upon religion, God and

---

3   Ray Henry, "Rhode Island Slavery Legacy Prompting Name Change," *Huffington Post*, http://1ref.us/b (accessed January 22, 2014).

4   White, *Patriarchs and Prophets*, 717.

His word have been blasphemed, souls have been hardened in unbelief, and many, under a cloak of piety, have become bold in sin.

But the history of David furnishes no countenance to sin. It was when he was walking in the counsel of God that he was called a man after God's own heart. When he sinned, this ceased to be true of him until by repentance he had returned to the Lord.[5]

This is why I choose not to gloss over the glaring faults in the reasoning or logic of even beloved Adventist leaders who are proponents of unconditional love, as will be discussed in the next chapter.

So, the most important virtue upholding genuine history is demonstrated in the act of objective research. Proper research will help one arrive at the truth if the researcher is willing to alter the premise driving the research once sufficient evidence indicates that such a premise is faulty. Such was the case when John Cornwell wrote Eugenio Pacelli's biography titled *Hitler's Pope: The Secret History of Pius XII*. Cornwell describes his altering premise experience as a "moral shock" when he had initially hoped to vindicate Pius XII's reputation.[6] Such a change maintains the integrity of history and is often made with great courage in the face of sacrificial cost.

Once one has arrived at the truth, and begins to understand it for what it is, the natural consequence is emotional sincerity in communicating that truth. Therefore, to properly understand the meaning of unconditional love, one must research the history pertaining to the conceptualization of the term unconditional love, and one must strive to understand how it was first used. Contextual meaning is everything when coming to grips with understanding this

> *Doublethink means the power of holding two contradictory beliefs in one's mind simultaneously, and accepting both of them.*

scriptural revelation of God and His love. To misapply a derived definition of unconditional love—based upon simple convenience of personal meaning—and then force it upon Scripture is to misconstrue the truth, which can only result in misleading others to their ultimate destruction. Such an act is disingenuous doublethink, even though it may not be as consciously deliberate as, for instance, German guards deceiving their Jewish prisoners to their death with their assurances of hygiene and personal sanitation. We should take care to avoid doublethink, for, as George Orwell succinctly put it, "Doublethink means the power of holding two contradictory beliefs in one's mind simultaneously, and accepting both of them."

It is anyone's guess as to when the term "unconditional love" was first used. However, there can be no doubt as to who claims the origin of the concept. In her book, *Isis Unveiled*, Helena Blavatsky teaches that paganism, or, more specifically—Hinduism with its pagan "trinity"—believed in a mysterious, never-to-be-revealed highest deity who is "boundless and unconditioned." Note just exactly how the comprehension of this belief is expressed:

---

5   Ibid., 722, 723.

6   John Cornwell, *Hitler's Pope: The Secret History of Pius XII* (London: Viking Penguin, 1999), viii.

The "three Heads," superposed above each other, are evidently taken from the three mystic triangles of the Hindus, which also superpose each other. The highest "head" contains the *Trinity in Chaos*, out of which springs the manifested trinity. En-Soph, the unrevealed forever, who is boundless and unconditioned, cannot create, and therefore it seems to us a great error to attribute to him a "creative thought," as is commonly done by the interpreters. In every cosmogony this supreme Essence is *passive*; if boundless, infinite, and unconditioned, it can have no *thought* nor *idea*. It acts not as the result of volition, but in obedience to its own nature, and *according to the fatality of the law of which it is itself the embodiment*....

When the time for an active period had come, then was produced a natural expansion of this Divine essence from within outwardly, obedient to eternal and immutable law; and from this eternal and infinite light (which to us is darkness) was emitted a spiritual substance. This was the First Sephiroth, containing in herself the other nine Sephiroth, or intelligences.[7]

No doubt can exist for long when considering how the pagan infiltration of this concept might affect Christian theology over the centuries. Gnostic teaching taints Christian theology with antinomian conclusions, leading millions to reject God's law as a standard for judgment, which will conclude in the destruction of those whom a loving God created. Over the centuries many Christian theologians have debated the nature of God's love and whether or not God's love allows Him the option of anger toward rebellious creatures expressed by their complete and irrevocable destruction by purifying fire. But when pantheistic ideas were introduced to the Seventh-day Adventist Church by Dr. John Harvey Kellogg, the association of these theories to Hinduism clearly could not be helped within the mind of William Ambrose Spicer who had just returned to Battle Creek, Michigan in 1901, after serving as a missionary in India.

As he recalled the crisis Kellogg was creating and perpetuating by his stubborn refusal to repent, Spicer wrote,

Poets can make this philosophy look very refined. But the philosophy in its native oriental home does not hesitate to go the whole way of this kindergarten lesson. Jack not only has hair, but he has thoughts, good thoughts and evil thoughts. If God is within sending out the hair, then is He within sending out the good thoughts—and the evil thoughts. And the doctrine of pantheism strikes out the distinction between good and evil. It is all divine. While appearing to exalt all natural life to the divine, it really drags the divine down to the level of the natural.

"There is nothing supernatural about religion," the Delineator interviewer [of Kellogg] was given to understand. "It is a perfectly natural thing."

There is where the pantheistic philosophy has ever left man—with only natural forces, notwithstanding all the talk of the divine and of Personality and Intelligence and God. Man

---

7   Helena Blavatsky, *Isis Unveiled*, vol. 2, 6th ed. (New York: J. W. Bouton, 1891), 212, 213.

himself is as much divine as anything. The great saying of the Hindu philosophy was "Tat twam asi," meaning, "That thou art." You yourself are the mystical Absolute. Man is the same as God. "We speak without hesitation of our body as the temple of God," wrote Max Müller, "yet we shrink from adopting the plain and simple language of the Upanishads that the self of God and man is the same."–"Six Systems of Indian Philosophy," p. 254.[8]

Please keep in mind as we review this history that I, as the author, have nothing personal against the individuals mentioned hereafter. My hope is to remain courteous and respectful while attempting to sort out the issues arising from their teachings. Many are highly respected, well-known people within and without Seventh-day Adventist circles. I am simply trying to arrive at unvarnished truth regarding the nature of God's love, which is so pervasive an attribute of His character. We must not allow ourselves to idolize the teachings of any person to such an extent that we fail to be faithful to the truth as revealed in God's Word–which also embraces the Holy Spirit's influence and authority within the scriptural teaching on the Spirit of Prophecy.

The earliest published mention of unconditional love that has been brought to my attention is found in Matthew Clark's *Two Sermons, One On 2 Timothy ii. 15. Preach'd at the Rev. Mr. Nesbitt's, The Other On 1 Cor. iii. 6. At Girdlers Hall, At the setting apart the Reverend Mr. Hurrion, to the Office and Work of a Pastor in Mr. Nesbitt's Church; and the Reverend Mr. Wright, in the late Mr. Foxon's*: "And some can't bear any thing but what is just to their mind. If the law be preached, though for Gospel *ends*; if duties are pressed, though from Gospel *principles*, some may be so weak as to cry out against this, and condemn it as legal preaching. And on the other hand, when the eternal, sovereign, unconditional love and grace of God is insisted on, others may be ready to quarrel with it as a libertine doctrine, that leads men to sin, though the whole drift and design of it is to bring them to deny all ungodliness and worldly lusts."[9]

Unfortunately, Clark doesn't elaborate on whether or not he is for or against unconditional love, although inclination appears to be in favor of it because he states it to have a "drift and design" to "deny all ungodliness and worldly lusts." He certainly gives no biblical support for that "drift and design."

What becomes obvious is the recognition that unconditional love is something of a libertine doctrine. Libertines considered themselves freethinkers, unconfined by conventional or traditional morals and seekers of that which pleased the five senses of sight, sound, smell, taste, and touch, although Moravian pastors sought to change this perception by focusing on God as not being willing that the wicked should perish.[10] However, the libertine doctrine has become the teaching of the Universalist, as James White demonstrated when he quoted from one of their sermons:

In a word, we are constrained by the love of Christ to ridicule everything like practical piety, and to give ourselves up to the unqualified gratification of time and sense, under

---

8   W. A. Spicer, *How the Spirit of Prophecy Met a Crisis: Memories and Notes of the "Living Temple" Controversy* (1938), 61, 62.

9   Matthew Clark, *Two Sermons, One On 2 Timothy ii. 15. Preach'd at the Rev. Mr. Nesbitt's, The Other On 1 Cor. iii. 6. At Girdlers Hall, At the setting apart the Reverend Mr. Hurrion, to the Office and Work of a Pastor in Mr. Nesbitt's Church; and the Reverend Mr. Wright, in the late Mr. Foxon's* (London: Bible and Crown, 1725), 28.

10   2 Peter 3:9

the full assurance that however we live, whatever may be our crimes, we shall all finally be saved.

We do not believe that God requires his creatures to live such strict lives; we believe he intends that we shall enjoy ourselves in this world. We do not believe that heaven is as holy a place as the orthodox represent it, if it is, we shall soon wish ourselves back again: and as for singing the praises of the Lamb, we think it all downright fanaticism. We have *no heart* NOW for such consummate nonsense, and it is not very likely we shall feel any different THEN. Why should WE praise the "Lamb of Calvary," as they call him? He has not, in reality, done anything for US. *We* suffer the just penalty of our sins *in this life*; and we therefore expect to *claim* heaven, as a matter of *right*. But if it is such a place as the orthodox say it is, we had better be in hell; for we never could stand it in the midst of such glowing piety.[11]

In 1751 John Roche authored a book titled *Moravian Heresy*. His purpose was to set forth Moravian teachings, prove what was true, and refute what was error—in addition to giving a brief history of the sect. He commences with "Error I: That all things necessary for Christians to do hath been actually done for them by Christ, and their pardon then absolutely sealed.... [Herein is an absolute acquitance, not conditional, and to prevent understanding it so, another of these teachers in a letter sent from Wales to the Society at the tabernacle in London, and bound up in this collection, says, page 3. of his letter, speaking with respect to this point]–'That is a free and unconditional love.' [And immediately after, in the same page, says] 'Death can have no sting when he (Christ) answered all the demands of the law for you.'"[12]

Roche proceeds to give evidence that this is an "Antinomian Doctrine"—any doctrine that does away with the law, and consequently does away with all justice. "'Laying it [sin] upon him [Christ] is a full discharge, and a general release and acquitance unto thee; that there is not any one Sin [past, present, or future] now to be charged upon thee.'"[13] Such a "general release and acquitance" corresponds to a judge dropping charges against the accused in such a way that the charge can never again be brought against the defendant—a practice that amounts to an unconditional pardon—and shall never again be levied regardless of the future behavior of the accused! An unconditional pardon requires no redress, penalty, or negative consequence of any kind—absolutely no remittance to right the wrong.

Note the connection made between the concept of unconditional acquitance (or pardon) and unconditional love. We cannot refrain from asking, what does Ellen G. White have to say about unconditional pardon and/or unconditional love?

Satan deceives many with the plausible theory that God's love for His people is so great that He will excuse sin in them; he represents that while the threatenings of God's word are to serve a certain purpose in His moral government, they are never to be literally fulfilled. But in all His dealings with his creatures God has maintained the principles of righteousness by revealing sin

11　　James White, "A Universalist Sermon," *Advent Review and Sabbath Herald*, January 7, 1862.
12　　John Roche, *Moravian Heresy* (Dublin, Ireland, 1751), 128, 129.
13　　Ibid., 130.

in its true character—by demonstrating that its sure result is misery and death. The unconditional pardon of sin never has been, and never will be. Such pardon would show the abandonment of the principles of righteousness, which are the very foundation of the government of God. It would fill the unfallen universe with consternation. God has faithfully pointed out the results of sin, and if these warnings were not true, how could we be sure that His promises would be fulfilled? That so-called benevolence which would set aside justice is not benevolence but weakness.[14]

Clearly, God's pardon is conditional. Someone has to pay the penalty, and pardon is granted upon that redeeming payment—in the case of sin, it is life for life—as long as one also believes that future obedience to the law demanding the penalty is a necessary condition for receiving pardon. On the other hand, a presidential pardon granted by the president of the United States is unconditional to the extent that future adherence to the law of the land is expected of the one being pardoned. In other words, with a presidential pardon, a murderer could go free without anybody paying the penalty for the murder—except the victim's family who must live out their lives mourning the loss, and all the while questioning the justice of the president granting the pardon. God's justice demands death as the consequence of transgressing the law. If God granted unconditional pardon, then there would have been no need for the death of the Lord Jesus Christ on our behalf.

As for the term unconditional love, Ellen White never once used it to describe God's love, or any other kind of love for that matter. Could it be that she had never heard of the term? After all, if the Moravians were using and teaching the term as early as 1751, it must have been well enough known by the time her ministry began. What significance might there be if Ellen White deliberately avoided the use of the term "unconditional love" in her writings when others of her contemporaries were using it? Yet we must be careful not to superimpose undue significance, or else we might miss the truth and perpetuate error.

One such contemporary of her time, Augustus Neander (1853), stated, in reference to John's first epistle, "The Apostle requires only this: that God should be the single object of man's unconditional love."[15] Ellen White wrote similarly: "Our consecration to God must be unreserved, our love ardent, our faith unwavering."[16] The assumption is this: Neander was making a connection between man's unconditional surrender to God by voluntarily loving God without reservation and acknowledging God's wisdom expressed in His law by explicit obedience to it, thereby fulfilling duty and obligation in a manner that pleases God. So, while avoiding the term "unconditional love," Ellen White appears, in this case, to convey similar sentiments by other means.

A few years earlier, in 1828 (although the text was revised in 1870), Thomas Erskine announced: "This proclamation of free unconditional mercy, manifested in the gift of Christ, is the blessed gospel of the grace of God." But in the margin, he contradicts himself: "God's free love requires absolute self-sacrifice on Man's part in order to take it in."[17]

---

14   White, *Patriarchs and Prophets*, 522.
15   Augustus Neander, *The Scriptural Expositions of Dr. Augustus Neander: III. The First Epistle of John Practically Explained* (New York: Lewis Colby and Co., 1853), 94.
16   Ellen G. White, "The Duty of Confession," *Review and Herald*, December 16, 1890.
17   Thomas Erskine, *The Unconditional Freeness of the Gospel* (Edinburgh: Edmonston and Douglas, 1870), 136.

Why should "unconditional freeness of the gospel," "free unconditional mercy," or "free love" require anything of man? How could all those superlatives be true if demands or requirements are laid out as something man has to do? What Erskine was really trying to do was revise Calvinism by utilizing constructive theology, which embraced the universal atonement of Christ. This leads to the concept of universal reconciliation, or universal salvation, which is simply called "universalism" today. Very little difference exists between universalism and Unitarian Universalism—Unitarians fully understand that unconditional love means universal salvation without the need of faith in a blood sacrifice as depicted by Christ's crucifixion.

Furthermore, what distinction is made between the "free love" of God and the free love of the spiritualist? We will return to this point later.

Next, we turn to Alford Brown Penniman (1898) who taught: "Another mode of spiritual decline is found when the soul consents to substitute conditional for unconditional love, the Jewish law of justice for the Christian law of love."[18] Penniman cannot be addressing any other law of justice than that which is connected to the moral law of the Ten Commandments as spoken by God, written by His finger, and expanded by precepts and judgments recorded by Moses so that all might understand how justice ought to be executed with fairness and mercy. He certainly is not addressing the traditions (or commandments) of the Pharisees, scribes, and rulers that Jesus accused as being taught for the commandments of God.[19]

Penniman also indicates that there is no lasting law but the law of sacrifice, because the moral law definitely is conditional. He also used the pagan language of Helena Blavatsky previously quoted, when he wrote, "A man abides in grace, and grace abides in him, as long as he extends to his brother what he sees himself to need and get from God. 'The mercy of God endureth forever' because He never fails to obey all law. He is the law personified. He is happy under the law of sacrifice to make His creatures happy. He knows no first love. He is Himself the first and the last the unconditioned and unconditional love."[20]

But Ellen White gives differing reasons for spiritual decline other than the Jewish law of justice: "There are ministers and workers who will present a tissue of nonsensical falsehoods as testing truths, even as the Jewish rabbis presented the maxims of men as the bread of heaven. These are given to the flock of God, as their portion of meat in due season, while the poor sheep are starving for the bread of life. Even now there seems to be a burning desire to get up something startling, and bring it in as new light. Thus men are weaving into the web as important truths a tissue of lies. This imaginary food that is being prepared for the flock will cause spiritual consumption, decline, and death."[21]

This warning is consistent with that given to us by the apostle Paul, when he wrote to the Colossians, "Beware lest any man spoil you through philosophy and vain deceit, after the tradition of men, after the rudiments of the world, and not after Christ."[22]

I have had many discussions over the years with proponents of unconditional love. One, who I consider

---

18   Alford Brown Penniman, *The Fruit of the Spirit and Other Sermons from a Greylock Pulpit* (Adams, MA: Freeman Book and Job Print, 1898), 142.

19   Matthew 15:6, 9; Mark 7:7–9

20   Penniman, *The Fruit of the Spirit and Other Sermons from a Greylock Pulpit*, 142.

21   Ellen G. White, "An Appeal for the Canvassing Work," *Review and Herald*, January 22, 1901.

22   Colossians 2:8

a friend, stated in an Internet forum post dated November 21, 2004, that "universalism is the teaching that through the atonement of Jesus, every person who has ever lived will ultimately be saved. In other words, Universalism = Unconditional Salvation. Universalism does not = Unconditional Love. The Bible plainly teaches that Salvation is conditional." I believe that he would be as astonished as I was when I found out that most of the writings on unconditional love during the 1800s were directly linked by context to universalism, especially as taught by the Unitarians of the time period. Two years later my friend posted on May 15, 2006, the following: "Since the terms 'unconditional love' and 'unconditional salvation' are utilized interchangeably by our Christian friends, to avoid confusion, it would seem best to avoid the term 'unconditional' in conjunction with 'love' altogether." Not only would we avoid confusion, we will avoid deception.

Another author from the 1800s, Stopford Augustus Brooke, a Unitarian (1898), proclaimed: "But the theologians and the doctrine-mongers limited God's [universal] Fatherhood; made it true only on conditions which they themselves, for the sake of keeping their power, imposed on men.... It seems of late, and here especially in England, that these limits put to the universal love of God are less insisted on ... that we are finding a common ground of faith and conduct in the recognition of the unconditional love of God."[23]

Truer words were never spoken regarding the nature of the ecumenical movement in these times. Unconditional love, as well as tolerance for what should be intolerable doctrinal errors, is the motivational glue cementing the movement together as truth is sacrificed for the sake of universal unity at all costs. But most significantly, we see confusion between the self-oriented conditions imposed by religious leaders for the sake of their own convenience—or for the sadistic inconvenience of others—and the others-oriented conditions God established to manifest a mercy-justice relationship ultimately resulting in the eternal happiness of all His created beings.

> *Universalism and spiritualism were created by Satan for the purpose of deceiving, if possible, the very elect.*

The first Seventh-day Adventist foreign missionary, John Nevins Andrews, refuted the Unitarian concept of universalism as early as 1853, when he wrote, "If the death of Christ destroyed the moral law, then the human family are delivered from its fearful sentence, whether they repent or not. This makes the atonement unconditional; hence, it is the real foundation of Universalism.... The doctrine that temporal (instead of the second) death is the ultimate penalty of God's law, is the real foundation of the non-resurrection of the wicked. For after the penalty of the law has been inflicted, those who have suffered it, cannot be raised to suffer something else."[24]

The connection between unconditional love and unconditional atonement (aka unconditional pardon) is inferred by Andrews' argument since we previously established that connection with what John Roche wrote in 1751.

23   Stopford Augustus Brooke, *The Gospel of Joy* (New York: Dodd Mead & Company, 1898), 344.

24   John Nevin Andrews, *A Review of the Remarks of O.R.L. Crozier on the Institution, Design and Abolition of the Sabbath* (Rochester, NY: James White, 1853), 46.

Ellen White has also written to show universalism to be a fatal error. Her clearest statements can be found in *The Great Controversy*. In the chapter "The First Great Deception," she addresses two great deceptions of Satan, showing the connection of both heresies to the lie Satan told Eve regarding the natural immortality of the human soul—an eternally burning hell fire that torments unrepentant sinners for as long as God shall live and a merciful God of love who cannot destroy the objects of His love.

> A large class, to whom the doctrine of eternal torment is revolting are driven to the opposite error. They see that the Scriptures represent God as a being of love and compassion, and they cannot believe that He will consign His creatures to the fires of an eternally burning hell. But holding that the soul is naturally immortal, they see no alternative but to conclude that all mankind will finally be saved. Many regard the threatenings of the Bible as designed merely to frighten men into obedience, and not to be literally fulfilled. Thus the sinner can live in selfish pleasure, disregarding the requirements of God, and yet expect to be finally received into His favor. Such a doctrine, presuming upon God's mercy, but ignoring His justice, pleases the carnal heart and emboldens the wicked in their iniquity....
>
> God has given in His word decisive evidence that He will punish the transgressors of His law. Those who flatter themselves that He is too merciful to execute justice upon the sinner, have only to look to the cross of Calvary. The death of the spotless Son of God testifies that "the wages of sin is death," that every violation of God's law must receive its just retribution. Christ the sinless became sin for man. He bore the guilt of transgression, and the hiding of His Father's face, until His heart was broken and His life crushed out. All this sacrifice was made that sinners might be redeemed. In no other way could man be freed from the penalty of sin. And every soul that refuses to become a partaker of the atonement provided at such a cost must bear in his own person the guilt and punishment of transgression....
>
> God does not force the will or judgment of any. He takes no pleasure in a slavish obedience. He desires that the creatures of His hands shall love Him because He is worthy of love. He would have them obey Him because they have an intelligent appreciation of His wisdom, justice, and benevolence. And all who have a just conception of these qualities will love Him because they are drawn toward Him in admiration of His attributes.[25]

The connection between universalism and spiritualism is readily exposed by the commonality of their doctrines on the natural immortality of the human soul and the emphasis on the nature of God's love, which appeals to their unrenewed hearts. Universalism and spiritualism were created by Satan for the purpose of deceiving, if possible, the very elect.

---

25   Ellen G. White, *The Great Controversy* (Mountain View, CA: Pacific Press Publishing Association, 1911), 537, 539, 540, 541.

If there were no other evidence of the real character of spiritualism, it should be enough for the Christian that the spirits make no difference between righteousness and sin, between the noblest and purest of the apostles of Christ and the most corrupt of the servants of Satan....

...Love is dwelt upon as the chief attribute of God, but it is degraded to a weak sentimentalism, making little distinction between good and evil. God's justice, His denunciations of sin, [and] the requirements of His holy law, are all kept out of sight. The people are taught to regard the Decalogue as a dead letter. Pleasing, bewitching fables captivate the senses and lead men to reject the Bible as the foundation of their faith. Christ is as verily denied as before; but Satan has so blinded the eyes of the people that the deception is not discerned.[26]

How have contemporary authors arrived at the conclusion that God's love is unconditional? Does the Bible really teach this concept? Most theologians teaching this concept, upon parishioners' queries as to its origin, will tell you that the Greek word *agape* means God's love is an unconditional love. But they cannot tell you how they know this conclusion to be truth. They will say, "God is love. It is His essence, so it must be unconditional." But when one looks at how *agape* is used in the New Testament, we get some surprises.

Dean VanDruff studied out the use of *agape* and *phileo* in the New Testament. As he shared his observations, he made some revealing, clarifying points that I have come to appreciate. Let us take time to look at a few.

We have already looked at John 3:16, which says, "For God so loved the world, that he gave his only begotten Son, that whosoever believeth in him should not perish, but have everlasting life." Of course, the Greek is *agapao*. And here the proponents of unconditional love smile quite knowingly, until one points out to them that *agapao* is also the word used three verses later: "And this is the condemnation, that light is come into the world, and men loved darkness rather than light, because their deeds were evil."[27] Now, based upon their conclusions, we see darkness loved unconditionally! What is quite obvious, however, is that the darkness is loved more than light. If the love were unconditional, both darkness and light would be equally loved rather than one being loved more than the other in any hierarchal or exclusive sense.

John's meaning cannot be confused, because he said the same thing, only in a different way: "For they loved the praise of men more than the praise of God."[28] Again, the Greek word is *agapao*. But John was not alone in this use of *agapao*. Peter wrote of those who walk after the flesh, "which have forsaken the right way, and are gone astray, following the way of Balaam the son of Bosor, who loved the wages of unrighteousness."[29] Again, the Greek word for love in this text is *agapao*.

Paul wrote to Timothy about Demas, saying, "For Demas hath forsaken me, having loved this present world, and is departed unto Thessalonica."[30] For this reference of love, the Greek word is once more *agapao*.

---

26   Ibid., 556–558.
27   John 3:19
28   John 12:43
29   2 Peter 2:15
30   2 Timothy 4:10

So, *agapao* has a meaning other than "God's unconditional love," and the definition, by context, is such that the term can be used to show the type of love sinners have for sinful attitudes.

"But surely," protest the proponents of unconditional love, "agape-love is the only love God expresses." Really? Then would *phileo* also mean "unconditional love" since the New Testament also reveals this to be an expression of God's love? Many theologians teach that *agapao* is God's love, and *phileo* is human brotherly love. But the Bible doesn't support this conclusion! The apostles sometimes interchanged the two words.

In referring to himself as the disciple Jesus loved, John used both words: "Then she runneth, and cometh to Simon Peter, and to the other disciple, whom Jesus loved [*phileo*], and saith unto them, They have taken away the Lord out of the sepulchre, and we know not where they have laid him."[31] "Therefore that disciple whom Jesus loved [*agapao*] saith unto Peter, It is the Lord."[32] "Then Peter, turning about, seeth the disciple whom Jesus loved [*agapao*] following; which also leaned on his breast at supper, and said, Lord, which is he that betrayeth thee?"[33] "Now there was leaning on Jesus' bosom one of his disciples, whom Jesus loved [*agapao*]."[34]

John wrote, "For the Father loveth the Son, and sheweth him all things that himself doeth: and he will shew him greater works than these, that ye may marvel."[35] Here John uses the Greek word *phileo*, which has a different meaning than *agape*. When he recorded Christ's words to the disciples during the last supper, John again used the Greek word *phileo* for both references of love in the following text: "For the Father himself loveth you, because ye have loved me, and have believed that I came out from God."[36]

Luke also interchanged the two words: "Woe unto you, Pharisees! for ye love [*agapeo*] the uppermost seats in the synagogues, and greetings in the markets."[37] "Beware of the scribes, which desire to walk in long robes, and love [*phileo*] greetings in the markets, and the highest seats in the synagogues, and the chief rooms at feasts"[38]

Dean VanDruff, in showing from Scripture these differences in usage by the apostles, also provides concise and adequate definitions for these Greek words far more appropriate than those of theologians teaching unconditional love: *agape* is an abstract or spiritual love, a willful love; *phileo* is a heartfelt or spontaneous love, an affectionate love.[39] But will these definitions gain universal acceptance? Not if the secular humanist has his or her way!

The reality is more insidious than many proponents of unconditional love care to admit. Error has crept into Christian theology in such a manner that its acceptance, over the expanse of time, makes the multiple historical occurrences a tradition of men that in turn is passed on as the essence of God. How well, then, is Isaiah's prophecy fulfilled even today: "Forasmuch as this people draw near me with their mouth, and with their lips do honour me,

---

31   John 20:2
32   John 21:7
33   John 21:20
34   John 13:23
35   John 5:20
36   John 16:27
37   Luke 11:43
38   Luke 20:46
39   Dean and Laura VanDruff, "UnConditional Love? A Critical Review of a Pop Religious Truism," Dean and Laura VanDruff's Dialogs & Commentary, http://1ref.us/c (accessed October 27, 2013). Materials quoted or paraphrased are used by permission. See also "Agapao & Phileo in Peter's Restoration," Acts 17:11 Bible Studies, http://1ref.us/d (accessed January 22, 2014).

but have removed their heart far from me, and their fear toward me is taught by the precept of men: Therefore ... the wisdom of their wise men shall perish, and the understanding of their prudent men shall be hid."[40]

We have seen the progression of unconditional love, as directly tied to unconditional mercy and pardon, transform into an ecumenical motivational force within the Christian community from 1751 to the late 1800s. But how has the secular world viewed or used this term?

In 1922 Emil Lucka published *The Evolution of Love*. It was his expressed purpose to "demonstrate that what psychology has shown to be the necessary phases of the evolution of love, have actually existed in historical time and characterised a whole period of civilization."[41] While critiquing the works of German composer and essayist Wilhelm Richard Wagner, Lucka wrote, "Sexual love has undergone a change, it is no longer love in the true sense, but the unconditional love of the mystic."[42] One might conclude that Lucka is referring to the term unconditional love as an obfuscation of the mystic rather than a clarification of truth. And in the context of sexual love, or *eros*, we have no difficulty in understanding how unconditional love is the motivational force behind the incredible growth of polyamory—a term which describes the lifestyle philosophy of the "swingers" (a term from which polyamorists attempt to distance themselves) in their efforts to justify their illicit relationships without committing the illegalities of the polygamist (but more on that subject later).

One begins to wonder, however, if there is any consistent definition to the term unconditional love because of the numerous ways it has been utilized. In 1948 Patrick Mullahy stated, "The neurotic demands unconditional love."[43] Here we see a clear application of unconditional love as something demanded by one who is diagnosed as mentally ill. This application would pose a conflict within the circles of psychology because not all psychoanalysts used the term in the same way.

Much earlier, in 1937, Karen Horney wrote something similar: "The main expressions are jealousy and demands for unconditional love.... The form in which this demand most often appears in the conscious mind is, 'I want to be loved for what I am and not for what I am doing.' "[44] Another psychoanalyst, a protégé of Horney who was to eclipse her, gave unconditional love a much grander purpose than some obfuscation of the mystic, or something demanded by the neurotic.

Erich Fromm was an only child who experienced "anxious solicitousness" from his father, and from his mother a "possessive motherly love."[45]

> The Fromm family was steeped in Jewish tradition and the young Fromm was an avid scholar of the Talmud and the old Testament, particularly the prophets Isaiah, Amos, and Hosea with their emphasis on justice, righteousness, and universal peace, motifs which would echo through all of Fromm's later writings. In 1926, however, at the age of 26 he officially

---

40   Isaiah 29:13, 14
41   Emil Lucka, *The Evolution of Love* (London: George Allen & Unwin Ltd., 1922), 3.
42   Ibid., 347.
43   Patrick Mullahy, *Oedipus Myth and Complex: A Review of Psychoanalytic Theory* (New York: Grove Press, 1955), 221.
44   Karen Horney, *The Neurotic Personality of Our Time* (London: Kegan Paul, Trench, Trubner & Co., Ltd., 1937), 129, 131.
45   Erich Fromm, *The Art of Loving, Fiftieth Anniversary Edition, P.S.* (New York: Harper Perennial Modern Classics, 2006), 11, 12.

abandoned his Jewish faith....

    ... Fromm described himself as "an atheistic mystic, a Socialist who is in opposition to most Socialist and Communist parties, a psychoanalyst who is a very unorthodox Freudian."[46]

When asked why he gave up his orthodox convictions and practices, he explained, "I just didn't want to participate in any division of the human race, whether religious or political."[47] So we see the tendency of his secular approach to the religious convictions of the Unitarian's concept of love.

Fromm left Germany with his first wife and headed for Switzerland in 1931, where he contracted and battled tuberculosis until April 1934. He never returned to Germany, most likely because of the rising backlash against Jews and communists made possible by the Reich concordat negotiated between Adolf Hitler and Eugenio Pacelli, the cardinal secretary of state for the Vatican who later became Pope Pius XII, aka "Hitler's Pope" in July 1933. (With Pacelli's guidance, his brother, Francesco, had previously negotiated and drafted the Lateran Treaty with Mussolini in February of 1929, thereby establishing Fascism in Italy and gaining recognition for Vatican sovereignty.[48])

In 1934, after divorcing his first wife, Fromm immigrated to the United States, where he met Karen Horney. Though intimate in their relationship, they never married. After his second marriage, Fromm started using the term unconditional love in his lectures with application as a virtue of motherly love. (Later on his lectures formed the basis for his book *The Art of Loving*, which was originally published in 1956.) Because of his second wife's illness, he moved to Mexico in 1950. After her suicide in the summer of 1952, Fromm believed he would never be able to find love because of his deep depression rooted in a keen sense of failure, helplessness, and abandonment. But around Christmas of 1953, he fell in love with Annis Freeman, and married her. They continued to live in Mexico until 1973, when they moved to Switzerland where he died in 1980.

Having witnessed untold suffering during World War I and the destructive power demonstrated in the worst of human nature found in the Third Reich during World War II, one can understand how the modern humanist-socialist, which Fromm had become, would be disillusioned, and consequently metamorphose into a postmodern skeptic. If that was not enough, add the devastating confrontation with apparent personal failure at human love in the event of spousal suicide, and one begins to see why he draws the intellectual, rational conclusions that he does in his book. Though many of his personal friends described him as a very loving person, they do not arrive at that conclusion based upon the very strong influence of his early upbringing, despite his attempts to escape those authoritarian experiences. As an atheist he chose to exult in humanistic self-realization that separated love from justice by denying a benevolent perspective of the authoritarianism he attributed to God. We cannot afford to ignore these underlying premises in determining why he began to use the term "unconditional love."

When writing about the love between parent and child, he describes love developing in the child as initially

---

46   Hugh Gillilan, "In Appreciation: Erich Fromm," Humanists of Utah, http://1ref.us/e (accessed October 28, 2013).
47   Fromm, *The Art of Loving, Fiftieth Anniversary Edition, P.S.*, 2.
48   Cornwell, *Hitler's Pope: The Secret History of Pius XII*, 114, 115, 130, 131.

from a "state of narcissism" inherently connected to the "positive stimulation of warmth and food." During this stage of the relationship, the mother's love is unconditional while the infant's situation is merely passive, or receptive.

> There is nothing I have to do in order to be loved.... All I have to do is *to be*—to be her child. Mother's love is bliss, is peace, it need not be acquired, it need not be deserved. But there is a negative side, too, to the unconditional quality of mother's love. Not only does it not need to be deserved—it also *cannot* be acquired, produced, controlled. If it is there, it is like a blessing; if it is not there, it is as if all beauty had gone out of life—and there is nothing I can do to create it.... Motherly love by its very nature is unconditional.[49]

Then he qualifies his statements by stating that not all mothers love in that way.

Fromm proceeds to explain how the child transmogrifies from utter dependence upon mother's unconditional love to independence where the father's conditional, or "deserved," love becomes more important.

> Fatherly love is conditional love. Its principle is "I love you because you fulfill my expectations, because you do your duty, because you are like me."... The negative aspect is the very fact that fatherly love has to be deserved, that it can be lost if one does not do what is expected. In the nature of fatherly love lies the fact that obedience becomes the main virtue, that disobedience is the main sin—and its punishment the withdrawal of fatherly love. The positive side is equally important. Since his love is conditioned, I can do something to acquire it, I can work for it; his love is not outside of my control as motherly love is.[50]

Such a love as Fromm describes enables the child to obtain an ever-growing awareness of competence and self-confidence that results in the child's ability to dispense with the authority of the father and establish self-autonomy. Furthermore, Fromm proposes that the unconditional love of the mother must tolerate the separation and support that separation by encouraging it.

The dilemma with such self-autonomy is found in the tension created by the development of the mother/father conscience. "Motherly conscience says: 'There is no misdeed, no crime which could deprive you of my love, of my wish for your life and happiness.' Fatherly conscience says: 'You did wrong, you cannot avoid accepting certain consequences of your wrongdoing, and most of all you must change your ways if I am to like you.'"[51] Such a contradiction of consciences within the individual's thinking must result in spiritual decline and mental illness because of high anxiety or no anxiety at all. But Fromm apparently overlooks some of the consequences of his rationale, if he isn't blind to them altogether.

Fromm declares that man's concept of God's love—even his love for God—is derived from an evolutionary

---

49   Fromm, *The Art of Loving, Fiftieth Anniversary Edition, P.S.*, 36–39, italics original.
50   Ibid., 40, italics original.
51   Ibid., 41.

process in which the determination of the nature of God's love is directly influenced by "the degree of maturity reached by the individual."[52] No wonder he sets such an impossible standard for originating—or acquiring—unconditional love, yet powerfully suggests the possibility of achieving it. Unconditional love is within the reach of humanity simply by growing to an undeterminable level of maturity. No one knows precisely how mature one has to be in order to achieve unconditional love! Therefore, he reasoned that not all mothers are able to demonstrate unconditional love for one cannot demonstrate that kind of love when one has not achieved that level of maturity. Apparently fathers never attain that maturity, for fatherly love is always conditional.

Only once does Fromm attempt to link unconditional love to forgiveness. Yet forgiveness should only be linked to conditional love by reason of the power of choice exercised by the victim. The fatherly conditional love of Fromm's theory is the only one that can be wronged—the only one that bears negative consequences since it is "deserved"—therefore, the father is the only one whereby a decision might be made to exercise forgiveness or extend mercy. The unconditional love of the mother simply does not care if the child has sinned or not.

In other words, unconditional love is apathetic toward justice. Note how Fromm contradicts himself by his own logic:

> The patriarchal aspect makes me love God like a father; I assume he is just and strict, that he punishes and rewards; and eventually that he will elect me as his favorite son; as God elected Abraham-Israel, as Isaac elected Jacob, as God elects his favorite nation. In the matriarchal aspect of religion, I love God as an all-embracing mother. I have faith in her love, that no matter whether I am poor and powerless, no matter whether I have sinned, she will love me, she will not prefer any other of her children to me; whatever happens to me, she will rescue me, will save me, will forgive me. Needless to say, my love for God and God's love for me cannot be separated.[53]

By his own words Fromm proves that unconditional love is merely a humanistic ideal—a figment of mature imagination extrapolated from a perceived need in an infantile being, as yet a cognitively-unformed-but-now-developing self-awareness.

> In a non-theistic system, there exists no spiritual realm outside of man or transcending him. The realm of love, reason and justice exists as a reality only because, and inasmuch as, man has been able to develop these powers in himself throughout the process of his evolution. In this view there is no meaning to life, except the meaning man himself gives to it; man is utterly alone except inasmuch as he helps another. Having spoken of the love of God, I want to make it clear that I myself do not think in terms of a theistic concept, and that to me the concept of God is only a historically conditioned one, in which man has

---

52   Ibid., 41.
53   Ibid., 62, 63.

expressed his experience of his higher powers, his longing for truth and for unity at a given historical period. But I believe also that the consequences of strict monotheism and a non-theistic ultimate concern with the spiritual reality are two views which, though different, need not fight each other.[54]

Shortly after Fromm wrote *The Art of Loving*, C. S. Lewis published his book titled *The Four Loves*. There is no apparent connection between the two works. One can only imagine it possible that a childhood Christian turned atheist (at the age of fifteen) and reluctantly reconverted to Christianity (aged thirty-three) was responding to a former Orthodox Jew converted to mystic atheism simply by the timing of the publications because Lewis stated "every love has its *art of love*."[55] Lewis uses the phrase "art of love" on one other occasion in *The Four Loves*.[56] It must be coincidental that both men wrote books about love at a time when both lost wives to which they were very much devoted. But my primary objective in sharing Lewis' book with you has more to do with the operation of revisionism than anything else.

While researching the etymology of the term unconditional love, I came across its use in a review of Lewis' use of charity in *The Four Loves*. "Caritas (agapē, ἀγάπη) is an unconditional love directed towards one's neighbor which is not dependent on any lovable qualities that the object of love possesses. Agape is the love that brings forth caring regardless of circumstance. Lewis recognizes this as the greatest of loves, and sees it as a specifically Christian virtue. The chapter on the subject focuses on the need of subordinating the natural loves to the love of God, who is full of charitable love."[57]

Herein is the problem: Lewis never used the term unconditional love in *The Four Loves*. In fact, in that book he used the word unconditional a mere three times: "We may give our human loves the unconditional allegiance which we owe only to God."[58] "We must not give unconditional obedience to the voice of Eros when he speaks most like a god."[59] "But Eros, honoured without reservation and obeyed unconditionally, becomes a demon. And this is just how he claims to be honoured and obeyed. Divinely indifferent to our selfishness, he is also demoniacally rebellious to every claim of God or Man that would oppose him."[60] In fact, he is addressing the inherent problems of free love, which is directly linked to unconditional love as it relates to the physical intimacy claimed by polyamorists.

How then does the revisionist extrapolate that Lewis is implicitly referring to unconditional love? Quite

---

54 Ibid., 67.
55 Lewis, *The Four Loves*, 44.
56 Ibid., 55.
57 "The Four Loves," Wikipedia, http://1ref.us/f. This direct quote no longer appears on the Wikipedia page referenced in this footnote. Because Wikipedia may be edited by article contributors at any time without warning to those who access or cite their research, the original quote that the author cited months ago has been modified to state the following: "Charity (agapē, ἀγάπη) is the love that brings forth caring regardless of the circumstance. Lewis recognizes this as the greatest of loves, and sees it as a specifically Christian virtue. The chapter on the subject focuses on the need of subordinating the natural loves—as Lewis puts it, 'The natural loves are not self-sufficient'—to the love of God, who is full of charitable love, to prevent what he termed their 'demonic' self-aggrandisement" (accessed December 24, 2013).
58 Lewis, *The Four Loves*, 8.
59 Ibid., 109.
60 Ibid., 110.

likely because Lewis also wrote the following:

> In reality, however, they express the continually renewed, because continually necessary, attempt to negate that misconception of ourselves and of our relation to God which nature, even while we pray, is always recommending to us. No sooner do we believe that God loves us than there is an impulse to believe that He does so, not because He is Love, but because we are intrinsically lovable. The Pagans obeyed this impulse unabashed; a good man was "dear to the gods" because he was good. We, being better taught, resort to subterfuge. Far be it from us to think that we have virtues for which God could love us. But then, how magnificently we have repented! As Bunyan says, describing his first and illusory conversion, "I thought there was no man in England that pleased God better than I." Beaten out of this, we next offer our own humility to God's admiration. Surely He'll like that? Or if not that, our clear-sighted and humble recognition that we still lack humility. Thus, depth beneath depth and subtlety within subtlety, there remains some lingering idea of our own, our very own, attractiveness.[61]

Did Lewis implicitly refer to unconditional love as coined by Fromm, or did he take for granted some fine quality about the relationship between justice and charity that revisionists have opportunistically usurped to further their cause in the realm of Christianity—just like what Fromm started in the sphere of atheism? After all, Fromm and those like him are trying to bring about a tolerant environment for two mutually exclusive belief systems by attempting to harmonize them in an ecumenical fashion. I would stress that the point Lewis was attempting to show was the distinctions between four loves and the conditions by which one might adhere to those distinctions.

> *Rejection is a form of hate, as is apathy, a passive expression of rejection.*

One cannot speak on behalf of Lewis because the man is deceased and cannot correct any misrepresentations. However, the so-called Christian proponents of unconditional love must acknowledge that God could only continue to love fallen man if Christ—superior to Lucifer/Satan in every way—lived a perfectly obedient life in fulfillment of the conditions upheld by both justice and love, and then by a bloody death paid the penalty on behalf of those who were already condemned by their disobedience to a law of love. Grace is not God seeing our good in us. Any good we attempt to generate for ourselves is nothing but filthy rags.[62] Rather, it is God seeing the good of Christ in us because we believe on Him, are connected to Him, and, in a cognitive awareness of our great need, claim His righteousness as our only hope for love and acceptance. Only by faith in Jesus and His righteousness is any good imputed and imparted to us. It is only because of Christ that we can obtain justification. Then follows the acceptance made

---

61   Ibid., 130, 131.
62   Isaiah 64:6

possible through repentance—that is, a sanctification empowering obedience by faith because of that connection of divine power with human instrumentality, which is also a gift from God.

In the evolution of the humanist usage of unconditional love, another prominent psychoanalyst, Carl Ransom Rogers, added his significant influence to the debate. Rogers at one time seriously considered the ministry, but in 1922, while on a trip to China, he began to harbor doubts regarding his religious convictions. A couple of years later he left the seminary to pursue a career in psychology.

In 1961 he published what is perhaps his most famous book, *On Becoming A Person*. In this work he elaborates on the concept of unconditional acceptance, modeling acceptance of the client no matter how bad his or her feelings, values, or behaviors are so that the client might learn self-acceptance. The Neo-Rogerian will argue that the only deficiency with Rogers' method is that genuine unconditional acceptance doesn't truly exist as long as the therapist is the only source of acceptance. Until the client learns unconditional self-acceptance—whether the psychotherapist provides acceptance or not—rejection by self and others will continue to be the end result.

The natural conclusion of these theories springs from the concept of unconditional love. How can anyone loving unconditionally ever reject the object of that love? After all, rejection is a form of hate, as is apathy, a passive expression of rejection. Since rejection is out of the question because the health and progress of the patient is paramount, unconditional acceptance becomes necessary in the minds of Rogerian and Neo-Rogerian therapists. Unfortunately, unconditional self-acceptance never leads to a change of feelings, values, or behaviors. Those changes can only be achieved when accepting a commonly valued, absolutely unchanging standard by which the need for change and subsequent modifications, improvements, or advances can be consistently measured. The success of the therapist is directly proportional to his or her ability to instill a desire to accept rules of relationship that are healthy and beneficial while rejecting those attitudes and behaviors that tend to destroy relationships because they willfully ignore those established rules held in common.

As far as Christian psychology is concerned, perhaps there is no greater influence than Dr. James C. Dobson, founder of Focus on the Family, a Christian family based ministry. A firm believer in unconditional love, he has written several books emphasizing the need for discipline, respect, and accountability in every aspect of our lives. Yet he appears to be blind to the doublethink so evident in his rationale, so clearly communicated in this question and answer section.

Q. It has always been my understanding that marriage was supposed to be based on *unconditional* love. That is, the commitment to one another should be independent of behavior, no matter how offensive or unfaithful. But your concept of accountability in marriage seems to be saying, "I will love you as long as you do what I want."

A. You've misunderstood my point. The limitations of language make it very difficult to explain this concept adequately, but let me try again. I certainly believe in the validity of unconditional love, and in fact, the mutual accountability I have recommended is an expression of that love!... I'm trying to say that *unconditional* love is not synonymous with permissiveness, passivity, and weakness. Sometimes it requires toughness and discipline and accountability.[63]

But once more we see an attempt to allow unconditional love to be something it is not: conditional. Tough is a binary word. If it isn't tough, it is weak or tender. If it is tough, then there must be an underlying condition upholding a specific standard by which we may make an accurate determination for our final conclusion. What is the standard? When Ford builds a truck "Ford Tough," the implication is that Ford has a standard to which their trucks are inspected, measured, and judged. Quality control determines whether or not the truck is worthy of the Ford name, and only then is it supposed to be shipped out for sale to the consumer. Ford's reputation must be upheld, and that is why the vehicle must be subjected to judgment. The same goes for Chevy, Dodge , or any other company making any other product where pride is associated with the brand name.

Those who claim to believe in the God portrayed in both testaments of the Bible must know that God has a reputation associated with an unselfish character that must remain intact, or else He never would have written the third commandment: "Thou shalt not take the name of the Lord thy God in vain; for the Lord will not hold him guiltless that taketh his name in vain."[64]

Unconditional love has no conditions. Therefore, it has no standard. Conditions imply exclusivity. But unconditional love is all inclusive. Quality control goes out the window, and we end up with anything goes. What kind of accountability do we have when a "player" comes home and tells his wife how much he missed her while he was enjoying his mistress if the wife must choose to "forgive" him for breaking a vow to exclude all others? Tough luck to those who are too weak to impose their own will over those they love unconditionally while the "strong" get to exercise their will in any fashion they please.

Dobson apparently wants unconditional love to mean unconditional accountability. But unconditional love can only mean there are no bad consequences that might arise when trying to hold someone accountable for wrong behavior. Why? Because, as we have already read in the teachings of the universalists, unconditional love also implies that unconditional forgiveness and unconditional pardon must be granted if one can even distinguish between good and bad behavior. It will be a sad day when Christ returns and people realize the error of their doublethink—that black is white, wrong is right, and all will ultimately go to heaven because God is too loving to destroy His created beings in the lake of fire. The sad fact is that Dobson does not see the contradiction between his belief in unconditional love and his teachings on morality upheld by discipline and accountability. We cannot defend the relativity of unconditional love and still uphold an absolute, immutable moral code. The one simply cannot

> *The overwhelming message of unity in diversity is glued with the adhesive of unconditional love.*

---

63   James C. Dobson, *Love Must Be Tough: New Hope For Families In Crisis* (Waco, TX: Word Books, 1983), 80, 81, italics original.

64   Exodus 20:7

exist in harmony with the other.

Yet our fascination with unconditional love continues to grow. Since the 1960s the concept of unconditional love has swept through virtually every gamut of global culture. Various symbols designed to convey the concept are being marketed everywhere in an effort to build unity and tolerance on a global scale. Those who adhere to the New Age idea of "yin and yang"—an ancient symbol denoting the eternal coexistence and balance between good and evil—teach unity in duality, or unity in diversity. Christians have morphed the cross with yin and yang as a symbol of unconditional love, thereby amalgamating pagan symbols that otherwise have no correlation with each other in an effort to incorporate their understanding of unity in diversity. Lately, I have seen bumper stickers using the various symbols representing the religions of the world to spell out "coexist." The overwhelming message of unity in diversity is glued with the adhesive of unconditional love.

Atheists are flocking to the concept by the hundreds of thousands.

> Stephanie posted a message on Stan's forum of practical spirituality, telling us how unconditional love works for her: "First, accept very logically, that there is no god. Then invent a god. The name of this god is unconditional love. Pray to this god.... I do not believe that this god is real. It is obviously part of my mind that has created a comforting illusion. The love that pours back to me is just a reflection of my own thoughts and feelings."[65]

At the end of the blog entry, Stan concludes by emphasizing the importance of "I" as distinct from the Freudian concept of ego while asserting the centrality of self's influence and power. He also declares that "I" is independent of body, immortal, and invincible to the extent that self cannot be injured or destroyed.[66]

So we see the connection made by unconditional love between New Age mysticism and atheism to self-centeredness and to the false doctrine of the natural immortality of the soul. All of these examples point toward modern spiritualism and are linked to Helena Blavatsky's Hindu trinity. We also see within their teachings that unconditional love is invincible to the degree that it cannot be injured, thereby logically removing the option to forgive or the need of forgiveness. Without injury there simply is no need for forgiveness!

What happens when self becomes the center and expresses itself as unconditional love within Christian circles? Then polyamory relationships can be formed and maintained so long as two or more self-centered individuals mutually agree to be intimate unconditionally according to mutually established rules. This tangent of polygamy began when the United States Federal Government incorporated Utah, with its overwhelming Mormon influence, into its territories. Bigamy and polygamy, which were previously practiced legally, were then declared illegal in a territory now amenable to federal jurisprudence; however, the practice continued to exist in various communes as an underground subculture.

As time went on, the movement that overwhelmingly replaced multiple marriages became known as polyamory. The *Boston Phoenix* had this to say in an article titled "Free love grows up. Free love might sound

---

65 "Unconditional Love: Ursula journal," Power to Share: The Practical Spirituality of Unconditional Love, http://1ref.us/g (accessed October 29, 2013).
66 Ibid.

like a euphemism for group sex, but to Boston's polyamory community, it's just like marriage—only bigger": "Polyamory is the philosophy and practice of loving more than one person at a time. It's different from polygamy—the practice of taking more than one wife—in that polyamory is legal, has nothing to do with Mormonism, and spans a whole range of commitment levels besides marriage." Further on in the article, reporter Alicia Potter quoted Deborah M. Anapol, the author of *Polyamory: The New Love Without Limits*: " 'Swinging is impersonal sex,' says Deborah M. Anapol ... 'And while I'm not judging that, I don't consider it polyamory, because it doesn't focus on the relationship.' "[67]

Boldly recognized and denounced in the nineteenth century for what it is, free love—on every level: spiritual, emotional, physical—is nothing less than "bestial" and spiritualism. Such were the expressions heard when President Lincoln appointed a Day of National Humiliation, Fasting and Prayer in 1863 and 1864.[68] Another author gives us the contextual understanding of bestial as it was used at that time.

> Professor Quackenbos, who made a special study of the system, pronounced this verdict: "The teachings of Spiritism regarding marriage are subversive of all respect for the sacredness of the institution as ordained by God. It takes the ground that every person has an 'affinity' to whom he or she will eventually be united in the world to come, no matter how disappointing the search for this affinity may be on earth. The evils of wedded life are due to the union of persons who are not such spiritual affinities. Ill-assorted married couples are at liberty to separate. Divorce is justified as soon as companionship becomes for any reason disagreeable or undesirable. Thus the union of hearts after God's holy ordinance is degraded to a living together like beasts in a lair: and a man may break his marriage vows *ad infinitum* in the pursuit of his spiritual affinity. In this way encouragement is given to licentiousness; a formal marriage finally becomes unnecessary, and men and women literally wrap themselves in the filthy skirts of Ashtoreth. Spiritism asserts that every one will be married in the next world, and that the mates or affinities of those who remain single on earth live in waiting in the spirit-land. Hence it affects to solemnize the marriage of women with demons.... 'Those in communion with a class of spirits above them run no risk of forming uncongenial matrimonial relations, as a spirit out of the form can perceive affinities more readily than a person in the natural body; consequently, marriages formed by them will be happy ones, and the offspring of such, gentle and loving, harmonizing the future.' " (Quoted in *Lehre und Wehre*, 1900, p. 146 f.)[69]

Yet another author clearly stated:

---

67 Alicia Potter, "Free Love Grows Up," The Phoenix Media/Communications Group, http://1ref.us/h (accessed October 29, 2013).

68 Samuel Phillips Day, *Life and Society in America* (London: Newman and Co., 1880), 256, 257; John H. Clifford, *The Works of Abraham Lincoln*, vol. 3, ed. Marion M. Miller (New York: Newton & Cartwright, 1908), 156, 157, 162–164.

69 Theodore Graebner, *Spiritism: A Study of Its Phenomena and Religious Teachings* (St. Louis, MO: Concordia Publishing, 1919), 125, 126.

There is no one particular wherein Spiritualism is proving itself a curse to the age and to the race more than in this. "Free Love" is a common phrase with a certain class of "Reformers," who wish to abolish not only the Bible, but all its institutions. Some Spiritualists deny being Free Lovers; but this denial cannot screen the system from the charge of upholding the abomination; for, 1. We have never known a Free Lover who was not a Spiritualist, and if Spiritualism and Free Lovism are not identical, they at least have a wonderful "affinity" for each other! 2. It is well known that a large proportion of Spiritualists are Free Lovers, both theoretically and practically; and they go, not only unrebuked, but indorsed as Spiritualist laborers, in lecturing and writing. It avails nothing for an individual to deny the charge as applying to himself, as long as he associates and fraternizes with, and upholds, those who are openly committed to it. He gives it all the aid of his influence and association, which is sometimes much stronger than that of practice.[70]

While polyamorists claim that unconditional love is the ability to be inclusive and intimate with more than one person at a time, David Cloutier would have us believe that the exclusive vow of marriage is unconditional love. "First, married love is unconditional. Most agreements we make in our lives have conditions: if I do my job, you pay me my salary; or I will pay rent on this apartment until the end of the lease. These agreements have conditions. Marriage does not. Marriage vows, by indicating that the love will be present 'for better or worse, for richer or poorer,' mean that our commitment does not depend on the spouse's job, health, or anything else."[71]

Never mind that faithfulness is a condition when marriage is an exclusive relationship, or that this condition is often explicitly incorporated into the marriage vow. No distinction is made between unilateral conditions and the mutual conditions of a bilateral covenant. Cloutier, by his doublethink, simply has confused us as to the meaning of unconditional love.

From a historical view, none appear to be more completely revisionist by their doublethink than Roman Catholics. Revisionists appear to make the introduction of the term unconditional love to be earlier than it really was. David Richo attempts to assert that Benedict XV believed in the concept by his reference to the attribute of peace. "Queen of Peace is the title appended by Pope Benedict XV in World War I. 'Blessed are the peacemakers' is a reference to the feminine pacific quality of the Self so unlike the bellicose ego that thrives on discord and competition. The style of the feminine is the foundation for peace-making: a primacy granted to unconditional love, wisdom, and healing power. This is the opposite of military, retaliatory, and warlike styles of behavior. Peace is the harmony of masculine and feminine, a warrior spirit for justice and an heroic soul for mercy."[72]

If there is any indication that Pope Benedict XV actually was inclined to believe the concept of "unconditional love," it has yet to surface from the sublime waters of secrecy. In all likelihood, the first pope to use

---

70   J. H. Waggoner, *The Nature and Tendency of Modern Spiritualism*, 4th ed. (Battle Creek, MI: Steam Press of the Seventh-day Adventist Publishing Association, 1872), 137.

71   David Cloutier, *Love, Reason, and God's Story* (Winona, MN: Saint Mary's Press, Christian Brothers Publications, 2008), 173.

72   David Richo, *Mary Within Us: A Jungian Contemplation of Her Titles and Powers* (Berkeley, CA: Human Development Books, 2007), 57, 58.

the term "unconditional love" was John Paul II. In a homily delivered while in San Francisco at the Mission Dolores Basilica on September 17, 1987, he declared that God "does not love us because we have merited it or are worthy of it. God loves us, rather, because he is true to his own nature.... God's love has many aspects. In particular, *God loves us as our Father*.... It is also true to say that *God's love for us is like that of a mother*.... God loves you all, without distinction, without limit.... He loves us all with an unconditional, everlasting love."[73]

Then consider the Catholic sanctity of the Virgin Mary that—as upheld by the cult of Mary and promoted by John Paul II—depicts her as the "embodiment of unconditional love, devoid of any judgment."[74]

Confusion increases as one recalls the history of the Roman Catholic Church with centuries of pogroms against Jews, inquisitions against Christians denounced as heretics, and crusades aimed at Muslims, which holocausts included recriminations toward various priestly orders as they fell into disfavor with the popes.

Yet revisionists would have us believe that "The core of the teaching of the Church, therefore, is the free love received from God and given to others without any discrimination. Love is more than an ethical principle: it is a life which has a concern to have unconditional respect for human life, it is the Kingdom which is coming in the hearts of men and women."[75]

But here again, we must see John Paul II's meaning within the context of previous papal pronouncements. What better pope to study, than the one reigning during the Holocaust? Even as millions of Jews and Orthodox Serbs were brutally executed, Pius XII proclaimed a theology so very consistent with Roman Catholic doctrine that it is difficult to comprehend unless connected with John Cromwell's understanding of it.

> "Not every sin, even the most grievous, is of such a kind, nor does all life depart from those who, though by sin they have lost charity and divine grace, and are consequently no longer capable of a supernatural reward, nevertheless retain Christian faith and hope." In other words, Catholics, no matter how grievous their sins, could rest assured that they were part of the people of God, while those who refused to pay allegiance to the Pope, however good and decent, were to be regarded as excluded. "It is therefore a dangerous error," he [Pius XII] concludes, "to hold that one can adhere to Christ as head of the Church without loyal allegiance to his Vicar on earth."[76]

John Paul II's use of unconditional love raises other questions rooted in other important doctrinal concerns. One such question touching upon God's own nature is: If God is true to His own nature, then why do Catholics give Mary the title of co-Redemptrix or Mediatrix? Perhaps Michael Carroll provides the most accurate reason when he wrote, "Orthodox tradition recognizes Mary in her role as *Theotokos* (or God-bearer), but distinguishes her from *Sophia*, or Heavenly Wisdom, the female personification of the divine principle,

73   Pope John Paul II, *Address of His Holiness John Paul II*, Libreria Editrice Vaticana, http://1ref.us/i (accessed October 29, 2013).

74   Shmuley Boteach, *Hating Women: America's Hostile Campaign Against the Fairer Sex* (New York: HarperCollins, 2005), 44.

75   Maurice Nyunt Wai, *Pañcasila And Catholic Moral Teaching: Moral Principles As Expression Of Spiritual Experience in Theravada Buddhism And Christianity* (Roma: Editrice Pontificia Università Gregoriana, 2002), 72.

76   Cornwell, *Hitler's Pope: The Secret History of Pius XII*, 276.

whereas the Roman Catholic tradition has merged these two concepts and has in the process deified Mary."[77]

Mary could not have a competitor in the minds of Roman Catholic adherents. She and Sophia must be one and the same. So deification of Mary then provides God's fatherly nature with that sublime quality John Paul II calls "unconditional, everlasting love," which then appears to be consistent with Fromm's philosophy of unconditional love as it relates to the more mature matronly qualities.

Again, if God is true to His own nature, then why do popes and prelates include the practice of indulgences within their belief system? James Philipps tries to explain the inconsistency by referring to the three stages of the communion of saints: pilgrimage, perfection, and the intermediary state of purgation, from which the word purgatory is derived.

> Ironically, the concept of an indulgence is grounded in that same Christian experience of the unconditional love of God we have just explored....
>
> How an expression of God's unconditional love and the enduring nature of Christian community became the horrid mess that sparked the Protestant Reformation involves a combination of poor theology, bad habits, and greed. It's important to remember that no Christian Church—either Protestant or Roman Catholic or Eastern Orthodox—teaches that God's grace through indulgences or any other practices can be "earned." Just as the members of any loving family do, we pray and make sacrifices and repent for the sake of one another, not to earn the other's love, but *because* we are caught up in the relationship of love.[78]

The problem is that the insertion of unconditional love does nothing to solve the quandary that folks find themselves in when they feel the need to resort to indulgences, or any other like practices, in order to obtain assurance of grace for themselves and beloved relatives or friends. Something about the ordinance of indulgences is causing these unsettled minds to comprehend that grace is somehow lacking. The insufficiency must somehow be determined; therefore, the cause is judgment in one degree or another. The determination of one needing a purgation that involves the purchase of indulgences reveals that judgment is made by someone with the qualification and authority to judge. Therefore, the state of perfection that did not occur during the process of pilgrimage, delineated by a probationary period, indicates that the suddenly deemed hopeless might obtain from the repentance of a loved one what their own experience was powerless to achieve—that state of perfection which must be declared by a judge!

Note that indulgences have conditions with which one must comply in order for benefit to be received.

> While indulgences granted either generally or by special rescript remain in force during the Great Jubilee, it should be noted that the Jubilee indulgence also can be applied in suffrage to the

---

77   Michael P. Carroll, *The Cult of the Virgin Mary: Psychological Origins* (Princeton, NJ: Princeton University Press, 1992), 19.

78   James Philipps, *Turning Points: Unlocking the Treasures of the Church* (New London, CT: Twenty-Third Publications, 2006), 85, 86.

souls of the deceased: such an offering constitutes an outstanding act of supernatural charity, in virtue of the bond which, in the Mystical Body of Christ, unites the faithful still on pilgrimage here below and those who have already ended their earthly journey. Then too, the rule that a plenary indulgence can be gained only once a day remains in force during the entire Jubilee year....

After worthily celebrating sacramental confession, which ordinarily, according to the norm of Canon 960 of the Code of Canon Law and of Canon 720 § 1 of the Code of Canons of the Eastern Churches, must be individual and complete, each member of the faithful, having fulfilled the required conditions, can receive or apply the gift of the plenary indulgence during a suitable period of time, even daily, without needing to go to confession again. It is fitting however that the faithful should frequently receive the grace of the Sacrament of Penance, in order to grow in conversion and in purity of heart. Participation in the Eucharist, which is required for all indulgences, should properly take place on the same day as the prescribed works are performed.[79]

Other conditions are listed. One wonders why unconditional love would implement a plan involving such extensive conditions in order to receive benefit from God's grace, which admittedly is free! Where is the consistency between belief and practice?

It is no small wonder, then, that proponents of unconditional love would fantasize about a pope who would one day declare, "Here then are the eleven new words I am adding to the Nicene Creed.... We believe in one Lord, Jesus Christ, the only Son of God, eternally begotten of the Father, God of God, Light of Light, and true God of true God, begotten not made, one in being with the Father, who because of God's unconditional love for each *one of us and for our salvation came down from Heaven*."[80]

Yet the connection to unconditional salvation is readily made just a few sentences later, with this rationalization: "'Vengeance is mine,' saith the Lord. 'I will repay!' This view is anthropocentric, namely, a human view of God. In fact, there is no vengeance in God."[81]

The spiritual battle lines are taking shape. Soon there will be no middle ground—no neutral position—as one can see from the writings of Sarah Young in her book *Jesus Calling*, which is styled as though Jesus is speaking directly to the reader. After reminding her readers that "the evil one is *the father of lies*," she writes, "One of his favorite deceptions is to undermine your confidence in My unconditional Love. Fight back against these lies! Do not let them go unchallenged. *Resist the devil in My Name, and he will slink away from you. Draw near to Me*, and My Presence will envelop you in Love."[82]

How does she bring the reader to this point? She tells them to "bring every thought captive to Me. Whenever your mind wanders, lasso those thoughts, and bring them into My Presence. In My radiant Light ... Judgmental thoughts are unmasked as you bask in My unconditional Love."[83] In this devotional, she appears to

79   William Wakefield Card. Baum, "Decree of the Sacred Penitentiary on the Conditions for Gaining the Jubilee Indulgence," Eternal Word Television Network, Inc., http://1ref.us/j (accessed October 29, 2013).

80   John Cantwell Kiley, *The Final Restoration* (Lincoln, NE: iUniverse, Inc., 2004), 71, 72, emphasis added.

81   Ibid., 72.

82   Sarah Young, *Jesus Calling: Enjoy Peace in His Presence* (Nashville, TN: Thomas Nelson, Inc., 2012), 283.

83   Ibid., 30.

be pointing the reader to the Scriptures, but, in the process, she fails to emphasize that the thoughts brought into captivity must be in accordance with the obedience of Christ—obeying every word of God who is able to destroy both the body and the soul.[84]

One can have no doubt, having established earlier the positions of Fromm and Rogers, that her theology is skewed by her training in psychology and counseling, which is notably steeped in the concepts of unconditional love and unconditional acceptance.[85] She writes again as though Jesus Himself is addressing the reader, "Stop judging and evaluating yourself, for this is not your role.... The only source of real affirmation is My unconditional Love. Many believers perceive Me as an unpleasant Judge, angrily searching out their faults and failures. Nothing could be farther from the truth!"[86] Then she directs the reader to Luke 6:37, which tells us, "Judge not, and ye shall not be judged: condemn not, and ye shall not be condemned: forgive, and ye shall be forgiven." She uses this Scripture to tell readers that we are not to judge ourselves; however, this position contradicts the counsel Paul gives, "And herein do I exercise myself, to have always a conscience void of offence toward God, and *toward* men."[87] "Knowing therefore the terror of the Lord, we persuade men; but we are made manifest unto God; and I trust also are made manifest in your consciences."[88]

> *The spiritual battle lines are taking shape. Soon there will be no middle ground—no neutral position.*

Throughout her book, Sarah Young continually reminds the reader that "you don't have to perform to receive My Love. I have boundless, unconditional Love for you."[89] "Whenever you start to feel fearful or anxious, repeat this unconditional promise: 'Nothing can separate me from Your Love, Jesus.'"[90] "I am the Gift that continually gives—bounteously, with no strings attached. Unconditional Love is such a radical concept that even My most devoted followers fail to grasp it fully. Absolutely nothing in heaven or on earth can cause Me to stop loving you."[91] "I love you for who you are, not for what you do."[92]

Those who counsel others must be careful as to what they are teaching about God. Jeremiah wrote the following to unfaithful priests and prophets who were leading people to forget God:

> The anger of the Lord shall not return, until he have executed, and till he have performed

---

84   2 Corinthians 10:5; Matthew 10:28
85   Sarah Young has graduate degrees in psychology and counseling from Tufts University, Covenant Theological Seminary, and Georgia State University according to an interview by The Christian Broadcasting Network. http://1ref.us/k (Accessed 2/28/2014.).
86   Young, *Jesus Calling: Enjoy Peace in His Presence*, 61.
87   Acts 24:16
88   2 Corinthians 5:11
89   Young, *Jesus Calling: Enjoy Peace in His Presence*, 270.
90   Ibid., 224.
91   Ibid., 377
92   Ibid., 66.

the thoughts of his heart: in the latter days ye shall consider it perfectly.... But if they had stood in my counsel, and had caused my people to hear my words, then they should have turned them from their evil way, and from the evil of their doings.... Behold, I am against them that prophesy false dreams, saith the Lord, and do tell them, and cause my people to err by their lies, and by their lightness; yet I sent them not, nor commanded them: therefore they shall not profit this people at all, saith the Lord.... Therefore, behold, I, even I, will utterly forget you, and I will forsake you, and the city that I gave you and your fathers, *and cast you* out of my presence: And I will bring an everlasting reproach upon you, and a perpetual shame, which shall not be forgotten.[93]

Likewise, Hosea wrote the following to a people who rebelled against God: "The days of visitation are come, the days of recompence are come; Israel shall know it: the prophet is a fool, the spiritual man is mad, for the multitude of thine iniquity, and the great hatred.... They have deeply corrupted themselves, as in the days of Gibeah: therefore he will remember their iniquity, he will visit their sins.... All their wickedness is in Gilgal: for there I hated them: for the wickedness of their doings I will drive them out of mine house, I will love them no more: all their princes are revolters."[94]

> *When one removes power of choice, the exercise of judgment becomes moot.*

When asked by Christian Broadcast Network about her practice of dialoging with Jesus, Sarah Young stated, "Let me begin with some cautions. It's essential to remember that the Bible is the only infallible record of God's speaking. Always subordinate your personal listening to absolute biblical truth. If something you 'hear' is inconsistent with biblical teaching, don't write it down—it's not from God. New Christians, especially, need to be cautious about listening to God in this way. I had been a Christian for 20 years before I began this practice."[95]

If we don't take time to judge our conclusions or our consciences, how can we then know whether or not they are flawed by departing from what the Scriptures are actually teaching us about the nature of God's love? Can one safely "command" another, as though it came directly from Jesus, to "fight back against these lies" when in reality one is simply exposing the deception of the unconditional love concept by using the very Bible texts overlooked, neglected, or ignored? Why do so many avoid those difficult passages in Scripture that point out the error of these teachings?

Can there be any doubt as to the origin and application of the concept of "unconditional love" when seen in its theological and historical context? Clearly, some who used it went to an opposite extreme when confronted with the "poor theology" of their religious leaders. Others simply outright believed their own bad theology while embracing a concept of God's love that emasculates Him by reducing His omnipotence and

---

93   Jeremiah 23:20, 22, 32, 39, 40
94   Hosea 9:7, 9, 15
95   "Author Profile: Q & A with Sarah Young," The Christian Broadcasting Network, http://1ref.us/k (accessed October 30, 2013).

eliminating His power of choice. When one removes power of choice, the exercise of judgment becomes moot. Why bother upholding justice while extending grace if love has no conditions? Yet their conclusions do not so much as mention the many neglected or ignored Scriptures which indicate that their conclusions about the nature of God's love are simply off target.

Any mathematician or scientist will tell you that successful research testing must have pre-determined conditions or proofs to establish success or failure rates. Since God is love, and His law is love, then for God to prove and try His creatures in order to give them opportunity to develop character to see whether or not they are obedient to His law of love only provides evidence that God's love has conditions. They are unselfish and others-oriented, but none-the-less they exist.

The history of love as revealed in the Bible indicates that a day of judgment is coming. Mercy has been demonstrated, but not at the expense of justice. Mercy will triumph over justice, but justice will be magnified. Because love upholds the law, justice will be served, for God will by "no means clear the guilty."[96]

The persuasive power of spiritualistic theories makes the gospel of Christ of no effect. Consider these thoughts on the vain theories and philosophies of humans in their attempt to preach a form of the gospel that denies the power of God to choose whom He will continue to love and those whom He will reject:

> Our condition through sin has become preternatural, and the power that restores us must be supernatural, else it has no value. There is but one power that can break the hold of evil from the hearts of men, and that is the power of God in Jesus Christ. Only through the blood of the Crucified One is there cleansing from sin. His grace alone can enable us to resist and subdue the tendencies of our fallen nature. This power the spiritualistic theories concerning God make of no effect. If God is an essence pervading all nature, then He dwells in all men; and in order to attain holiness, man has only to develop the power that is within him.
>
> These theories, followed to their logical conclusion, sweep away the whole Christian economy. They do away with the necessity for the atonement and make man his own savior. These theories regarding God make His word of no effect, and those who accept them are in great danger of being led finally to look upon the whole Bible as a fiction. They may regard virtue as better than vice; but God being removed from His position of sovereignty, they place their dependence upon human power, which, without God, is worthless. The unaided human will has no real power to resist and overcome evil. The defenses of the soul are broken down. Man has no barrier against sin. When once the restraints of God's word and His Spirit are rejected, we know not to what depths one may sink.
>
> Those who continue to hold these spiritualistic theories will surely spoil their Christian experience, sever their connection with God, and lose eternal life.
>
> The sophistries regarding God and nature that are flooding the world with skepticism

---

96   Exodus 34:7

are the inspiration of the fallen foe, who is himself a Bible student, who knows the truth that it is essential for the people to receive, and whose study it is to divert minds from the great truths given to prepare them for what is coming upon the world.

I have seen the results of these fanciful views of God, in apostasy, spiritualism, and free-lovism. The free love tendency of these teachings was so concealed that at first it was difficult to make plain its real character. Until the Lord presented it to me, I knew not what to call it, but I was instructed to call it unholy spiritual love.[97]

This was written at a time when the universalist, atheist, secularist, and polyamorist were—and still are—calling what Ellen White refers to as "unholy spiritual love" unconditional love.

The same author also wrote the following:

God requires at this time just what he required of the holy pair in Eden, perfect obedience to his requirements. His law remains the same in all ages. The great standard of righteousness presented in the Old Testament is not lowered in the New. It is not the work of the gospel to weaken the claims of God's holy law, but to bring men up where they can keep its precepts....

The true follower of Christ will make no boastful claims to holiness. It is by the law of God that the sinner is convicted. He sees his own sinfulness in contrast with the perfect righteousness which it enjoins, and this leads him to humility and repentance. He becomes reconciled to God through the blood of Christ, and as he continues to walk with him he will be gaining a clearer sense of the holiness of God's character and the far-reaching nature of his requirements. He will see more clearly his own defects, and will feel the need of continual repentance, and faith in the blood of Christ. He who bears with him a continual sense of the presence of Christ, cannot indulge self-confidence or self-righteousness. None of the prophets or apostles made proud boasts of holiness. The nearer they came to perfection of character, the less worthy and righteous they viewed themselves. But those who have the least sense of the perfection of Jesus, those whose eyes are least directed to him, are the ones who make the strongest claim to perfection.[98]

We are not to rush into the acceptance of the gospel without any fixed stability of purpose. If we receive Jesus Christ, we must receive all the conditions, all the requirements, and make it our life business in everything to make the kingdom of God our first consideration. Difficulties will present themselves as obstructions. *But the greatest difficulties originate with self.* It will cost all there is of the man, for Christ demands the heart, the soul, the strength, and the mind of every human agent. 'Ye are not your own for ye are bought with a price; therefore glorify God in your body and in your spirit which are God's.' It will cost

97   Ellen G. White, *Testimonies for the Church*, vol. 8 (Mountain View, CA: Pacific Press Publishing Association, 1904), 291, 292.
98   Ellen G. White, "The Conference in Sweden," *The Review and Herald*, October 5, 1886.

self-humiliation, self-denial, self-sacrifice, a constant conflict with human passions. *Our natural temperaments can not be carried along in the road, cast up for the ransomed of the Lord to walk in.* Shame and weakness and disgrace are the sure result of professedly following Christ while walking in the ways and practices of the unrenewed, unconverted men.[99]

Hopefully, this journey through the history and development of the concept of unconditional love will help all to see the truth about its origins and its evolving nature. To ignore the meaning of unconditional love as established by historical context must result in the acceptance of a different history—one established by fable, lies, and fraud.

99   White, "Christianity," *Bible Training School*, October 1, 1916, italics original.

Chapter 3

From the Seeds of the Alpha to the Fruit of the Omega: The Dangerous Deception

Infallibility is a tough sell. For that matter, discussion on reasons why infallibility is so difficult to achieve has much to do with vindication, which takes varying amounts of time—from mere seconds to infinity. Dr. John Tillotson, Archbishop of Canterbury from April 1691 until his death on November 22, 1694, addressed the matter of infallibility within the context of miracles, stating these three main weaknesses: "Infallibility is an impossibility of being deceived... it is possible our senses to deceive us, I think nobody will deny; and if so, then the testimony of witnesses, and the report of history, which depends originally upon senses, may deceive us."[1]

While Bible history doesn't deceive, except those who misinterpret and misconstrue the facts of the Bible, we regard it as beneficial for the instruction it contains regarding the fallibility of humanity, and the infallibility of God.

You might easily recall the story of the commands given to Israel not to make covenants with the inhabitants of Canaan because God wanted to destroy them for their wicked ways—their probation having come to a close according to His word to Abraham.[2] But upon hearing of the Israelites crossing the Jordan River at flood stage and the destruction of strongholds near the Jordan, the Gibeonites were most alarmed about their precarious position. Considering the annihilation of Bashan, Midian, and Moab, the miraculous overthrow of Jericho, and the complete destruction of Ai, they resorted to deceit aimed at the tangible senses in order to obtain peace at any cost.

---

1   Ralph Barker, ed., *Sermons on Several Subjects and Occasions, by the Most Reverend Dr. John Tillotson, Late Archbishop of Canterbury, Volume the Eleventh* (London, 1757), 227.

2   Genesis 15:17; Exodus 23:23

From Shechem the Israelites returned to their encampment at Gilgal. Here they were soon after visited by a strange deputation, who desired to enter into treaty with them. The ambassadors represented that they had come from a distant country, and this seemed to be confirmed by their appearance. Their clothing was old and worn, their sandals were patched, their provisions moldy, and the skins that served them for wine bottles were rent and bound up, as if hastily repaired on the journey.

In their far-off home—professedly beyond the limits of Palestine—their fellow country-men, they said, had heard of the wonders which God had wrought for His people, and had sent them to make a league with Israel. The Hebrews had been specially warned against entering into any league with the idolaters of Canaan, and a doubt as to the truth of the strangers' words arose in the minds of the leaders. 'Peradventure ye dwell among us,' they said. To this the ambassadors only replied, 'We are thy servants.' But when Joshua directly demanded of them, 'Who are ye? and from whence come ye?' they reiterated their former statement, and added, in proof of their sincerity, 'This our bread we took hot for our provision out of our houses on the day we came forth to go unto you; but now, behold, it is dry, and it is moldy: and these bottles of wine, which we filled, were new; and, behold, they be rent: and these our garments and our shoes are become old by reason of the very long journey.'

These representations prevailed. The Hebrews 'asked not counsel at the mouth of the Lord. And Joshua made peace with them, and made a league with them, to let them live: and the princes of the congregation sware unto them.' Thus the treaty was entered into. Three days afterward the truth was discovered.[3]

Given the fallibility of men, even righteous men like Joshua, how careful must we be to imitate the Bereans in searching the Scriptures and asking God earnestly for correct understanding to see if what we read, hear in church or over the radio, or see on television is truthful. We especially ought to exercise caution because of warnings given us through the Spirit of Prophecy regarding the schemes Satan wants to throw at God's people. Note her concern as she writes about the dangers of universalism, spiritualism, pantheism, etc. that will take the church by storm.

The warnings of the word of God regarding the perils surrounding the Christian church be-long to us today. As in the days of the apostles [when] men tried by tradition and philosophy to destroy faith in the Scriptures, so today, by the pleasing sentiments of higher criticism, evolution, spiritualism, theosophy, and pantheism, the enemy of righteousness is seeking to lead souls into forbidden paths. To many the Bible is as a lamp without oil, because they have turned their minds into channels of speculative belief that bring misunderstanding

3   White, *Patriarchs and Prophets*, 505.

and confusion. The work of higher criticism, in dissecting, conjecturing, reconstructing, is destroying faith in the Bible as a divine revelation. It is robbing God's word of power to control, uplift, and inspire human lives. By spiritualism, multitudes are taught to believe that desire is the highest law, that license is liberty, and that man is accountable only to himself.

The follower of Christ will meet with the 'enticing words' against which the apostle warned the Colossian believers. He will meet with spiritualistic interpretations of the Scriptures, but he is not to accept them. His voice is to be heard in clear affirmation of the eternal truths of the Scriptures. Keeping his eyes fixed on Christ, he is to move steadily forward in the path marked out, discarding all ideas that are not in harmony with His teaching. The truth of God is to be the subject for his contemplation and meditation. He is to regard the Bible as the voice of God speaking directly to him. Thus he will find the wisdom which is divine.[4]

Unfortunately, we suffer from the lukewarm condition of Laodicea. We think we are rich when we are in need of everything God desires to give us—gold tried in fire, white raiment, and spiritual eyesalve.[5] Instead of being alert to our danger, "the sensibilities of many are blunted; false excitement has destroyed their discernment and spiritual eyesight. It is of the highest importance now for them to move understandingly, that Satan's object may not be fully accomplished in overthrowing those whom he has had power to deceive."[6]

So, then, how did unconditional love make inroads into Seventh-day Adventist theology? If Ellen White never used the term, did any of the pioneers of our movement use it? The answer appears to be a decided affirmative, but the questions must be asked Under what circumstances did this philosophy creep in? And just how did it develop? We must delve into the history of the Adventist movement in order to satisfy our inquiries, and for the same reasons given by Ellen White's grandson when he wrote her biography: "Not alone as a matter of history is the fanaticism met in early years recounted here. Because on several occasions Ellen White was shown in vision that the history of the past would be repeated and God's people would be called upon to meet elements of fanaticism before the end of time, we delineate in considerable detail the involvements of that first critical year in the history of the Seventh-day Adventist Church."[7]

But before engaging in a study of the early Adventist Church, we need to understand what was going on in the northeast of America in order to grasp the significance of the nature of fanaticism that emerged after the Great Disappointment of October 22, 1844.

New England in the late 1740s, especially in the region of Blackstone Valley of Rhode Island and Massachusetts, began hearing about a strange teaching we now know as "spiritual wifery" that persisted there

---

4   Ellen G. White, *The Acts of the Apostles* (Mountain View, CA: Pacific Press Publishing Association, 1911), 474, 475.
5   Revelation 3:18
6   Ellen G. White, *Testimonies for the Church*, vol. 1 (Mountain View, CA: Pacific Press Publishing Association, 1868), 323.
7   Arthur L. White, *Ellen G. White: The Early Years: 1827–1862*, vol. 1 (Washington, D.C.: Review and Herald Publishing Association, 1985), 72.

for about two decades. The concept included ideas that a spiritual confirmation could overrule and overthrow all civil recognized authority regarding traditional marriage for the happiness derived from a spiritual connection, otherwise known as "affinities" or "soul mates," formed by individuals and often approved by their spiritual leaders. Incidences of free love among various Christian Congregationalists in this region became so notorious as to lead to the Rhode Island General Assembly passage of the law "Against Adultery, Polygamy, and Unlawfully Marrying Persons; and for the Relief of Such Persons as Are Injured by the Breach of Marriage Covenants" in October 1749.

The penalty for such infractions included being hung for an hour, then publicly receiving no more than thirty lashes on their naked body before being hustled off to jail for an unspecified duration. "Dozens of families and several ministers were caught up in scandals over the next twenty years. It is more than likely that the Rhode Island law against breaches of marriage covenants was a direct response to the rapid spread of spiritual wifery in this period."[8]

The efforts of various state assemblies never fully uprooted the growing phenomenon of free-lovism, for wherever it was prosecuted with vigor the proponents simply relocated elsewhere. American history is replete with the notoriety of several individuals and their disciples, such as: Jacob Cochran, founder of the Cochranites in Saco, Maine, in 1818; Joseph Smith, Jr., founder of the Mormon faith who practiced plurality of wives from as early as 1831 until his death in 1844; and John Humphrey Noyes, founder of the Oneida Community in Oneida, New York, in 1848 after being hounded out of Vermont for adultery.

What is so intriguing about these movements is their connection to spiritual reawakening. "It is a recurrent phenomenon in western religious history. The incident in Cumberland [Rhode Island] can be adequately explained only in terms of these broader patterns of religious behavior. Any study of the documents in this case reveals at once that it was directly related to that astounding outburst of religious excitement in the years 1734–1755 which is known as the first great awakening, and any student of this awakening can cite a dozen or more similar incidents

> *Under a religious guise, Satan will seek to extend his influence over the Christian world.*

of sexually aberrant behavior in other parts of New England. What is more, these 'free love' movements, generally described as 'perfectionism,' have cropped up in later great awakenings in American history,"[9] such as those just listed.

But of these events we have an explanation supplied to us by Ellen White. She describes the phenomenon in this manner:

---

8   William G. McLoughlin, "Free Love, Immortalism, and Perfectionism in Cumberland, Rhode Island, 1748–1768" in *Rhode Island History*, vol. 33 (Providence, RI: The Rhode Island Historical Society, August and November 1974), 70, see also 67–85.

9   Ibid., 70. This passage cites C. C. Geen in *Revivalism and Separatism In New England, 1740-1800* (New Haven, 1962), 200–203.

Before the final visitation of God's judgments upon the earth there will be among the people of the Lord such a revival of primitive godliness as has not been witnessed since apostolic times. The Spirit and power of God will be poured out upon His children. At that time many will separate themselves from those churches in which the love of this world has supplanted love for God and His word. Many, both of ministers and people, will gladly accept those great truths which God has caused to be proclaimed at this time to prepare a people for the Lord's second coming. The enemy of souls desires to hinder this work; and before the time for such a movement shall come, he will endeavor to prevent it by introducing a counterfeit. In those churches which he can bring under his deceptive power he will make it appear that God's special blessing is poured out; there will be manifest what is thought to be great religious interest. Multitudes will exult that God is working marvelously for them, when the work is that of another spirit. Under a religious guise, Satan will seek to extend his influence over the Christian world.

In many of the revivals which have occurred during the last half century, the same influences have been at work, to a greater or less degree, that will be manifest in the more extensive movements of the future. There is an emotional excitement, a mingling of the true with the false, that is well adapted to mislead. Yet none need be deceived. In the light of God's word it is not difficult to determine the nature of these movements. Wherever men neglect the testimony of the Bible, turning away from those plain, soul-testing truths which require self-denial and renunciation of the world, there we may be sure that God's blessing is not bestowed. And by the rule which Christ himself has given, 'Ye shall know them by their fruits,' (Matthew 7:16), it is evident that these movements are not the work of the Spirit of God.

In the truths of His word, God has given to men a revelation of Himself; and to all who accept them they are a shield against the deceptions of Satan. It is a neglect of these truths that has opened the door to the evils which are now becoming so widespread in the religious world. The nature and the importance of the law of God have been, to a great extent, lost sight of. A wrong conception of the character, the perpetuity, and obligation of the divine law has led to errors in relation to conversion and sanctification, and has resulted in lowering the standard of piety in the church. Here is to be found the secret of the lack of the Spirit and power of God in the revivals of our time.[10]

So, it really should not come as any surprise that this fanaticism should attempt to find its way into the remnant of believers who chose to believe that the Great Disappointment of October 22, 1844, came about because of a fulfillment of prophecy[11] and a mistaken interpretation of the event marked by that date. Then let us proceed with the facts as they relate to the Adventist movement.

10   White, *The Great Controversy*, 464, 465.
11   Revelation 10:10

On July 24, 1844, Joshua V. Himes published, "We had several faithful brethren to assist in the meeting, among whom was Bro. J. G. Bennet [sic], of Claremont, N. H. He was formerly a distinguished member of the Methodist Conference, and though always brought up, and educated in that society, and highly esteemed among them, yet, when he saw this mighty truth, of our coming King at the door, he laid all upon the altar, and went forth to proclaim, 'Behold the Bridegroom cometh.' He is associated with Bro. A. M. Billings, formerly a sheriff, and an infidel, in Claremont, but now a Christian and minister of Christ. They are a part only of the fruits of the Claremont Tent Meetings. They are now holding Conferences and Camp-meetings continually, and with many others in that region, are doing all they can for the cause."[12]

On August 10, 1844, Bennett and Billings would hold meetings in Tunbridge, Vermont.[13] By August 19 they were encouraged by committee action to assist with the camp meeting scheduled to be held on September 4.[14] Such activity would only indicate that Bennett and Billings were trusted preachers of integrity and beloved by their coworkers in spreading the Advent message started by William Miller. Yet, after the Great Disappointment, they yielded to the fanaticism of "perfectionism" and "holy flesh" so prevalent in that region. "In the early records we find the names of some who at some point were involved in fanaticism: Joseph Turner, Israel Damman, a Mr. Bennett [sic], John Andrews, William Hyde."[15]

Early in her ministry, while still an unmarried minor, Ellen G. White traveled from Maine through New Hampshire and met the false doctrines of a "higher spiritualty" (aka "perfectionism," "holy flesh"), which included much talk about charity and living above all sin. She makes the connection of this early period with the pantheism in Kellogg's book *Living Temple*.

> In Living Temple the assertion is made that God is in the flower, in the leaf, in the sinner. But God does not live in the sinner. The Word declares that He abides only in the hearts of those who love Him and do righteousness. God does not abide in the heart of the sinner; it is the enemy who abides there.[16]

> As we read [*Living Temple*], I recognized the very sentiments against which I had been bidden to speak in warning during the early days of my public labors. When I first left the State of Maine, it was to go through Vermont and Massachusetts, to bear a testimony

12   Joshua V. Himes, "Behold! The Bridegroom Cometh!! Go Ye Out To Meet Him!!!" *The Advent Herald and the Signs of the Times Reporter*, vol. VII, no. 25, July 24, 1844.

13   Ibid., vol. VIII, no. 1, August 7, 1844.

14   Ibid., vol. VIII, no. 4, August 28, 1844.

15   White, *Ellen G. White: The Early Years: 1827–1862*, vol. 1, 71.

16   Ellen G. White, *Sermons and Talks*, vol. 1 (Silver Spring, MD: Ellen G. White Estate, 1990), 343; see also pages 341–344.

against these sentiments. *Living Temple* contains the alpha of these theories.[17] I knew that the omega would follow in a little while; and I trembled for our people. I knew that I must warn our brethren and sisters not to enter into controversy over the presence and personality of God.... The scripture used to substantiate the doctrine there set forth, is scripture misapplied.

I am compelled to speak in denial of the claim that the teachings of *Living Temple* can be sustained by statements from my writings. There may be in this book expressions and sentiments that are in harmony with my writings. And there may be in my writings many statements which, taken from their connection, and interpreted according to the mind of the writer of *Living Temple*, would seem to be in harmony with the teachings of this book. This may give apparent support to the assertion that the sentiments in *Living Temple* are in harmony with my writings. But God forbid that this sentiment should prevail.

Few can discern the result of entertaining the sophistries advocated by some at this time. But the Lord has lifted the curtain, and has shown me the result that would follow. The spiritualistic theories regarding the personality of God, followed to their logical conclusion, sweep away the whole Christian economy. They estimate as nothing the light that Christ came from heaven to give John to give to His people. They teach that the scenes just before us are not of sufficient importance to be given special attention. They make of no effect the truth of heavenly origin, and rob the people of God of their past experience, giving them instead a false science.[18]

The connection between pantheism and this false species of charity that has its roots in spiritualism—a charity that would lead apparently pious men to have wrongful relationships by leaving their wives for other

---

17   Regarding the nature of the heresies associated with pantheism, Lewis Walton provides interesting insights that tie in with Helena Blavatsky's connection of unconditional love to the Hindu religion in the previous chapter: "*But the real crisis for the church, so terrible that Ellen White would openly wonder whether she could live through it, involved something deeper than money. Few could see it, but it had already arrived. Hidden in Dr. Kellogg's new book were all the elements of an unparalleled crisis in doctrine. *For several years Kellogg had been making some rather odd statements about the nature of God. 'God is in me,' he had told a General Conference meeting recently, 'and everything I do is God's power; every single act is a creative act of God.' (*GC Bulletin*, 2d Quarter, 1901, 497.) It was a fascinating idea that seemed to bring the Deity very near, and it quickly captured the interest of some well-known denominational thinkers. There was a peculiar charm about Kellogg's suggestion that the air we breathe is the medium through which God sends His Holy Spirit physically into our lives, that the sunlight is His visible 'Shekinah.' And even well-trained minds responded to the new concept, catching fire from Kellogg's evangelical enthusiasm. Now these sentiments were appearing even more persuasively in the galley sheets of the new book he had chosen to call The Living Temple. In the human body, he asserted, was 'the Power which builds, which creates—it is God Himself, the divine Presence in the temple.' (J. H. Kellogg, *The Living Temple* [Battle Creek, MI: Good Health Pub. Co., 1903], 52). *Few people realized that this idea could take one clear out of Christianity, into the realm of religious mysticism that had no room for the Divine Being or a place called heaven. One man who saw the danger was William Spicer, a recently returned missionary from India, now a General Conference officer, who instantly recognized in Kellogg's new theology the same ideas he had seen in Hinduism. Alarmed, Spicer went to Kellogg to straighten it all out with a personal chat. The two men sat down on the veranda of the rambling twenty-seven-room house that Kellogg called The Residence, and Spicer, to his surprise, found himself 'at once in the midst of a discussion of the most controversial questions'" (Lewis R. Walton, *Omega* [Hagerstown, MD: Review and Herald Publishing Association, 1981], 21, 22). The asterisks are in the original quote. I assume they are used by Walton to denote paragraph breaks.

18   Ellen G. White, *Selected Messages*, book 1 (Washington, D.C.: Review and Herald Publishing Association, 1958), 203, 204.

women—could only be the free-lovism, unqualified, unconditional love already proven to be the counterfeit birthed in paganism, swaddled in modern spiritualism, nourished by universalism, and yet fully unsupported by the Bible. However, we have not paid close enough attention to the history of its infiltration into the Seventh-day Adventist denomination. Read from Ellen White's testimony of her ministry, written at the time of Kellogg's pantheism, regarding her early work so as to get the full picture of the crisis the church was then experiencing:

> At this time visions were given me to correct the errors of those who had taken the extreme view of some texts of Scripture, and refrained wholly from labor, and rejected all those who would not receive their views on this point, and some other things which they held to be religious duties. God revealed these errors to me in vision, and sent me to his erring children to declare them; but many of them wholly rejected the message, and charged me with conforming to the world. On the other hand, the nominal Adventists charged me with fanaticism, and I was falsely, and by some, wickedly, represented as being the leader of the fanaticism that I was laboring to do away....
>
> ... We next visited Bro. Nichols' family in Dorchester, and had a meeting there of the deepest interest. Again H. testified that the Lord had abundantly blessed him, and that he could go forty days on the strength he there received. But T. was exerting his influence to discourage and close up my way by spreading lying reports concerning me. H., who had been made so happy as he received my testimony, fell under the influence of T., and as his mind turned, he became unsettled, then unstable. It was evident that he was rejecting the counsel of God against himself. He seemed unhappy, and finally went into the spiritual view of the second advent, and received the grossest errors, neglected his family, took a spiritual wife, and his lawful wife died of a broken heart.[19]

Following is additional insight into the counsel that Mrs. White gave to Mr. Bennett and Mr. Billings as a young girl:

> When but a girl I went to New Hampshire to bear warning against these same doctrines. There was a man by the name of Billings and another by the name of Bennet [sic] who were preaching a higher spirituality. I was asked to meet these men, and I did so, giving them the light that God had given me. In the meeting a great distress came upon me. I was taken off in vision. The men began to triumph, thinking that things were going their way. When I got up to bear my testimony, they began to shout. I stopped and did not say a word until they had finished. Then I went on and told them plainly where the doctrines they were advocating would lead to.[20]

19   Ellen G. White, *Spiritual Gifts*, vol. 2 (Battle Creek, MI: Seventh-day Adventist Publishing Association, 1860), 58, 68.
20   White, *Sermons and Talks*, vol. 1, 341, 342.

These doctrines led to free-loveism, and my heart was sorely grieved as I saw the result they brought to those who accepted them. One family who for years had lived happily together was broken up. A man and his wife, well advanced in years, were separated. The husband left his wife and children, and established other family relations. We seemed to be able to do nothing to break the spell upon these persons. The precious truths of the Bible had no influence over them.[21]

I saw that the spirit that both Bennet and Libby possessed while Brother and Sister Phillips were in union with them, was an unclean spirit and an unholy spirit, and Brother and Sister O have not as yet realized and admitted and shaken it off. The spirit moved strongly on the feelings, and these feelings, many of them, are yet cherished as sacred, [indited by] the Holy Ghost.

But many times when it was upon Brother and Sister Phillips, they knew not what spirit they were of. At the time these men were professing so much of the Holy Ghost, especially Bennet, his life was corrupt, his heart vile. I was shown that a great many have been entirely thrown off their balance by not understanding the spirit that some of these [seemingly] very good and professedly holy men possessed. That they have felt the influence of and received great blessings through the influence of their prayers and apparent faith.

It has stumbled many an honest soul, and here they have grounded and made shipwreck of faith. They trusted to feeling, to an influence or power that was brought to bear upon their feelings. I saw that many, very many had been truly converted through the influence of persons who were living in open violation of the commandments of God, their lives vile and corrupt....[22]

In the vision at Grand Rapids I was shown something of your case. I saw that Brother P had not abstained from all appearance of evil, had been too familiar with the sisters, and had not always behaved with discretion and comeliness with his own wife in the presence of others. These things have brought a reproach upon the cause.

Dear Bro. P you have been indiscreet in practicing the salutation and have made but little difference as to the time and place, whether you were surrounded by unbelievers or not, and have been ready to practice it too frequently, and no good but evil has resulted from it.

I saw that you had dwelt too much upon little things, non-essentials, had entered too largely into others' business affairs, and were too precise to bring them to your views and ideas and the result has been bad. You have been too severe upon others, noticed their faults too much and dwelt upon them, have dwelt too much on articles of dress, etc., etc.

21   Ellen G. White, *Manuscript Releases*, vol. 11 (Silver Spring, MD: Ellen G. White Estate, 1990), 248.
22   Ellen G. White, *Manuscript Releases*, vol. 5 (Silver Spring, MD: Ellen G. White Estate, 1990), 228, 229.

I saw that you had done very wrong, and been exceedingly unguarded in taking sisters upon your knees. God's word does not allow it and you have no right to do it and you have sinned in so doing.

I saw you could not be too careful and reserved with the sisters. No married man has any right to sit another woman upon his knee, or allow it in a woman, but his own wife. You must be more judicious, more guarded.[23]

In looking back upon the early history of the Millerite and Advent movements, Ellen White exhorted the church as follows:

Brethren, look well to the character of your religion. Do not forget that Christ is to be your pattern in all things. You may be sure that his religion is not a sensational religion. A religion of this kind I learned to dread in my very earliest experience in the cause of present truth. I was at that time, before I was seventeen years old, bidden to warn those who were cherishing fanciful ideas, and who declared that their strange movements were inspired of God.

In New Hampshire there were those who were active in disseminating false ideas in regard to God. Light was given me that these men were making the truth of no effect by their ideas, some of which led to free-lovism. I was shown that these men were seducing souls by presenting speculative theories regarding God.

I went to the place where they were working, and opened before them what they were doing. The Lord gave me strength to lay plainly before them the danger of their course. Among other views, they held that those once sanctified could not sin, and this they were presenting as gospel food. Their false theories, with their burden of deceptive influence, were working great harm to themselves and to others. They were gaining a spiritualistic power over those who could not see the evil of these beautifully clothed theories. Great evils had already resulted. The doctrine that all were holy had led to the belief that the affections of the sanctified were never in danger of leading astray. The result of this belief was the fulfillment of the evil desires of hearts which, though professedly sanctified, were far from purity of thought and practice.

> *In the future, truth will be counterfeited by the precepts of men. Deceptive theories will be presented as safe doctrines.*

---

23   Ellen G. White, *Manuscript Releases*, vol. 7 (Silver Spring, MD: Ellen G. White Estate, 1990), 208.

This is only one of the instances in which I was called upon to rebuke those who were presenting the doctrine of an impersonal god diffused through nature, and the doctrine of holy flesh.

In the future, truth will be counterfeited by the precepts of men. Deceptive theories will be presented as safe doctrines. False science is one of the agencies that Satan used in the heavenly courts, and it is used by him today. The false assertions that he made to the angels, his subtle scientific theories, led many of them from loyalty. And, having lost their place in heaven, they prepared temptations for our first parents. Adam and Eve yielded to the enemy, and by their disobedience, humanity was estranged from God, and the earth was separated from heaven.[24]

The importance of establishing the vileness of these fanatics is so great that it is essential to read one more piece of communication from Ellen White during this early period in church history. Carefully consider the points she draws out in this sketch of her ministry to meet the confusion Satan had hoped to sow:

"It was difficult to accomplish much good in New Hampshire. We found little spirituality there. Many pronounced their experience in the movement of 1844 a delusion; it was hard to reach this class, for we could not accept the position they ventured to take. A number who were active preachers and exhorters in 1844, now seemed to have lost their moorings, and did not know where we were in prophetic time; they were fast uniting with the spirit of the world.

"Upon one occasion when I was delivering the message that the Lord had given me for the encouragement of his people, I was interrupted several times by a certain minister. He had been very active in preaching definite time; but when the appointed period passed, his faith utterly failed, and he wandered in darkness, doubting and questioning everything. He was ever ready to array himself against any one who claimed more light than he possessed. The Spirit of the Lord rested upon me, as I related what he had shown me. This minister interrupted me several consecutive times; but I continued speaking, when he became very angry and excited, violently opposing what I said. He raised his voice to a high key, and abused me till he was forced to stop from sheer exhaustion. In a few moments he left the house, being seized with hemorrhage of the lungs. He rapidly failed from that time, and died not long after.

"Our testimony was welcomed by some, but many received us suspiciously. Fanaticism and spiritual magnetism seemed to have destroyed the spirit of true godliness. Many appeared unable to discern or appreciate the motives that led me in my feebleness, to travel and bear my testimony to the people. Those who had little interest for the salvation of souls,

---

24   Ellen G. White, "Beware of Fanciful Doctrines," *The Review and Herald,* January 21, 1904.

and whose hearts had turned from the work of preparation, could not comprehend the love of God in my soul that quickened my desire to help those in darkness to the same light that cheered my path. Could they also have seen what had been revealed to me of God's matchless love for men, manifested in giving his only Son to die for them, they would not have doubted my sincerity.

"I believed all that had been shown me in vision. Truth was to me a living reality, and my labor was for eternity. However others might view my work, the weight of its importance was heavy on my soul. In feeble health I was toiling to do good to others unto eternal life. Moments seemed precious to me, delays dangerous.

"In New Hampshire we had to contend with a species of spiritual magnetism, of a similar character with mesmerism. It was our first experience of this kind, and happened thus: Arriving at Claremont, we were told there were two parties of Adventists; one holding fast their former faith, the other denying it. At other places we had visited and labored with this latter class, and found that they were so buried in worldliness, and had so far adopted the popular view in regard to our disappointment that we could not reach nor help them.

"But we were now pleased to learn that there was a little company here who believed that in their past experience they had been led by the providence of God. We were directed to Elders Bennett and Bellings [sic] as persons holding similar views with ourselves. We discovered that there was much prejudice against these men, but concluded that they were persecuted for righteousness' sake. We called on them and were kindly received and courteously treated. We soon learned that they professed sanctification, claiming they were above the possibility of sin, being entirely consecrated to God. Their clothing was excellent, and they had an air of ease and comfort.

"Presently a little boy about eight years old entered, literally clad in dirty rags. We were surprised to find that this little specimen of neglect was the son of Elder Bennett. The mother looked exceedingly ashamed and annoyed; but the father, utterly unconcerned, continued talking of his high spiritual attainments without the slightest recognition of his little son. But his sanctification had suddenly lost its charm in my eyes. Wrapped in prayer and meditation, throwing off all the toil and responsibilities of life, this man seemed too spiritually minded to notice the actual wants of his family, or give his children the least fatherly attention. He seemed to forget that the greater our love to God, the stronger should be our love and care for those whom he has given us; that the Saviour never taught idleness and abstract devotion, to the neglect of the duties laying directly in our path.

"This husband and father declared that the heavenly attainment of true holiness carried the mind above all earthly thoughts. Still he sat at the table and ate temporal food; he was not fed by a miracle, and some one must provide that food, although he troubled himself little about that matter, his time was so devoted to spiritual things. Not so his wife, upon whom rested the burden of the family. She toiled unremittingly in every department of household labor to keep up the home. The husband declared that she was not sanctified, but allowed worldly things to draw her mind from religious subjects.

"I thought of our Saviour as a constant worker for the good of others. He said 'My Father worketh hitherto, and I work.' The sanctification that he taught was shown in deeds of kindness and mercy, and the love that counteth others better than themselves.

"While at this house a sister of Elder Bennett requested a private interview with me. She had much to say concerning entire consecration to God, and endeavored to draw out my views in regard to that subject. I felt that I must be guarded in my expressions. While talking, she held my hand in hers, and with the other softly stroked my hair. I felt that angels of God would protect me from the unholy influence this attractive young lady was seeking to exercise over me, with her fair speeches, and gentle caresses. She had much to say in regard to the spiritual attainments of Elder Bennett, and his great faith. Her mind seemed very much occupied with him and his experience. I was glad to be relieved at length from this trying interview.

"These persons, who made such lofty professions, were calculated to deceive the unwary. They had much to say of love and charity covering a multitude of sins. I could not unite with their views and feelings; but felt that they were wielding a terrible power for evil. I wished to escape from their presence as soon as possible.

"Elder Bennett, in speaking of faith, said, 'All we have to do is to believe, and whatever we ask of God will be given us.'

"Elder White suggested that there were conditions specified. 'If ye abide in me, and my words abide in you, ye shall ask what ye will, and it shall be done unto you.' Said he, 'Your theory of faith must have a foundation; it is as empty as a flour-barrel with both heads out. True charity never covers up unrepented and unconfessed sins. She only drops her mantle over the faults that are confessed and renounced. True charity is a very delicate personage, never setting her pure foot outside of Bible truth.' As soon as the views of these people were crossed, they manifested a stubborn, self-righteous spirit that rejected all instruction. Though professing great humiliation they were boastful in their sophistry of sanctification, and resisted all appeals to reason. We felt that all our efforts to convince them of their error were useless, as they took the position they were not learners but teachers.

"While in New Hampshire we visited at the house of Brother Collier, where we proposed to hold a meeting. We supposed this family were in union with those whom we had met at Elder Bennett's, mentioned in the preceding chapter. We asked some questions in reference to these men; but Brother Collier gave us no information. Said he, 'If the Lord sent you here, you will ascertain what spirit governs them, and will solve the mystery for us.'

"Both of these men attended the meeting at Brother C's. While I was earnestly praying for light and the presence of God, they began to groan and cry 'Amen!' apparently throwing their sympathy with my prayer. Immediately my heart was oppressed with a great weight, the words died upon my lips, darkness overshadowed the whole meeting.

"Elder White arose and said, 'I am distressed. The Spirit of the Lord is grieved. I resist this influence in the name of the Lord! O God, rebuke this foul spirit!'

"I was immediately relieved, and rose above the shadows. But again, while speaking words of encouragement and faith to those present, their groanings and amens chilled me. Once more Elder White rebuked the spirit of darkness, and again the power of the Lord rested upon me, while I spoke to the people. These agents of the evil one were then so bound as to be unable to exert their baneful influence any more that night.

"After the meeting Elder White said to Brother Collier, 'Now I can tell you concerning those two men. They are acting under a Satanic influence, yet attributing all to the Spirit of the Lord.'

"'I believe God sent you to encourage us,' said Brother Collier. 'We call their influence mesmerism. They affect the minds of others in a remarkable way, and have controlled some to their great damage. We seldom hold meetings here, for they intrude their presence, and we can have no union with them. They manifest deep feeling, as you observed tonight, but they crush the very life from our prayers, and leave an influence blacker than Egyptian darkness. I have never seen them tied up before tonight.'

"During family prayer that night the Spirit of the Lord rested upon me, and I was shown many things in vision. These professed ministers were presented to me as doing great injury to the cause of God. While professing sanctification they were transgressing the sacred law. They were corrupt at heart and all those in unison with them were under a Satanic delusion and obeying their own carnal instincts instead of the word of God. These two men exerted a marked and peculiar power over the people, holding their attention and winning their confidence through a baneful mesmeric influence that many who were innocent and unsuspecting attributed to the Spirit of the Lord. Those who followed their teachings were terribly deceived and led into the grossest errors.

"I was shown that the daily lives of these men were in direct contrast with their profession. Under the garb of sanctification they were practicing the worst sins and deceiving God's people. Their deception was all laid open before me, and I saw the fearful account that stood against them in the great book of records, and their terrible guilt in professing entire holiness, while their daily acts were offensive in the sight of God. Some time after this, the characters of these persons were developed before the people and the vision given in reference to them was fully vindicated.

"These men claimed to be sanctified, and that they could not sin. 'Believe in Jesus Christ,' was their cry, 'only believe and this is all that is required of us; only have faith in Jesus.' The words of John came forcibly to my mind: 'If we say that we have no sin, we deceive ourselves, and the truth is not in us.' I was shown that those who triumph, and claim that they are sinless, show in this very boasting that they are far from being without the taint of sin. The more clearly fallen man comprehends the character of Christ, the more distrustful will he be of himself, and the more imperfect will his works appear to him in contrast with those which marked the life of the spotless Redeemer. But those who are at a great distance from Jesus, whose spiritual senses are so clouded by error that they cannot comprehend the divine character of the great Exemplar, conceive of him as altogether such an one as themselves, and talk of their own perfection of holiness with a high degree of satisfaction. They really know little of themselves, and less of Christ. They are far from God."[25]

The attack upon the remnant through violation of the seventh commandment with free-loveism affected many ministers in Ellen White's lifetime, and it has affected others throughout the years, but at this time we will examine the lives of three other men of prominent influence who served the church during Ellen White's ministry: Moses Hull, J. H. Waggoner, and E. J. Waggoner.

Accepting the Adventist messages in 1857, Moses Hull began preaching what he learned. Ordained a minister of the gospel in 1858, he gained popularity and influence because of his debating style when preaching Bible truths that were contrary to many doctrines held by nominal Protestants of the time. On occasion, Ellen White wrote Hull warnings that he was too reliant upon himself and that he preached with his own reputation forefront in his mind. Such thoughts of self-flattery were dangerous, especially when in conjunction to the praise from young women. Ellen White penned,

> I saw that you would be tempted to feel that your brethren want to gauge you, that they want to put too much restraint upon you. But your brethren only want you to live according to the instructions of God's word, and God wishes to bring you there, and angels are watching you with the deepest solicitude. You must conform your life to the word of God, that you may be blessed and strengthened of Him, or you will fall out by the way, and while you preach to others, you yourself will be a castaway. But you may be an overcomer, and may win eternal life. You are recovering yourself from the snare of Satan, but he is preparing other snares for you. God will help and strengthen you if you seek Him earnestly. But study yourself. Try every motive; let it not be your aim to preach brilliant discourses to exhibit Moses Hull, but seek to exhibit Christ. Simplify the truth to your hearers so that small minds may comprehend it. Make your discourses plain, pointed, and solemn. Bring the people to a decision. Make them feel the vital force of truth. If any speak one word of flattery to you, rebuke them sharply. Tell them that Satan has troubled you with that for some time, and they need not help him in his work.
>
> When among the sisters, be reserved. No matter if they think you lack courtesy. If sisters, married or unmarried, show any familiarity, repulse them. Be abrupt and decided, that

25   Ellen G. White, *Life Sketches of James White and Ellen G. White 1880* (Battle Creek, MI: Seventh-day Adventist Publishing Association, 1880), 205–211.

they may ever understand that you give no countenance to such weakness. When before the young, and at all times, be grave, be solemn.[26]

As time passed, Moses Hull continued engaging in debates with spiritualists. Again, Mrs. White warned him of his danger:

> "Satan has looked on and witnessed the heavy blow Bro. Hull has dealt to Spiritualism in Battle Creek. Spiritualists have understood his organization, and felt assured it would not be in vain to make a determined effort to overthrow him who injured their cause so much. In discussing with Spiritualists you have not merely to meet the man and his arguments, but Satan and his angels. And never should merely one man be sent forth alone to engage with a Spiritualist. If the cause of God really demands that Satan and his host be confronted through a spiritual medium, if enough is at stake to call for such a discussion, then one should never go forth alone, but several together, that with prayer and faith the host of darkness may be driven back, and the speaker shielded by angels that excel in strength.
>
> "Bro. Hull, you was [sic] shown me under the soothing influence of a fascination which will prove fatal, unless the spell is broken. You have parleyed with Satan, and reasoned with him, and tarried upon forbidden ground, and have exercised your mind in things which were too great for you, and by indulging in doubts and unbelief, have attracted evil angels around you, and driven from you the holy and pure angels of God. If you had steadfastly resisted Satan's suggestions, and had sought strength from God with a determined effort, you would have broken every fetter, and driven back your spiritual foe, and come closer and nearer to God, and triumphed in his name. I saw that it was presumption in you to go forth to meet a Spiritualist when you were enshrouded in clouds of unbelief, and bewildered. You went to battle with Satan and his host without an armor, and have been grievously wounded, and are insensible to your wound. I fear, greatly fear, that the thunders and lightnings of Sinai would fail to move you. You are in Satan's easy chair, and do not see your fearful condition and make any effort. If you do not arouse, and recover yourself from the snare of the Devil, you must perish. The brethren and sisters would save you, but I saw that they could not. You have something to do. You have a desperate effort to make, or you are lost. I saw that those who were under the bewitching influence of Spiritualism, know it not. You have been charmed, and mesmerized, and yet know it not, and do not make the least effort to come to the light."[27]

Moses Hull had previously confided to Ellen White that the spiritualists predicted his apostasy from truth to join their cause. "Brother Hull has told me recently what the spiritualist medium told him (also a lady

---

26   White, *Testimonies for the Church*, vol. 1, 437.

27   Ellen G. White, "Communications to Elder M. Hull," *The Review and Herald*, January 19, 1864.

medium), that the spirits had informed them that Brother Hull would soon leave the Adventists and become a spiritualist, confirming what had been shown me in vision, as I have written you."[28]

Should we be amazed, then, that he finally did leave the Adventist church? "For the remainder of his life Moses Hull was a spiritualist. By the early 1870s he had left his wife and not only advocated 'free love' but practiced it. The last 35 years of his life he lived in a common-law marriage with a spiritualist medium, Mattie E. Sawyer."[29] It is believed by some that Mattie E. Sawyer is the very lady medium that communicated Hull's departure from the faith of Jesus.

Hull went on to preach unabashedly that free-lovism was not adultery, and that he was unashamed of the lifestyle, going so far as to write, "Many think they are improved physically and spiritually by a change of climate and scene, when their principal improvement is caused by a separation from their old sexual mate, and sometimes by the substitution of a new one. Several years have passed since ... and I have never regretted the step, but have continued to repeat the offense against man-made institutions...."[30]

But apparently he did grow to regret his decision. According to his great nephew, "Before Uncle Moses died he was a most miserable man. He is reported to have told one of our loyal members—my father, I believe— that he would be willing to crawl on his hands and knees from ____ to ____ (two large cities of that time—I fail to remember the names) if by so doing he could be back where he once was in the church and in favor with God."[31]

Joseph H. Waggoner also became an influential preacher of Adventism, beginning his ministry in the early 1850s. He was a member of the Baptist Church when he heard about the three angels' messages of Revelation 14. He also accepted the temperance message, tossing his tobacco into the stove and resolving to never be found using it at the time Christ should return.[32] Serving in a number of capacities over the course of his ministry, and authoring several books, he had a wide influence over many people through the years. So did his wife, Maryetta, only not necessarily for the better.

No worse influence can be exerted against the gospel than an unbelieving spouse married to a minister, as Ellen White wrote: "An unsanctified wife is the greatest curse that a minister can have. Those servants of God that have been and are still so unhappily situated as to have this withering influence at home, should double their prayers and their watchfulness, take a firm, decided stand, and let not this darkness press them down. They should cleave closer to God, be firm and decided, rule well their own house, and live so that they can have the approbation of God and the watchcare of the angels. But if they yield to the wishes of their unconsecrated companions, the frown of God is brought upon the dwelling. The ark of God cannot abide in the house, because they countenance and uphold them in their wrongs."[33]

Apparently testimonies were sent to Maryetta Waggoner concerning her course as a minister's wife—testimonies she rejected. The May 14, 1861, issue of *The Review and Herald* contains a confession admitting her

---

28   Ellen G. White, *Manuscript Releases*, vol. 6 (Silver Spring, MD: Ellen G. White Estate, 1990), 100.

29   James R. Nix, "The Tragic Story of Moses Hull," *Adventist Review*, August 27, 1987, 16.

30   Moses Hull, *Woodhull & Claflin's Weekly*, August 23, 1873.

31   Lewis R. Ogden, "My Uncle Moses," *Review and Herald*, July 5, 1973.

32   Woodrow W. Whidden II, *E. J. Waggoner: From the Physician of Good News to Agent of Division* (Hagerstown, MD: Review and Herald Publishing Assn., 2008), 21.

33   White, *Testimonies for the Church*, vol. 1, 139.

doubts over, disbelief in, and despising of the testimonies sent her by Ellen White. Having admitted her faults and regrets, she promised to make amends.[34] But it seems she was never quite able to make full repentance. At some point in time, Maryetta had a moral fall. In a letter to J. H. Waggoner dated February 1, 1872, sent from Battle Creek, Ellen White plainly stated that Maryetta was "a medium of darkness" that had "imbued" her children "with her spirit, thoroughly educated in deception and falsehood and self-sufficiency.... Finally she [Maryetta] was left to pursue her own course, following the promptings of her unconsecrated heart; then you could have been free from her and God designed that you should be free from her.... The law of God and the laws of the land freed you from your wife, but this golden opportunity you let pass, and you voluntarily went back to your wife, fastening the chains of bondage upon yourself.... You began to look to yourself, talk of yourself—of your weakness, your infirmities, your feebleness, your aches, your pains. In short, your mind is in danger of running the same channel that your wife had so long been in."[35] And that channel he did run in!

In 1876 while working in California, Joseph Waggoner met Mrs. Chittenden. Over the intervening years, this woman would have just as dangerous a hold over him as Maryetta. Their affinity for each other started out benignly, but as the months and years passed by, the friendship went beyond a singular transgression of the heart and became a scandal and a byword. Attention to the whole affair brought to church leadership a vexation of spirit that could not be diminished by passiveness or inaction. At last, in apparent exasperation at Waggoner's silence regarding her personal attempts to intervene on his behalf and bring about repentance in his conduct as well as conversion of heart, Ellen White wrote to Elder Butler on September 6, 1886, from Basel, Switzerland (citing the cases of two other ministers as examples):

> I am troubled in regard to Elder [J. H.] Waggoner. He writes me nothing, and I feel deeply pained on his account. It seems sometimes to me that the Lord is testing us to see whether we will deal faithfully in regard to sin in one of our honored men. The time is close at hand when the General Conference will have to decide the point, whether or not to renew his credentials....
>
> The persistency in Elder Waggoner to accept and claim Mrs. Chittenden as his—what shall I call it—his affinity? What is this? Who can name it? Is Elder Waggoner one who has hated the light God has given him, showing that his preferences for Mrs. Chittenden's society and his intimacy with her, was sinful as in the light of the Word of God? Or did he accept the message and act upon it?
>
> Notwithstanding, I went to Elder Waggoner with the testimony given me of God, yet he did not reform. His course has said, "I will do as I please in the matter; there is no sin in it." He promised before God what he would do, but he broke his promise, made to Brother C. H. Jones, W. C. White, and myself, and his feelings did not decidedly change; but he seemed to act like a man bewitched, under the spell of the devil, who had no power over his own inclinations. Notwithstanding all the light given, he has evidenced no real conviction

---

34   Whidden, *E. J. Waggoner: From the Physician of Good News to Agent of Division*, 23, 24.
35   Ibid., 27, 28.

or sense of sin, no repentance, no reformation. Hearts have ached sorely over this state of things, but they had no power to change his heart or his purposes....

The plague of sin is upon Elder Waggoner, and pain and sorrow are upon the souls of all who are aware of this chapter in his experience. Christ is dishonored. A man blessed with superior light and knowledge, endowed with great capacity for good, that he may by a life of obedience and fidelity to God become equal with angels, [and] his life measure with the life of God, has perverted his God-given power to administer to lust, coveting the wife of another. God finds Elder Waggoner setting at naught the most costly lessons of experience, violating the most solemn admonitions of God, that he may continue in sin.

I have hoped and prayed that he would restore reason to its right throne and break the fetters that for years Satan has been weaving about him, soul and body, and that the clouds that have shadowed his pathway be removed and Christ come to his soul to revive and bless it. Christ will lift the heavy burden from weary shoulders, and give rest and peace to those who will wear His yoke and lift His burdens....

Your case has been shown me to be worse than that of Elder Cornell, because you had greater light, capacity, and influence; and his course is a beacon to warn you off from following in his steps. Elder Cornell's credentials were taken away from him; he is a deeply repenting man, humbled in the dust....

I have felt, for your sake, restrained from opening the matter of Mrs. Chittenden's infidelity to her husband, but I fear I have neglected my duty. If we had dealt with this matter as if it had been the case of a lay member of the church, I believe God would have then sent you repentance that needed not to be repented of.

Our pity, our love, to save you from reproach, has hurt you. My heart is so sad and agonized at times for you, I can only weep. I say, Must he be lost? Must he after suffering for the truth's sake, after standing in its defense until he is old and gray-headed, become an idolater, as did Solomon? Will he, for the love of a woman, trample down the law of God and look about him as much as to say, I do no sin; I am all right?

Will we be clear to let such things be concealed and sins hidden, with no real evidence of repentance or reform? Your leaving California does not give you a new heart. You are out of sight of the infatuating influence of your "adorable charmer," but this does not change the affections or impulses of the heart. Elder Himes might have finished his course with joy had it not been for sensual practices, but he was led away of his own lusts and enticed. The days and years which might have been his very best were his worst....

Now the question is, Will those who profess the truth comply with the conditions? Will the characters of those who profess to believe the truth correspond with its sacredness? Satan's special efforts are now directed toward the people who have great light. He would lead them to become earthly and sensual. There are men who minister in sacred things whose hearts are defiled with impure thoughts and unholy desires. Married men who have children are not satisfied. They place themselves where they invite temptation. They take liberties which should only be taken with their lawful wives. Thus they fall under the rebuke of God, and in the books of heaven "Adultery" is written opposite their names.

There should be no approach to danger. If the thoughts were where they should be, if they were stayed upon God, and the meditations of the soul were upon the truth and the precious promises of God and the heavenly reward that awaits the faithful, they would be guarded against Satan's temptations. But, by many, vile thoughts are entertained almost constantly. They are carried into the house of God and even into the sacred desk.[36]

Why have I been so thorough in dredging up this particular scandal in Adventist history? Why is it so important? What is the point?

While J. H. Waggoner was involved in his affinity with Mrs. Chittenden, he wrote something that smacks of the language used by others who teach free love theology. He inserted the subtle departure from truth, laying a foundation for future and further departure, by stating:

The great question to be decided is this: In what respect is the gospel plan unconditional, and in what respect is it conditional? If there is anywhere such a distinction, and if we can clearly trace the line, the subject must thereby be relieved of much difficulty. Examining this, we find that,

1. The introduction of the gospel, or setting forth of Christ as the way of salvation, was unconditional. But,

2. The application of the gospel to individual salvation, is conditional.

We do not see how any, who believe the Bible, can dissent from either of these declarations. It is not said to the world, nor to any class in the world, that if they would do some certain thing Christ should die for them. But it is said that if they will believe and do certain things, they shall be saved by his blood so freely shed for the sins of the world. "God so loved the world, that he gave his only begotten Son, that whosoever believeth in him should not perish, but have everlasting life." John 3:16. *Freely and unconditionally he gave his Son to be a propitiation for the sins of the whole world, to die for all,* but not so that they will be saved from perishing if they refuse to repent and believe. Salvation was freely purchased by the death of Christ, but will never be given to those who neglect it. Hebrews 2:3. *Eternal life through Christ was freely and unconditionally brought to man,* Romans 6:23; yet, if they would not perish they must "lay hold on eternal life;" 1 Timothy 6:19; which they can only secure "by patient continuance in well-doing;" Romans 2:7; and so "work out their own salvation with fear and trembling." Philippians 2:12. But in uniting works to faith we detract nothing from the grace and glory of Christ, for we can do nothing in our own

---

36   Ellen G. White, *Manuscript Releases*, vol. 21 (Silver Spring, MD: Ellen G. White Estate, 1993), 378–385.

unassisted strength. John 15:5. With this distinction in view we find no difficulty in harmonizing all the Scriptures. But we will notice a few texts to further show the conditional nature of God's promises to man.[37]

Herein lies the problem: Jesus, though a gift from the Father, had conditions He had to meet on behalf of the fallen race in order to secure our salvation. And that plan included the work of sanctification, which we must engage in after accepting Christ so that we may become fully conformed to the character of Christ.

Not too long after Waggoner published his work, Ellen White made a number of statements that contradict his position.

> Christ would never have left the royal courts and taken humanity, and become sin for the race, had He not seen that man might, with His help, become infinitely happy and obtain durable riches and a life that would run parallel with the life of God.[38]

> Christ would never have given His life for the human race if He had not faith in the souls for whom He died. He knew that a large number would respond to the love He had expressed for humanity.[39]

Christ would never have given His life for the human race if He had not faith in the souls for whom He died.

When you look at the cross of Calvary, you cannot doubt God's love or His willingness to save. He has worlds upon worlds that give Him divine honor, and heaven and all the universe would have been just as happy if He had left this world to perish; but so great was His love for the fallen race that He gave His own dear Son to die that they might be redeemed from eternal death. As we see the care, the love, that God has for us, let us respond to it; let us give to Jesus all the powers of our being, fighting manfully the battles of the Lord. We cannot afford to lose our souls; we cannot afford to sin against God. Life, eternal life in the kingdom of glory, is worth everything. But if we would obtain this precious boon, we must live a life of obedience to all of God's requirements; we must carry out the principles of the Christian religion in our daily life.[40]

---

37   J. H. Waggoner, *The Atonement* (Mountain View, CA: Pacific Press Publishing Association, 1884), 339, 340, emphasis added.

38   Ellen G. White, *Testimonies for the Church*, vol. 3 (Mountain View, CA: Pacific Press Publishing Association, 1875), 540; Ellen G. White, "The Spirit of Christ," *The Review and Herald*, June 22, 1886.

39   White, *Manuscript Releases*, vol. 21, 370.

40   Ellen G. White, "The Government of God," *The Review and Herald*, March 9, 1886.

Christ was the one who consented to meet the conditions necessary for man's salvation. No angel, no man, was sufficient for the great work to be wrought. The Son of man alone must be lifted up; for only an infinite nature could undertake the redemptive process. Christ consented to connect himself with the disloyal and sinful, to partake of the nature of man, to give his own blood, and to make his soul an offering for sin. *In the counsels of heaven, the guilt of man was measured, the wrath for sin was estimated, and yet Christ announced his decision that he would take upon himself the responsibility of meeting the conditions whereby hope should be extended to a fallen race.* He understood the possibility of the human soul, and united humanity to himself, even as the vine knits the grafted branches and twigs into its being, until, vein by vein, and fiber by fiber, the branches are united to the living Vine.[41]

Who imposed the conditions that Jesus must meet to save humanity? The fallen? No. God, who is love, presented the conditions of an unselfish love that can never be separated from justice and righteousness.

One cannot separate the *introduction* of the gospel from its *application*, or *implementation*, as J. H. Waggoner attempted to do. As Ellen White wrote, in order to exonerate God and demonstrate His fairness before the universe, the plan of salvation has conditions firmly fixed in the foundation of unselfish love with its covenant relationships:

> It was in order that the heavenly universe might see the conditions of the covenant of re-demption that Christ bore the penalty in behalf of the human race. The throne of Justice must be eternally and forever made secure, even tho the race be wiped out, and another creation populate the earth. By the sacrifice Christ was about to make, all doubts would be forever settled, and the human race would be saved if they would return to their alle-giance. Christ alone could restore honor to God's government. The cross of Calvary would be looked upon by the unfallen worlds, by the heavenly universe, by Satanic agencies, by the fallen race, and every mouth would be stopped. In making His infinite sacrifice Christ would exalt and honor the law. He would make known the exalted character of God's gov-ernment, which could not in any way be changed to meet man in his sinful condition.[42]

Happily, Joseph H. Waggoner repented of his illicit relationship(s) before his death in 1889. At the end of his life of ministry, he was an editor of the publishing work established in Basel, Switzerland, and contributed to the notes prepared for Ellen G. White's book *The Great Controversy* (1888). But the concept of "free love"

---

41   Ellen G. White, "Divinity in Humanity," *The Signs of the Times*, March 5, 1896, emphasis added.

42   Ellen G. White, "A Crucified and Risen Saviour," *The Signs of the Times*, July 12, 1899. The language of this statement indi-cates that God had at least two options: destroy the rebellious race and create another in its place, or redeem the repentant rebels through the atoning blood of Jesus Christ, who meets all the conditions of love on behalf of those who believe and accept the peace Christ makes for us.

practiced all those years by both father and mother had its deleterious effects upon their son Ellet J. Waggoner. The seeds were sown; they lay dormant in the soil of his character, awaiting the right moment to germinate and grow.

Other books more adequately deal with the positive and powerful ministry of E. J. Waggoner leading up to and immediately following the General Conference session held in Minneapolis, Minnesota, in 1888.[43] However, to stay focused on the history of free love, unconditional love, and unqualified love, this text addresses how Ellet Joseph Waggoner slipped into mystic theology, which amounts to spiritualism, and applied and mingled his ideas about spiritual wifery and unqualified love with the gospel.

Shortly after a stinging defeat of his independent, congregational approach to church organization at the Swansea Conference in South Wales in 1903, he decided to accept a position at the newly formed Emmanuel Missionary College in Berrien Springs, Michigan. The steamship voyage found the Waggoner family divided between two berths—his wife, Jessie, and two daughters in one, and Ellet in another across the hall. Apparently Eddie Spicer, a former employee of the International Tract Society, and an acquaintance of Jessie's from either Sabbath school or one of the Sunday school groups in London, also made the transatlantic voyage at this time.[44] But if Jessie supposedly was infatuated with Eddie as Pearl Waggoner Howard (a daughter sharing her memory of the trip) alleges, Ellet definitely had an affinity for Edith Adams—most likely initiated long before their departure from Britain in 1903. To complicate matters, Ms. Adams moved to Battle Creek, Michigan, eighteen months later to begin a job with Good Health Publishing Company and became a boarder at the Waggoner's home.

Within six weeks of close habitation, for both Eddie and Edith were boarders in the Waggoner's modest house, Jessie filed for divorce without any claim to "interests in property, and not to obtain further relief" from the defendant.[45] Little more than two weeks later, after he failed to appear in court regarding the divorce within the time allotted, proceedings commenced without any input on his behalf, for he waived his rights to a rebuttal by his absence.

Ellet complacently believed Jessie would proceed with the divorce on grounds of incompatibility. But Jessie, apparently convinced by her attorney, wanted the divorce on biblical grounds, for much had been written by the Pen of Inspiration about the basis of divorce, including: "A woman may be legally divorced from her husband by the laws of the land, and yet not divorced in the sight of God and according to the higher law. There is only one sin, which is adultery, which can place the husband or wife in a position where they can be free from the marriage vow in the sight of God. Although the laws of the land may grant a divorce, yet they are husband and wife still in the Bible light, according to the laws of God."[46]

---

43   Eric C. Webster, *Crosscurrents in Adventist Christology* (New York: Peter Lang, 1984, republished by Andrews University Press, 1992); George R. Knight, *Angry Saints: Tensions and Possibilities in the Adventist Struggle Over Righteousness by Faith* (Hagerstown, MD: Review and Herald Publishing Assn., 1989); and Whidden, *E. J. Waggoner: From the Physician of Good News to Agent of Division*. These are just a few books written about E. J. Waggoner.

44   Whidden, *E. J. Waggoner: From the Physician of Good News to Agent of Division*, 332.

45   The circuit court records for Calhoun County show that Eddie Spicer served Ellet J. Waggoner with the subpoena on September 13, 1905, two days after it was issued.

46   Ellen G. White, *Manuscript Releases*, vol. 1 (Silver Spring, MD: Ellen G. White Estate, 1981), 159.

In her formal complaint, which was registered in the Circuit Court of Calhoun County on September 11, 1905, Jessie swears that she "has ever since marriage, demeaned herself to the said Ellet J. Waggoner, as a faithful chaste and affectionate wife," evidenced by the birth of two daughters, both in their early twenties by this time.[47] The complaint clearly placed the onus upon Ellet, charging him with multiple counts of adultery with persons unknown, in addition to Edith Adams, while absolving Jessie of any wrongdoing alleged by her younger daughter Pearl.

Ellet was annoyed at the results of the proceedings, notwithstanding the testimonies of Eddie Spicer and Johannes Hanson certified and deposed against him. The only recourse he believed he had open to him for the purpose of clearing the reputation of Edith Adams, if not his own, was by publishing a defense in both the Battle Creek *Morning Enquirer* and the Battle Creek *Daily Journal*. The articles appeared in the January 15, 1906, issues, which was more than two weeks after the divorce was finalized according to the circuit court records of the divorce.

However, in a letter to Alonzo T. Jones, dated April 9, 1906, Ellen White emphatically stated, "Elder Waggoner has been an injury. In the European field for a long time he has sown seeds that have and will bear evil fruit, leading some to depart from the faith, and to give heed to seducing spirits, doctrines of Satanic origin. Unless he is converted, he is not fitted to act any part in the ministry of the word. He is a decided transgressor of the seventh commandment."

Jessie never remarried, although she spent considerable time in the company of Eddie Spicer. She accompanied him to Kankakee, Illinois, and Toledo, Ohio, where Eddie apparently ended their association.[48]

Alonzo T. Jones, Waggoner's partner in preaching the righteousness by faith message in 1888, presided over Ellet's marriage to Edith Adams on September 17, 1906, in Ann Arbor, Michigan.[49] Waggoner never rejoined the ministry in the Seventh-day Adventist Church.[50]

Again, you may be wondering why we are examining the marriages and adulterous affairs of these Adventist pioneers. But it goes back to the thought process of free love or unconditional love. Waggoner departed from the faith he first preached because he began believing in "unqualified love" in relation to marriages formed for selfish reasons. It was imperceptible at first, but once he began to ignore the truth, he continued to slide down this perilously slippery slope. In the end he believed in mysticism and the pantheistic approach to the indwelling presence of God in all humanity, whether repentant or not.

The idea of free love was present in an article that appeared in *Present Truth* in 1898. While serving as editor of the magazine in Britain, Waggoner wrote the following extreme position on unselfish love, which is clearly contradicted by Scripture:

---

47   Although the document was signed by Jessie, the official complaint was apparently prepared by her attorney James L. Powers.

48   Whidden, *E. J. Waggoner: From the Physician of Good News to Agent of Division*, 333.

49   Dr. Whidden's book states that the exact date and place of their marriage is unknown, for the Calhoun County court records do not contain a marriage license for the couple (Ibid., 334, 343). However, after searching the court records in Washtenaw County, their marriage certificate was found. Apparently, Ellet and Edith did not wish further notoriety in Calhoun County so soon after making a public pronouncement of innocence after the scandalous divorce, they got married in another county. (I give profound thanks to Steve Emse of Scotland, Connecticut, for helping me locate this and other details regarding this history.)

50   See pages 354–369 in Dr. Whidden's book for an explanation of the theological reasons why Waggoner refused to reunite with the ministry.

Love Is Unselfishness. –This follows from the foregoing; for since love means service, and service means the doing of something for others, it is evident that love takes no thought of itself, and that he who loves has no thought but of how he may bless others. So we read, "Love suffereth long, and is kind; love envieth not; love vaunteth not itself, is not puffed up, doth not behave itself unseemly, seeketh not its own, is not provoked, taketh not account of evil." 1 Cor. xiii. 4, 5, R.V.

A Deplorable Error. –It is just on this vital point that everybody in the world is making or has made a mistake. Happy are they who have found out their mistake, and have come to the understanding and practice of true love. "Love seeketh not her own." Therefore self-love is not love at all, in the right sense of the word. It is only a base counterfeit. Yet the most of that which in the world is called love, is not really love for another, but is love of self. Even that which should be the highest form of love known on earth, the love which is used by the Lord as a representation of His love for His people,—the love of husband and wife,—is more often selfishness than real love. *Leaving out of the question, as unworthy of notice, marriages that are formed for the purpose of gaining wealth or position in society, it is a fact, which all will recognise when their attention is called to it, that in nearly every case the parties to a marriage are thinking more of their own individual happiness than of the happiness of the other.* Of course this condition of things exists in varying degrees, and in proportion as real, unselfish love exists, is there real happiness; for it is a lesson that the world is slow to learn, that true happiness is found only when one ceases to seek for it, and sets about making it for others.

"Love Never Faileth." –These are the words of Inspiration, found in 1 Cor. xiii. 8. Here, again, is a test which shows that much that is called love is not love. Love never ceases. The statement is absolute, never. There is no exception, and no allowance made for circumstances. Love is not affected by circumstances. We often hear about one's love growing cold, but that is something that can never happen. Love is always warm, always flowing: nothing can freeze the fountain of love. Presently we shall better understand why this is so; *but now it is sufficient for us to learn the fact that love is absolutely endless.* We have the Word of the Lord for this, and that should be enough. We may reject love, we may refuse to love, we may drive love from our hearts; but the quality of love is unchanging.

Love Is Subjective. –Perhaps this sub-title needs explanation. It means simply this, that *love depends upon the individual who loves, and not upon the one loved.* That is really to say, as already said, that *love does not depend on circumstances. Love is impartial and unlimited.* The word "neighbour" means whatever dwells near. Love, therefore, extends to everything with which it comes in contact. *He who loves must necessarily love everybody.*

Right here it may be objected that love does make distinctions, and the case of husband and wife, or of any of the members of a family, may be cited. But the objection does not hold, for the family relation, rightly understood, was institute in order that by a union love might the more effectually be manifested to others. On the principle that strength is not merely doubled, but increased tenfold, by union, as shown by the statement that "one shall chase a thousand, and two put ten thousand to flight," union multiplies the working value of love. If two persons, each of whom has this unselfish love to all mankind, unite in love, then their union makes them ten times better able to serve others. "That is too high an ideal," you say. Well, we are talking of a very great and high thing now; *we are talking of love, absolute and unqualified.* Poor, frail, needy human beings can not afford to accept anything but the best.

Why Love. –Sometimes when a declaration of love is made, the loved one asks, "Why do you love me?" Just as if anybody could give a reason for love! *Love is its own reason. If the lover can tell just why he loves another, then that very answer shows that he does not really love.* See; Whatever object he names as a reason for love, may sometime cease to exist, and then his supposed love ceases to exist; but "love never faileth." Therefore love can not depend upon circumstances. So the only answer that can be given to the question as to why one loves, is, "because;" because of love. Love *loves*, simply because it is love. *Love is the quality of the individual who loves, and he loves because he has love, irrespective of the character of the object.*[51]

Within this discourse Waggoner relies on the Revised Version Bible translation. This is probably because of Waggoner's acceptance of Wescott and Hort's take on unconditional love ("seeketh not its own, is not provoked, taketh not account of evil" [1 Cor. 13:5]) as opposed of the rendering given in the King James Version ("seeketh not her own, is not easily provoked, thinketh no evil"). This mystical, subjective approach to defining love lends itself to antinomianism because it does away with the objective principles and characteristics of love as set forth in God's moral law, which includes provocations and keeping record of wrongs within the context of long-suffering forbearance.

Waggoner would repeat these sentiments again in the book *The Glad Tidings*:

Sometimes when a declaration of love is made, the loved one asks, "Why do you love me?" Just as if anybody could give a reason for love! *Love is its own reason. If the lover can tell just why he loves another, then that very answer shows that he does not really love.* Whatever object he names as a reason for love, may sometime cease to exist, and then his supposed love ceases to exist; but "love never faileth." Therefore love can not depend upon circumstances. So the only answer that can be given to the question as to why one loves, is "because," because of love. *Love loves, simply because it is love.* Love is the quality of the individual who loves, and he loves because he has love, irrespective of the character of the object. *The truth of this is seen when we go back to God, the Fountain of love. He is love;*

---

51   E. J. Waggoner, "The Epistle to the Galatians. Love, the Fulfilling of the Law," *The Present Truth*, April 28, 1898, emphasis added.

love is His life; but no explanation of His existence can be given. The highest human conception of love is to love because we are loved, or because the object of our love is lovable. *But God loves the unlovely, and those who hate Him.* 'We also were aforetime foolish, disobedient, deceived, serving divers lusts and pleasures, living in malice and envy, hateful, hating one another. But when the kindness of God our Saviour, and His love toward man, appeared, not by works done in righteousness, which we did ourselves, but according to His mercy He saved us.' Titus 3:3,4, R.V. 'If ye love them which love you, what reward have ye? do not even the publicans the same?' 'Be ye therefore perfect, even as your Father which is in heaven is perfect.' Matt. 5:46,48....

"Love worketh no ill to his neighbor." The word "neighbor" means whoever dwells near. Love, therefore, extends to everything with which it comes in contact. He who loves must necessarily love everybody. It may be objected that love does make distinctions, and the case of husband and wife, or of any of the members of a family, may be cited. But the objection does not hold, for the family relation, rightly understood, was instituted in order that by a union love might the more effectually be manifested to others. On the principle that strength is not merely doubled, but increased tenfold, by union, as shown by the statement that "one shall chase a thousand, and two put ten thousand to flight," union multiplies the working value of love. If two persons, each of whom has this unselfish love to all mankind, unite in love, then their union makes them ten times better able to serve others. If any one thinks this is too high a standard, let him remember that we are considering a very high thing—the highest thing in the universe. *We are talking of love, absolute and unqualified, as it comes from heaven, and not that which has been dragged through the mire of earth.* Poor, frail human beings certainly need the very best.[52]

Three years before Ellen White wrote to A. T. Jones regarding the ill effect to be expected from Waggoner's pantheistic ideas and his lifestyle, which was consistent with a false theory on love, she wrote directly to Waggoner and shared her concerns with him about the path of his life:

You have been represented to me as being in great peril. Satan is on your track, and at times he has whispered to you pleasing fables and has shown you charming pictures of one whom he represents as a more suitable companion for you than the wife of your youth, the mother of your children.

Satan is working stealthily, untiringly, to effect your downfall through his specious temptations. He is determined to become your teacher, and you need now to place yourself where you can get strength to resist him. *He hopes to lead you into the mazes of spiritualism. He hopes to wean your affections from your wife, and to fix them upon another woman. He*

---

52   E. J. Waggoner, *The Glad Tidings* (Oakland, CA: Pacific Press Publishing Company, 1900), 215, 216, emphasis added.

desires that you shall allow your mind to dwell upon this woman, until through unholy affection she becomes your god.

The enemy of souls has gained much when he can lead the imagination of one of Jehovah's chosen watchmen to dwell upon the possibilities of association, in the world to come, with some woman whom he loves, and of there raising up a family. We need no such pleasing pictures. All such views originate in the mind of the tempter.

> *Satan is working stealthily, untiringly ... determined to become your teacher ... He hopes to lead you into the mazes of spiritualism.*

We have the plain assurance of Christ that in the world to come, the redeemed "neither marry, nor are given in marriage: neither can they die anymore: for they are equal unto the angels; and are the children of God, being the children of the resurrection."

It is presented to me that spiritual fables are taking many captive. Their minds are sensual, and, unless a change comes, this will prove their ruin. To all who are indulging these unholy fancies I would say, Stop; for Christ's sake, stop right where you are. You are on forbidden ground. Repent, I entreat of you, and be converted.[53]

Not long after Waggoner published *Glad Tidings* (1900), in which he discussed at length his association of unselfish love with unqualified love (which is by definition associated with spiritual affinities), the General Conference met in session at Battle Creek (April 2–23, 1901). Both Waggoner and Prescott requested an interview with Ellen White, which she refused to grant. Later, she wrote to Prescott about the reasons why she refused to meet with them:

> I have been shown your peril during the time of your connecting with Dr. E. J. Waggoner. You both came to the [General] Conference [session] of 1901 enthused with what you supposed to be precious spiritual light. You were desirous of presenting this light to me, but I was shown that much of that which you supposed to be precious light was dangerous, misleading fables, and that I must have no conversation with you regarding these ideas that were filling your minds.
>
> The theories held by Ellet Waggoner were similar in character to those we had met and rebuked in several places where we met fanatical movements after the passing of the time in 1844. *Dr. Waggoner was then departing from the faith in the doctrine he held regarding spiritual affinities.*[54]

---

53   White, *Medical Ministry*, 100, 101.
54   Ellen G. White, *Manuscript Releases*, vol. 12 (Silver Spring, MD: Ellen G. White Estate, 1990), 62, 63.

Ellen White had already made several strong statements regarding marriage and how fanciful views would distort the truth and lead people to commit the worst imaginable evils. The timing of these statements, sometimes in multiple publications with very close issuance dates, indicates just how seriously she took the matter of unconditional, unqualified love and its connection to spiritualism in the form of spiritual affinity, or spiritual wifery, like these statements vigorously upholding the standard of righteousness against such crimes as abortion:

> Marriage has received Christ's blessing, and it is to be regarded as a sacred institution. True religion does not counterwork the Lord's plans. God ordained that man and woman should be united in holy wedlock, to raise up families that, crowned with honour, would be symbols of the family in heaven. And at the beginning of His public ministry Christ gave His decided sanction to the institution that had been sanctioned in Eden. Thus He declared to all that He will not refuse His presence on marriage occasions, and that marriage, when joined with purity and holiness, truth and righteousness, is one of the greatest blessings ever given to the human family. Priests and popes have made laws forbidding people to marry, and secluding them in monasteries. These laws and restrictions were devised by Satan to place men and women in unnatural positions. Thus Satan has tempted human beings to disregard the law of marriage as a thing unholy, but at the same time he has opened the door for the indulgence of human passion. Thus have come into existence some of the greatest evils which curse our world,—adultery, fornication, and the murder of innocent children born out of wedlock.[55]

These evils, which spawned from spiritual wifery, spiritual affinity, unconditional/unqualified love, and free-lovism, were recognized by ministers outside the Seventh-day Adventist Church as well. One Presbyterian clergyman denounced the doctrine of devils prophesied as making headway within various denominations. Quoting from Revelation 16:14 and 1 Timothy 4:1, he stated:

> I have important facts to publish which show the fulfillment of this prophecy. My acquaintance with Spiritualism, so called, and various forms of delusion which have appeared among christians [sic.], enable me to furnish startling information to the professedly evangelical masses concerning the strange Satanic power which is now sweeping through the world in these last days....
>
> What I want is to show what this Spiritualism is so that all who have eyes can see it. The

---

55   Ellen G. White, "The Marriage in Galilee," *The Bible Echo*, August 28, 1899. Interestingly enough, Waggoner at one time wrote something similar: "The social relations exhibited, if possible, even deeper corruption. The sanctity of marriage had ceased. Female dissipation and the general dissoluteness led at last to an almost entire cessation of marriage. Abortion, and the exposure and murder of newly-born children, were common and tolerated; unnatural vices, which even the greatest philosophers practiced, if not advocated, attained proportions which defy description" (E. J. Waggoner, *Fathers of the Catholic Church* [Oakland, CA: Pacific Press Publishing Company, 1888], 25).

rapping and table tipping circles are only one of its developments. Its orthodox circles exist on a much larger and more dangerous scale because less suspected....

First, it is needful to remark that spiritualism like the father of lies, always appears as an angel of light. It is full of love, sympathy, tenderness in its professions. It is bland in its address, flattering, speaks well of everybody and every thing which is not opposed to itself. It apologizes freely for sin, preaches love, peace, and comfort to all classes, and lulls their consciences to sleep, and generally flatters the people with ideas of progress, that the world is getting better and better; in these respects it is directly the reverse of the religion, of Jesus Christ. This is hated because of its reproofs and utter conflict with all worldly desires and hopes of men....

You cannot attend its meetings without danger of being made insensible to its fatal errors, and drawn hopelessly under their influence....

All the reform movements of the day which are outside of simple gospel work are wholly in the Spiritualist drift, resulting directly from false views of sin. As though healing these physical evils could touch man's moral state! Such men show they don't know what sin is. They have no conscience; their idea of sin is only physical inconvenience. They hate it only on selfish, not on moral grounds. Hence they doctor it on selfish and carnal principles.

All religion which betrays this want of conscience which makes outward reform instead of righteousness the end, or which makes happiness and human convenience instead of God and his law the end is a spiritualist religion. All this seeking blessings and happiness at meetings, instead of seeking God and holiness is of the same nature. Going to meeting to have a good time, to have self-enjoyment is no better than going to the theatre. Hence many think meetings a total failure where they don't get happy, or where the truth makes confusion as it did in meetings where Christ, Steven, and apostles preached. Such christians [*sic*.] are spiritualists.

All who place peace before purity, who make union, love and harmony their end, instead of truth and righteousness, are on Spiritualist ground....

Spiritualism is always opposed to Judging. This follows of course from a loss of conscience. You never saw a regular spiritualist but would judge you sharply, if you judged any body for sin. If you reprove and disfellowship one for sin, it will always quote Matt 7: 1st. "Judge not." and preach as a charity which covers up sin, and fellowships as brethren all who practice it. It thus teaches a love which would send a brother to hell, just such love as Satan has for all sinners. No man who has a true sense of sin would ever thus pervert the

> *A love which is opposed to God's law is itself sin, and all there is of sin.*

texts of Scripture about judging.

The Bible does not prohibit judgment, but makes it a necessity of all gospel work, and says "Reprove, rebuke, exhort, &c." It only requires that we first pluck the beam from our own eyes, that is get converted ourselves before we undertake to convert others, and that we judge righteously, and that we judge not brethren in nonessentials....

[Free loveism, false charity] ... is the central and distinctive mark of Spiritualism. The life and power of this delusion is *Free Love*. It comprehends vastly more however than orthodox proffessors generally dream. Multitudes who are themselves Free-lovers, and leading advocates of the same, would be astonished and horified to have this reputation, just because they don't know what it means and are ignorant of the Spiritualist power they are under. But what is this *Free Love* by a gospel estimate? It is simply this: LOVE WITHOUT A CONSCIENCE, or LOVE REGARDLESS OF GOD'S LAW. This, and this only is the horrible sin and delusion. It is the whole of it, and this is the substance and whole of Spiritualism the damning moral epidemic of these lost days.

Any thing that is love is supposed to be virtuous, but this is a fatal mistake. Unholy love is the essence of sin, just as holy love is the substance of purity. A love which is opposed to God's law is itself sin, and all there is of sin. This only is what makes the devil vile, nothing else but unholy love. The life of sin is love, just, as the life of holiness is love. A love which fellowships sinners, which loves God's enemies as such, and treats them just as though they were innocent, is itself rebellion against God, and the very filth and scum of hell. But no one ever heard a Spiritualist medium lecture, but this idea of love would be brought out which treats sinners as innocent, and their sin as an infirmity to excite pity, and not displeasure. Love itself is made the panacea for all sin, its atonement, and sacrifice, the sole ground of pardon and the healing balm. That love which thus treats the sinner as if he were innocent, even loves him all the more for his sins, most manifestly conflicts with God's law which treats the sinner as infinitely deserving damnation. It is the vilest of all iniquity. And this is free-love, Spiritualism whether it is found is orthodox or heterodox meetings.... You hear no more the stern denunciations of God's law to sinners, and separation from their fellowship, purging out the buyers and sellers, having a holy church as formerly, but indiscriminate fellowship, and honied words of love every where to sinners, especially to business sinners or such as have money and social position. This love gospel is all there is of Spiritualism. It is *free loveism*. To give loose reins to adulterous passions cannot make a man any more vile....

The essential character of Spiritualism is also marked by either denying or subverting the atonement. Even the wicked world have in every age recognized the true nature of sin by offering sacrifice, and seeking to propitiate deity in times of peril. But Spiritualism, true to its nature, having no sense of sin discards this idea of sacrifice, and makes love take its place as the ground of atonement and reconciliation of God to the sinner.... They shrewdly employ orthodox words, but wholly reject that view of sin which requires a sacrifice to propipitate God or to satisfy justice. They base salvation on the *unqualified and unconditional love of God* to the sinner, but a love which turns God into a devil. The radical idea of the gospel, essential to its moral character and to infinite purity, is "Without the shedding of blood there is no remission of sins." That God could not forgive it, or even love the sinner without a sacrifice which righteous law demanded. O the depths of that subtlety which makes love the basis of the sinner's hope, and the cross only a farce sweeping justice and purity from the throne of God betrays more than any thing else the mind and genius of the father of lies! This theology of spiritualism pervades nearly the whole orthodox church.

There is another school of this same Spiritualism tenacious of the old theology who err on the opposite side. They make Christ's death so atone for sin that all sinners are free if they will only believe it, even while they continue in sin. Indeed they are taught that they cannot cease from sin, must sin a little, and yet they are free from its guilt and may rejoice in God if they can only so believe Christ. This is just as dangerous a class of free-lovers as the opposite. They turn the grace of God into lasciviousness, make Calvary a curse and a lie, and make the gospel and love of Christ the vilest iniquity. These perversions of the atonement betray the loss of conscience, and satanic power of Spiritualism....

Spiritualism repudiates any uniform law by which we can estimate the character of others. Each man has his own ideas, education or nature, so that we cannot tell absolutely what may be right for him, so that we cannot judge his character. Thus do they excuse sin or crime. Whoever you hear use this reason against condemning men for sin, you may know they are Spiritualists. This is a prominent and distinctive feature of this delusion.[56]

Clearly, this minister had a gift to discern the spirit behind the message of unqualified and unconditional, free love. Consistent with Johnson's conclusions we see what the apostle James wrote about discernment and wisdom: "This wisdom descendeth not from above, but *is* earthly, sensual, devilish.... But the wisdom that is from above is first pure, then peaceable, gentle, *and* easy to be intreated, full of mercy and good fruits, without partiality, and without hypocrisy."[57] In a later chapter we will see how this discernment regarding the penal substitution theory of atonement comes under attack, especially from theologians promoting the emerging church.

We cannot emphasize enough how dangerous these love-sick sentimental theories are when the soul is left unguarded. Again, Ellen White relates the burden of her soul as she worked in cooperation with God's Spirit to snatch souls as brands from the burning throughout her ministry, but especially early on:

Among them were brethren and sisters whom I loved and highly esteemed. They had believed the testimonies that I had borne to the people. But they had been led astray by

56   Lyman H. Johnson, "Spiritualism, Or Devil Worship," *The Stumblingstone*, vol. 2, no. 12, January 1872, emphasis added.
57   James 3:15, 17

spiritualistic ideas which were nothing less than a love-sick sentimentalism. The power of God came upon me as I warned them of their dangers, and some said they had never expected to see so much of the blessing of God this side of the Eden above. I bore them a message similar to the message I have been bearing for the last two months. I was instructed that the ideas they had accepted were but the alpha of a great deception. I had to meet similar delusions in Portsmouth and in Boston.

These doctrines led to free-loveism, and my heart was sorely grieved as I saw the result they brought to those who accepted them. One family who for years had lived happily together was broken up. A man and his wife, well advanced in years, were separated. The husband left his wife and children, and established other family relations. We seemed to be able to do nothing to break the spell upon these persons. The precious truths of the Bible had no influence over them.

This same hypnotic influence is seen working among our people today.[58]

What effect does this have on us today as individuals and as a denomination? Have we learned anything from our history, or do we walk around with the self-assurance that we are God's people and are therefore as infallible as God Himself? Sadly, it seems that far too many of us are ignorant and self-deceived on this issue. So let us continue with perseverance to learn more about what our contemporary history has to reveal on the subject.

The church must have received quite a shock to lose so many beloved ministers and physicians to the influence of Kellogg, Jones, Tenney, and Waggoner.[59] It appears that for a time all talk of free-loveism, or unqualified, unconditional love, died down, but only a few short years after Ellen White's death, we start to see the idea of free-loveism promoted once again, though sparingly.

John Orr Corliss enjoyed having J. H. Waggoner as a teacher and tutor in the biblical languages. "Amid his many and heavy duties, he found time to master Greek and Hebrew, that he might delve deeper into the Scriptures. Best of all, he could make plain to others what he himself had learned. He was indeed a natural teacher, as the writer can truthfully testify; for he was able to give him help in the last-named language that his regular teacher seemed unable to bestow. It mattered not how busy he might be as editor of the *Signs of the Times*, during the years he acted as such, he was always approachable, and ready to assist any one needing help."[60]

With such a relationship, one might conclude that he was influenced by both Waggoners' theology when he took a very subjective approach to the nature of God's love in his writing in *The Signs of the Times*:

---

58   White, *Manuscript Releases*, vol. 11, 247, 248.

59   "A. T. Jones, Dr. Kellogg, and Elder Tenney are all working under the same leadership. They are classing themselves with those of whom the apostle writes, 'Some shall depart from the faith, giving heed to seducing spirits and doctrines of devils.' In the case of A. T. Jones, I can see the fulfillment of the warnings that were given me regarding him" (Ellen G. White, *Loma Linda Messages* [Payson, AZ: Leaves-Of-Autumn Books, 1981], 276).

60   John Orr Corliss, "The Message and Its Friends—No. 7: J. H. Waggoner, Theologian and Editor," *The Advent Review and Sabbath Herald*, vol. 100, no. 39, September 27, 1923, 6.

Man was created for heavenly fellowship, and so was made in the very image of his Maker, that he might be fit for such relationship. Thus he came to be capable of understanding and enjoying intercourse with Jehovah—the I AM, and all-pervading One. This was to be a continued and unbroken fellowship so long as the conferred divine purity remained unsullied.

But sin entered to rob man of his inherited fellowship—his intercourse with the Divine. And yet, though fallen, nothing less than the original association can fully satisfy the sinner, nor is God willing to have him deprived of it; so this longing for fellowship has been, in a way, mutual. On God's part it was so strong as to cause Him to yield up His only begotten Son on man's behalf, that the restoration might be completely effected.

This earnest desire on God's side of the case is rightly accredited to His nature, which is unqualified love. (1 John 4:16.) True love is therefore a longing for fellowship, whether possessed by God or man, because all love is of God. So, he who loves God will surely long for His fellowship, and will, therefore, make diligent inquiry about how best to do His will. His sole ambition will be to walk with God daily, and to act in a way pleasing to Him, regardless of how the world moves....

What manner of longing can this be, that after the chosen spouse of God, formed in His own likeness for mutual fellowship, has forsaken the very fountain of life, that the craving for fellowship should follow the guilty to the lowest depths, in order to perpetuate the work of creation! It must indeed be the carrying out of an eternal purpose, since no other motive could compass such a work. It is therefore entirely beyond the limit of sin-darkened minds to comprehend so much; but thanks be to the wonderful plan of redemption, Christ can be brought to dwell in the heart of faith, and so cause it to know infinite love which passes knowledge, and thus fill it with all the fullness of God.[61]

Note the similarity to E. J. Waggoner's theology on the indwelling Christ and the emphasis on feelings rather than the more objective, biblical principles upon which those feelings should be grounded. True love is pure and righteous, long-suffering, and not easily provoked. But this subjective approach to defining love completely overlooks the simple fact that God's law is love. And, as long as we choose to be at enmity with God's law, we are at enmity with God's love. The persistence of that enmity can so rebuff God's love that God will choose to love no more—casting the unrepentant rebel out of His house.[62]

Although there were those who supported Waggoner's ideas about love, there were others who held firm to the teachings of the Bible and the Spirit of Prophecy. A. G. Daniells, the longest serving president of the General Conference of Seventh-day Adventists (1901–1922), and W. A. Spicer, who served as secretary of the General Conference and then succeeded Daniells as president (1922–1930), both strenuously opposed the pantheistic teachings of Kellogg and Waggoner (among others).

---

61   John Orr Corliss, "The Mystery of Divine Fellowship," *The Signs of the Times*, vol. 48, no. 36, September 13, 1921, 4.

62   "All their wickedness *is* in Gilgal: for there I hated them: for the wickedness of their doings I will drive them out of mine house, I will love them no more: all their princes *are* revolters" (Hosea 9:15).

Francis McLellan Wilcox, serving as editor of the *Review and Herald* (1911–1944), wrote a two-part symposium on how pantheism, atheism, mysticism, and spiritualism were so prevalent in the worldly institutions of higher learning that he feared these ideas might adversely affect, even infect, our own institutions with false philosophies related to the alpha of heresies. He wrote,

> We do not know in what varied forms and phases the omega of error will manifest itself in the future, but this warning needs to be burned into our very souls. The alpha of error against which we were warned twenty-five years ago involved the principles of pantheism, naturalism, and evolution. It was a teaching which destroyed faith in the inspiration of the divine word, in Christ the Saviour from sin, in the efficacy of the atonement, making man his own savior, and, exalting an intellectual philosophy to the supplanting of a living, transforming Christian faith in the miracle-working power of divine grace. And this is the very teaching, only in aggravated degree, emanating from the great universities today. This teaching well answers to the omega against which we were warned. It may, of course, assume other forms in the future and come to us from other sources. But we need to recognize it in its present form, and heed the warning we have received against its reception. Will we do it?...
>
> We may be assured of this, that the omega of error, whenever it comes, will present many plausible reasons as to why it should be accepted. On the subtle plea of broadmindedness, liberality, competent and efficient leadership, and conformity to the advanced thought of a new age, it will demand recognition. And from the standpoint of worldly policy and expediency it will have much to commend it for acceptance; but the evil fruit of its seductive power will be just as baneful. The omega will not come from professed enemies of our work, but rather from professed friends, even from Seventh-day Adventists who are still enrolled as members of the church, but who have lost out of their hearts the spirit of this message. Of this danger we are warned....[63]

Others have, through the years, tried to keep the dangers of the omega deception from entering the church as an overwhelming surprise.

- 1930 – Francis McLellan Wilcox, editor, *Review and Herald*
  - "Why Our Educational Symposium? The Alpha and the Omega of Deadly Error. (Part 1)," *Review and Herald*, October 16, 1930
  - "Why Our Educational Symposium? The Alpha and the Omega of Deadly Error. (Part 2)," *Review and Herald*, October 23, 1930
- 1935/1936 – Willie White
  - One page typed statement titled "The Alpha and the Omega"

---

63   Francis McLellan Wilcox, "Why Our Educational Symposium? The Alpha and the Omega of Deadly Error. (Part 2)," *Review and Herald*, vol. 107, no. 54, October 23, 1930.

- 1975 – Alfred S. Jorgensen, field secretary, Australasian Division
    - "The 'Omega' of Apostasy," *Ministry Magazine*, March 1975
- 1977 – Robert H. Pierson, president (1966–79), General Conference of Seventh-day Adventists
    - "As a leader you need to be well-acquainted with Satan's plans for the omega apostasy that will inevitably come—perhaps sooner than we have believed. Could the apostate 'angel of light' even now be sowing seeds that will bear the awful harvest the church will experience before the end?" ("The Alpha of Apostasy," *Ministry Magazine*, August 1977).
    - "The seeds of such apostasy are in the churches of Christendom all around us. Before Jesus returns, the Seventh-day Adventist Church may well be confronted with a crisis that will exceed in magnitude the Kellogg alpha apostasy. It 'will be of a most startling nature' " ("The Omega of Apostasy," *Ministry Magazine*, October 1977).
- 1979 – *SDA Adult Sabbath School Lessons*, April–June, author, Fernando Chaij
    - "Spiritualism and Bible Prophecy," Monday, May 21
- 1980 – Roger W. Coon, Ph.D., pastor, Takoma Park SDA Church, Takoma Park, Maryland
    - "How near is the 'Omega'?" *Ministry Magazine*, April 1980
- 1981 – Lewis R. Walton, SDA Attorney
    - Author of *Omega*, published by the Review and Herald Publishing Association
- 1981 – Neal C. Wilson, president (1979–90), General Conference of Seventh-day Adventists
    - Endorsed Lewis Waltons' book *Omega* in the November 5, 1981, issue of the *Adventist Review*
- 1995 – Lewis R. Walton, SDA Attorney
    - Author of *Omega II: God's Church at the Brink*, published by Orion Publishing
- 2005 – Thomas Mostert, president (retired in 2007), Pacific Union Conference
    - Author of *Hidden Heresy? Is Spiritualism Invading Adventist Churches Today?*, published by Pacific Press Publishing Association
- 2010 – Rick Howard, SDA Pastor
    - Author of *The Omega Rebellion*, published by Remnant Publications
- 2012 – Rick Howard, SDA Pastor
    - Author of *The Omega Rebellion, Revised and Updated*, published by Remnant Publications

In spite of the efforts of these men and others to speak out against the dangers of such ideas as unconditional or unqualified love, from the 1970s to present day, contributors to our church magazines have strongly influenced the readership in the direction of the free use of these terms. This is troubling because the terms are not biblical; instead they are spiritualistic assertions that strongly direct the reader to a nonjudgmental state where accountability for behavior becomes nonexistent.

Books published by church-recognized printing houses and associations from Ellen White's death to the present day show the same pattern. In 1965 Dr. LeRoy Edwin Froom published a two-volume work titled *The Conditionalist Faith of Our Fathers*. In an effort to bolster our belief in the death and resurrection of the personality and body of those subject to the wages of sin, Froom quoted Bishop John A. T. Robinson's attempt to expose the pantheistic nature of the mystic religions of Hinduism and Buddhism and their apparent similarities to Platonic and Neo-Platonic Immortal-Soulism:

> "Because its fundamental theological presupposition is pantheistic (the real, immortal part of a man is a 'bit' of divinity), this doctrine never really succeeds in establishing a personal immortality. The end of man is always reabsorption, the overcoming of individuality, which is generally viewed as evil. When pressed to its limits in the religions of the East, the doctrine promises a state of bliss for the individual which is indistinguishable from his annihilation."[64]

Therefore, Robinson observes the fallacy of the Christian doctrine of death and the state of the soul, which Froom documents in his book:

> "The exponent of [innate] immortality assumes too simply that immortality is in itself salvation. But that is to reckon without God and without sin. To be raised to live with God, without any possibility of surcease, may be the most unendurable torment.
>
> "But God wills nevertheless to have it so. For resurrection is His destiny for every man, whether he is worthy of it or not, whether he likes it or not. For it depends on God's *unconditional love*.... There is a further great point of difference between the doctrine of immortality and that of resurrection which requires a more extended treatment.... The Bible opposes the *immortality of the soul* with the *resurrection of the body*."[65]

One cannot conclude that Froom initiated a trend in the teaching of unconditional love within our denomination based upon this one quote, but it appears to be the first use of it in book form since E. J. Waggoner's *Glad Tidings*. We cannot claim Froom is in favor of the concept, although he omits certain observations Robinson makes that appear to connect unconditional love with natural immortality of the soul as it relates to pantheism. And it is interesting indeed that we can see its connection to the doctrine of resurrection when one understands that if God's love is unconditional simply because God is love, then one might also conclude that immortality of the soul is unconditional since God is the Originator of life everlasting. Unfortunately, the connection that Froom makes while quoting Robinson also provides no *direct* comment regarding the blending that notes only a resurrection of both the wicked and the righteous—those who are worthy and those who are not—because of God's unconditional love, which Robinson refers to as "strange" while at the same time acknowledging the point made by Paul Althaus of "inescapeable godlessness in inescapable relationship to God."[66]

Somewhere, somehow, the concept of unconditional love began to make its inroads amongst Seventh-day

---

64   LeRoy Edwin Froom, *The Conditionalist Faith of Our Fathers*, vol. 2 (Washington, D.C.: Review and Herald Publishing Association, 1965), 849, 850.

65   Ibid., 850, emphasis added.

66   John A. T. Robinson, *Honest to God* (Louisville, KY: Westminster John Knox Press, 2002), 80.

Adventists even though the term was not used by Ellen White or our early pioneers—excepting E. J. Waggoner. Rather, counsel has been given regarding the moral direction some take as they attempt to establish the basis for God's love as unconditional. Yet over the past decades, many ministers and authors within our denomination have preached it from the pulpit, over the airwaves in radio and television broadcasts, and published it in books. And it appears to be a direct result of revisiting the writings of E. J. Waggoner and A. T. Jones as we approached the centennial "celebration" of the 1888 General Conference session in Minneapolis, and the influential efforts of righteousness by faith proponents who failed to completely separate out the pantheistic/panentheistic ideas from Waggoner's publications.[67]

Jack Sequeira wrote a book about salvation by faith in which he incorporated the concept of unconditional love. Notice how he sets up his premise for what he calls "unconditional good news" by first establishing his teaching on the nature of God's love. "When the Bible says that 'God is love' (1 John 4:8, 16), it doesn't mean that one of His attributes is love. It means that He *is* love. It means that love is the essence of His nature."[68]

What immediately becomes apparent from Sequeira's teaching is that love *is* God's essence, and not merely an attribute of God's essence. The apostle John wrote, "God is light, and in him is no darkness at all."[69] Are we to proceed with the same premise as Sequeira stated regarding God's love and conclude that God is unconditionally light? What then do we do with the scriptures concerning the darkness encircling the cross while Christ was experiencing the wrath of God for our sins?[70] And knowing that God is judge, are we then to conclude that justice is God's essence? If love is the essence of God's nature, and love is not merely an attribute, are we then in error to call God an essence of love?

Furthermore, if the gospel is "unconditional good news," then why does Paul write to the Corinthians as he does? "Now thanks be unto God, which always causeth us to triumph in Christ, and maketh manifest the savour of his knowledge by us in every place. For we are unto God a sweet savour of Christ, in them that are saved, and in them that perish: To the one we are the savour of death unto death; and to the other the savour of life unto life. And who is sufficient for these things? For we are not as many, which corrupt the word of God: but as of sincerity, but as of God, in the sight of God speak we in Christ."[71]

Ellen White wrote along similar lines, stating, "Let ministers and people remember that gospel truth ruins if it does not save. The soul that refuses to listen to the invitations of mercy from day to day can soon listen to

---

67   "An edited version of this book [Glad Tidings] appeared in 1972 from Pacific Press (edited by Robert Weiland). Wieland, well aware of the pantheistic sentiments in the book, simply edited out many of Waggoner's 'most blatant pantheistic sentiments.' But in his foreword to the book he never bothered to inform his readers that he had done so. The reason for this is that Wieland felt that Waggoner's pantheistic sentiments were only mildly 'parasitic' in relationship to his central message of Christ and His righteousness" (Whidden, *E. J. Waggoner: From the Physician of Good News to the Agent of Division*, 309, footnote 58).

"The metaphor of a somewhat benign 'parasitism' comes from Robert J. Wieland, employed to try to protect the alleged orthodoxy of Waggoner's salvation views. In other words, Wieland has argued that Waggoner's pantheistic tendencies were an essentially harmless irrelevancy to Waggoner's already developed views on Christ as our righteousness" (Ibid., footnote 61).

I have personally heard Elder Wieland make remarks consistent with Dr. Whidden's conclusions. Interestingly enough, Waggoner's use of "unqualified" in context with love has been removed from the more recent editions of *Glad Tidings*.

68   Jack Sequeira, *Beyond Belief* (Nampa, ID: Pacific Press Publishing Association, 1993), 19.

69   1 John 1:5

70   Psalms 18:9, 11

71   2 Corinthians 2:14–17

the most urgent appeals without an emotion stirring his soul."[72] How can an unconditional gospel ruin anything unless there is a condition by which ruin can be attained or accomplished?

An unconditional gospel could never be counterfeited or replaced by "another gospel," yet Paul discovered that the Galatians had been bewitched by another gospel—albeit one consisting of works that denied Jesus![73]

But what is the danger today? The other gospel of today consists of faith that denies the law of love the Lord Jesus Christ lived and died to magnify, while atoning for the sins of the world. Unconditional love has no need of a Savior because with it there is no condition by which reconciliation and atonement between God and individuals becomes necessary—no condition by which God may choose to express wrath toward rebels, or the rebels enmity toward God. But the carnal nature has no desire for the Bible gospel as revealed in Paul's words to the Corinthians: "For if he that cometh preacheth another Jesus, whom we have not preached, or if ye receive another spirit, which ye have not received, or another gospel, which ye have not accepted, ye might well bear with him."[74]

The confusion and entanglements from venturing on holy ground—the nature of God's love—with nothing more than speculative, unsanctified imagination causes unnecessary debate and division. We should be content with what clear counsel we have received on this issue! "The question of the essence of God was a subject on which He maintained a wise reserve, for their entanglements and specifications would bring in science which could not be dwelt upon by unsanctified minds without confusion."[75] "But let us never undertake to define God as an essence. Never, never venture one step into the way of putting God in the place of the things of His creation."[76]

Those who state that love is God's essence go beyond what God has already revealed to us. "God is love, in himself, in his very essence."[77] Several times Ellen White calls love an attribute:

"Genuine love is a precious attribute of heavenly origin, which increases in fragrance in proportion as it is dispensed to others."[78]

"As the knowledge of God is enlarged, love is increased, because God is love. The love of God is unlike the carnal attribute which fastens the mind upon the human, and leads men to neglect the service of God."[79]

---

72   White, *Testimonies for the Church*, vol. 5, 134. Elsewhere, we read just how this ruination occurs. "Every act of transgression, every neglect or rejection of the grace of Christ, is reacting upon yourself; it is hardening the heart, depraving the will, benumbing the understanding, and not only making you less inclined to yield, but less capable of yielding, to the tender pleading of God's Holy Spirit.... Even one wrong trait of character, one sinful desire, persistently cherished, will eventually neutralize all the power of the gospel. Every sinful indulgence strengthens the soul's aversion to God. The man who manifests an infidel hardihood, or a stolid indifference to divine truth, is but reaping the harvest of that which he has himself sown. In all the Bible there is not a more fearful warning against trifling with evil than the words of the wise man that the sinner 'shall be holden with the cords of his sins.' Proverbs 5:22" (Ellen G. White, *Steps to Christ* [Mountain View, CA: Pacific Press Publishing Association, 1892], 33, 34).

73   Galatians 1:6, 7

74   2 Corinthians 11:4

75   Ellen G. White, *Upward Look* (Washington, D.C.: Review and Herald Publishing Association, 1982), 148.

76   Ibid., 347.

77   Ellen G. White, "No Union Between the Church and the World," *The Review and Herald*, February 26, 1895.

78   Ellen G. White, *Our High Calling* (Washington, D.C.: Review and Herald Publishing Association, 1961), 231.

79   Ellen G. White, "Bible Religion," *The Signs of the Times*, February 24, 1890.

"Let us ponder this divine love, that we may become changed, and may reflect this precious attribute of the character of our Redeemer. We shall be in less peril of placing our affections on unworthy objects."[80]

Since love is *in* His very essence, we can rest assured that God's essence has love as a precious attribute, but it also has other precious attributes such as justice and mercy, peace and joy.

In *Beyond Belief* Sequeira attempts to establish agape love as unconditional love because it is selfish to have conditions. He acknowledges that places in the New Testament use philos "at times to describe God's love, but always in the context of agape."[81] What context? We have already shown from Dean VanDruff's research just how interchangeable agape and philos are in respect to God's love, and we discovered that agape love was connected to the darkness that the carnal nature cherishes. Instead of elaborating as to what context he is referring to, Sequeira states that human love is selfish—therefore it is conditional—whereas God's love is unselfish, which he then concludes couldn't possibly have conditions. He fails to comprehend that unselfish love can have conditions if those conditions are in the best interests of all created beings. Obedience to God's commandments is best for all concerned. When all voluntarily submit to the conditions of love and life as established by God then all will live a life more abundant in peace and joy!

Sadly, Robert Wieland comes to Sequeira's defense when critical thinkers ponder whether or not his teachings are truth—or merely his opinions posed as truth. Wieland emphatically states, "Of course God's love for the sinner is unconditional!"[82] He attempts to reinforce his conclusion by referring to a partial passage: "Ellen White speaks thus of 'conditions': 'The question will come up, How is it? Is it by conditions that we receive salvation? Never by conditions do we come to Christ.'"[83]

But he stops short of what else Ellen White wrote about conditions. When we read a little further, we see, "And if we come to Christ, then what is the condition? The condition is that by living faith we lay hold wholly and entirely upon the merits of the blood of a crucified and risen Saviour. When we do that, then we work the works of righteousness."[84] The distinction Ellen White makes is lost to Wieland and his readers because he stops short of sharing the contrast that a condition exists for receiving salvation, but no conditions exist for coming to Christ to observe His love demonstrated upon the cross.

This is made clearer by her next statement: "But when God is calling the sinner in our world, and inviting him, there is no condition there; he is drawn by the invitation of Christ and it is not, 'Now you have got

---

80   Ellen G. White, "True Religion," *The Signs of the Times*, January 13, 1888.

81   Sequeira, *Beyond Belief*, 20.

     Robert S. Folkenberg echoes this same sentiment in his book *We Still Believe*: "Therefore, in and through Christ, we stand complete and perfect (see Romans 9:16; 1 Corinthians 6:11; Ephesians 1:3; Colossians 2:10). That is why the gospel is unconditional good news. Our assurance of salvation is based, not on our behavior, but on Christ's" ([Nampa, ID: Pacific Press Publishing Association, 1994], 41).

     Essentially, this concept means we are saved in our sins, and not from our sins despite Folkenberg's attempts to connect true obedience to "a repentant, humble response to God's unconditional love." It contradicts what Christ said about the love relationship: "If ye keep my commandments, ye shall abide in my love; even as I have kept my Father's commandments, and abide in his love" (John 15:10). If we don't keep the commandments as a faith and love response to God's incredible gift of salvation, we cannot abide in His love.

82   Robert J. Wieland, *Is Beyond Belief Beyond Belief?* (Paris, OH: The Committee, 1993), 16.

83   Ibid.

84   Ellen G. White, *The Ellen G. White 1888 Materials* (Washington, D.C.: Ellen G. White Estate, 1987), 537.

to respond in order to come to God.' The sinner comes, and as he comes and views Christ elevated upon that cross of Calvary, which God impresses upon his mind, there is a love beyond anything that is imagined that he has taken hold of."[85]

What does the sinner witness? Christ meeting all the conditions of love for us! Then God's love begets love in us! Christ's faith begets faith in us! The compelling response is to lay hold wholly and entirely upon the merits of the blood of a crucified and risen Savior by a living faith imparted to us—which faith will work the works of righteousness! But what do we read a little further on? "Christ is drawing everyone that is not past the boundary. He is drawing him to Himself today. No matter how great that sinner is, He is drawing him."[86]

Another one of Ellen White's quotes may be taken out of context and presented as potential support for unconditional love. Although Jack Sequeira and Robert Wieland did not use it to bolster their position, it must be presented in order to show that the conditions of God's love are not self-centered.

> Those who call themselves His followers may despise and shun the outcast ones; but no circumstance of birth or nationality, no condition of life, can turn away His love from the children of men. To every soul, however sinful, Jesus says, If thou hadst asked of Me, I would have given thee living water.
>
> The gospel invitation is not to be narrowed down, and presented only to a select few, who, we suppose, will do us honor if they accept it. The message is to be given to all. Wherever hearts are open to receive the truth, Christ is ready to instruct them. He reveals to them the Father, and the worship acceptable to Him who reads the heart. For such He uses no parables. To them, as to the woman at the well, He says, "I that speak unto thee am He."[87]

The very context reveals the selfish conditions that selfish men impose, thereby falsely witnessing to the true nature of God's love. The invitation must be given to all. Just as Jesus revealed in the fishing parable, the net must be cast. And when it is drawn in, all manner of fish are caught in it. Then comes a time of judgment where the fish are sorted. The good fish are placed in vessels to be sold, while the bad are thrown out.[88] However, there are times when we are to be silent, even as Christ was silent before King Herod.

> Herod had rejected the truth spoken to him by the greatest of the prophets, and no other message was he to receive. Not a word had the Majesty of heaven for him. That ear that had ever been open to human woe, had no room for Herod's commands. Those eyes that had ever rested upon the penitent sinner in pitying, forgiving love had no look to bestow upon Herod. Those lips that had uttered the most impressive truth, that in tones of tenderest entreaty had pleaded with the most sinful and the most degraded, were closed to the haughty

---

85   Ibid., 537.
86   Ibid., 537, 538.
87   White, *The Desire of Ages*, 194.
88   Matthew 13:47–50

king who felt no need of a Saviour.[89]

Wieland further defends his position by quoting from *Christ's Object Lessons*: "We do 'not work in order to earn God's love.' "[90] This attempt to establish the concept of unconditional love falls very short of the complete truth. What Wieland fails to help us comprehend is that any love that must be earned is not true love! Genuine love is given, by choice. And contrary to Waggoner's thought that love needs no reason to love, that choice is going to be consistent with righteousness as defined by the moral law, which is love expressed by God's lips and written by His finger. Otherwise, God, who is love, would have no reason to hate sin!

So, we see that the love of God is demonstrated in that He chose to accept the risks of redeeming humanity by implementing a foreordained plan to offer human beings undeserved (by added reason of betrayal) love—grace! "The atonement of Christ sealed forever the everlasting covenant of grace. *It was the fulfilling of every condition upon which God suspended the free communication of grace to the human family.* Every barrier was then broken down which intercepted the freest exercise of grace, mercy, peace, and love to the most guilty of Adam's race."[91]

To those who have always obeyed God, His love is accepted and returned as uninjured love. To those who have yielded to temptation and sinned, but now choose to repent, it is offered as an injured love that chooses to forgive because Jesus, as our Substitute, obeyed on our behalf, meeting the conditions of love for us!

> Where man stumbled and fell, Jesus came off more than conqueror. Had he failed on one point, in reference to the law, all would have been lost; he would not have been a perfect offering, nor could he have satisfied the demands of the law; but he conquered where Adam failed, and by loyalty to God, under the severest trials, became a perfect pattern and example for our imitation, and he is able to succor those who are tempted. There is enough in this idea to fill our hearts with joy and gratitude every day of our lives. He took our nature upon him that he might become acquainted with our trials and sorrows, and, knowing all our experiences, he stands as Mediator and Intercessor before the Father.[92]

To both classes, the conditions of God's love—as demanded by the law of love—remain the same as the conditions of a covenant relationship: obey and live, disobey and die. "God will not compel the service of any man, but he reveals to him his obligation, unfolds to him the requirements of his holy law, and sets before him the result of his choice—to obey and live, or to disobey and perish."[93] We respond to God's love by fulfilling the obligations borne of conditions, which are not grievous but are the voluntary response that love begets.

We should not hesitate to make the right choice in this matter.

---

89   White, *The Desire of Ages*, 730.
90   Wieland, *Is Beyond Belief Beyond Belief?*, 16.
91   Ellen G. White, "Sealed by Christ's Atonement," in *God's Amazing Grace* (Washington, D.C.: Review and Herald Publishing Association, 1973), 153, emphasis added.
92   Ellen G. White, "This Do and Thou Shalt Live," *The Signs of the Times*, November 24, 1887.
93   Ellen G. White, "Justification by Faith," *The Signs of the Times*, November 3, 1890. See also Romans 8:13.

The Lord has made it apparent that he proffers to the sinner the privilege of cooperating with God. He gives light, and furnishes evidence of the truth. He makes plain what are his requirements, and it is left with the sinner as to whether he will accept the truth, and receive grace and power by which he may comply with every condition, and find rest in giving willing service to Jesus Christ, who has paid the price of his redemption. If the sinner hesitates, and fails to appreciate the light that has reached his intellect and stirred the emotions of his soul, and refuses to render obedience to God, the light grows dim, has less and less force, and finally vanishes from his view. Those who fail to appreciate the first rays of light, will not heed more decided evidences of the truth. If the tender appeals of God fail to meet with a response in the heart of the sinner, the first impressions made upon his mind lose their significance, and he is finally left in darkness. The invitation is full of love. The light is as bright when he finally refuses it, as when it first dawned upon his soul; but through rejection of light, his soul becomes full of darkness, and does not realize what is the peril of disregarding the light. Christ says to such a soul, "Yet a little while is the light with you."[94]

We have already read this statement, but it bears repeating: "Let ministers and people remember that gospel truth ruins if it does not save. The soul that refuses to listen to the invitations of mercy from day to day can soon listen to the most urgent appeals without an emotion stirring his soul."[95] Surely a gospel that "ruins if it does not save" could never be called an "unconditional gospel"!

If Wieland had included the surrounding context of the *Christ's Object Lessons* quote, his attempt to establish his point would have been weakened! "God's great object in the working out of His providences is to try men, to give them opportunity to develop character. Thus He proves whether they are obedient or disobedient to His commands. Good works do not purchase the love of God, but they reveal that we possess that love. If we surrender the will to God, we shall not work in order to earn God's love. His love as a free gift will be received into the soul, and from love to Him we shall delight to obey His commandments."[96]

Consistent with this line of reason provided by Ellen White, Lewis R. Walton writes, in the way of astute observation, about the nature of the omega deception and an illustration involving the concepts found in contract law regarding "condition precedent and condition subsequent." He first draws our attention to potential confusion over works and sanctification as they relate to doctrines believed and held dear amongst various factions within the church:

If history teaches us anything, the omega will probably also involve some sort of confusion over the role of works and sanctification. We know that this has nearly always been involved in past apostasies, either by direct theological attack or by the behavior of those advocating change. Canright openly attacked the law. Those claiming to have holy flesh attacked

---

94   Ellen G. White, "Words to the Young," *The Youth's Instructor*, August 17, 1893.
95   White, *Testimonies for the Church*, vol. 5, 134.
96   Ellen G. White, *Christ's Object Lessons* (Washington, D.C.: Review and Herald Publishing Association, 1900), 283.

it in a disguised way, claiming to believe while indulging in all sorts of wrongdoing done in the name of holiness. Kellogg's era saw notorious immorality among some believers. Whenever Adventist either directly or indirectly have become confused over their behavioral responsibilities, great harm has always resulted. And so it is vital for us to understand what some have portrayed as a paradox in Adventism: the duty to expend human effort in bringing to fruition a gospel that, most Protestants argue, is a free gift from God that shouldn't require such human input.[97]

But, while works and sanctification may be causes for confusion, they are secondary in that both are deeply impacted by the chosen perspective one has regarding the nature of God's love as reflected by His law. Later in his book, Walton tells of another, more fully developed understanding that directly links a mystic spiritualism with a false view of love as the omega, writing, "In a theological setting, the term is almost unassailable. Use it cleverly, and you end the argument: the other person doesn't have 'love.' "[98]

Walton ably continues to argue his initial understanding of the omega deception with this wonderful illustration that is just as applicable to God's love as it is to the exercise of His grace as evidenced by the plan of salvation:

It is an apparently complex question that is remarkably easy to answer if one understands two principles of law called condition precedent and condition subsequent. A condition precedent is one that is imposed on a person before he or she receives property. In order for title to vest, the individual must *do* some specified act, after which the property belongs to that person. In a religious sense, this is a counterfeit of the true gospel—and it is the most common form of religion known to man. All paganism has its roots deep in this concept; taken to its extreme, it demands human sacrifices in order to bring people into favor with deity. In Christianity, the only condition precedent is faith—a faith so complete that it leads to the surrender of one's entire will to a loving God.

Condition subsequent is an apparently similar but operationally very different sort of rule. Here property is transferred outright, without the requirement of any prior act. But it, too, is transferred on conditions—conditions that operate *after* the transfer. A man might convey land to his neighbor, for example, upon condition that it never be used for the sale of alcoholic beverages; if the neighbor ever breaches that condition, the land reverts to the original grantor. And that is a striking example, in human law, of the operative mechanism for the plan of salvation. The gift is free; in no sense can the new owner be said to have 'earned' it; yet by his abuse of the conditions under which it was granted, he can make himself unfit for the neighborhood and thus unable to continue as an owner.[99]

---

97   Walton, *Omega*, 73, 74.
98   Lewis R. Walton, *Omega II – God's Church on the Brink* (Glennville, CA: Orion Publishing, 1995), 185.
99   Walton, *Omega*, 73, 74.

Seeing then how conditions are useful from a legal perspective, we should also understand how conditions are also useful in scientific work. When performing scientific experiments in the laboratory, certain controls, or conditions, are established to determine the varying degrees of success or failure. The same is true in the spiritual realm. But the universe is witness to a terrible conflict between good and evil, between Christ and Satan, and all are either the seed of the woman or the seed of the serpent.

Since delineating the facts of history to this point, in an attempt to clarify what the alpha of heresies is, and because both alpha and omega are integral parts of the alphabet forming the beginning and the end, it behooves us to state the facts regarding the development and exposure of the omega. Ellen White wrote the following to leading Adventist physicians in a letter dated July 24, 1904: "Be not deceived; many will depart from the faith, giving heed to seducing spirits and doctrines of devils. We have now before us the alpha of this danger. The omega will be of a most startling nature."[100]

> *In a theological setting, the term is almost unassailable. Use it cleverly, and you end the argument: the other person doesn't have 'love.'*

Again, I wish to express that I have nothing personal against those individuals who have promoted spiritualism and doctrines of devils because they have preached and published that God's love is unconditional and unqualified. The battle is not with an individual or individuals, "for we wrestle not against flesh and blood, but against principalities, against powers, against the rulers of the darkness of this world, against spiritual wickedness in high places."[101] In many cases, prominent and influential leaders have spoken or written about unconditional love in complete ignorance of just what exactly they have been promulgating. Over the course of time, the invention of computerized search engines combined with digitalized libraries have made the process of research so much more productive and efficient than the days of traveling to the libraries of the world in search of necessary information. Still, having accepted a thought as good and wholesome without further research, they presented what has tickled their ears, knowing full well that it will tickle the ears of others. But if they have willfully neglected the Spirit of Prophecy and church history to preach what feels good to them and being wise in their own eyes, then may they feel the woe that will be their portion if they fail to repent before it is too late.

Because it is spiritualism that teaches the concept of unconditional, unqualified love, or free-loveism, we must make comparisons between the writings and sayings of spiritualists with the writing and sayings of individuals holding official positions within the church as licensed, ordained ministers of the gospel who are held in high esteem. For certainly just as E. J. Waggoner had "sown seeds that have [borne] and will bear evil fruit, leading some to depart from the faith, and to give heed to seducing spirits, doctrines of satanic origin," the

---

100   White, *Manuscript Releases*, vol. 7, 188.
101   Ephesians 6:12

result will be the same if they are teaching the same doctrines.[102] These evil impressions must be exposed.

We must consider the "shaking" influence of these exciting, though spurious, teachings upon the church and the results that follow. As Lewis Walton ponders, we must also consider that:

> For generations we have accustomed ourselves to assuming that all this takes place mainly outside the Adventist Church and that we, safely inside God's remnant, will watch it in interested but detached security. And that assumption may leave us puzzled as to how the very elect in our midst could be threatened with deception. Is there a possibility that we have underrated the enemy, that the same delusion of a false revival may also present itself in the midst of Adventism, accompanied by all the sensory trappings that demand belief? If we answer that question in the negative, we are hard pressed to explain why some of our "brightest lights" will go out and will become our most formidable, articulate enemies. Men and women do not become *that* angry over petty intra-church issues. That level of anger is shown only when people convince themselves that the church has rejected some idea that they perceive as vital religious truth.
>
> So the shaking, which we have long expected and dreaded, will involve doctrine and—if history and logic are correct—will probably include the church's rejection of what some people feel is vital "new light." (Remember that Ellen White clearly says the shaking will result from "the introduction of false theories.") That leaves us with an important question: What will be attacked?[103]

And, after considering these things, we must then make a willful decision as to whether or not we will continue to believe what they are preaching. It is my hope that all will choose to follow after the truth as it is in Christ. For Paul has given to us an exhortation with a conditional promise that springs from God's unselfish love—a love that has conditions of acceptance with Him:

> Be ye not unequally yoked together with unbelievers: for what fellowship hath righteousness with unrighteousness? and what communion hath light with darkness? And what concord hath Christ with Belial? or what part hath he that believeth with an infidel? And what agreement hath the temple of God with idols? for ye are the temple of the living God; as God hath said, I will dwell in them, and walk in them; and I will be their God, and they shall be my people. Wherefore come out from among them, and be ye separate, saith the Lord, and touch not the unclean thing; and I will receive you. And will be a Father unto you, and ye shall be my sons and daughters, saith the Lord Almighty.[104]

---

102   Letter from Ellen G. White to A. T. Jones, April 9, 1906.
103   Walton, *Omega*, 71.
104   2 Corinthians 6:14–18

All must consider the wise counsel of Ellen White regarding making decisions and determine what is truth:

> There is a lack with some men of thorough decision and defined positions as to what is truth. Nothing but most earnest, clear, determined decision, and full surrender to God, will break the spell. With some their own course of action in thought and purpose is deciding their eternal destiny. Some have become confused by a continued course of action of men in responsible positions, because they know them not to be true and decided for truth and righteousness. Do they turn from idols which they have created? No, no. Old habits come in and are invited to stay and rule the heart.
>
> The tempter presents matters in such a very seducing way that men love the presentation. Satan says, as he did to Adam and Eve, "Ye shall be as gods," and the poor souls come under Satan's mesmeric influence, and they are among the number of those who depart from the faith and begin to weave them beautiful allurements to charm the senses. They love and adore nature, talk science, and all is a fine gossamer picture, pleasing to the fancy of the worldly but an abomination in the sight of the Lord. Each heart has its own idol unless that heart is cleansed. It loves, adores, and worships the beautiful theories spun, but there is death in these things.
>
> I ask men ... What are you worshiping? Are you converted? Do you profess to believe the truth of Daniel and Revelation? Have you become nearly insane over your own specious theories? Has the living God taken possession of heart, mind, and soul? Have you been critically examining your own life by the Word of God, and has it had its influence to break you from the idolatry and imagery you have framed to make of none effect the Word of the living God?[105]

We must also keep in mind, even as we consider our own spiritual condition and what idols we may harbor in our hearts, the warning Ellen White raised that "*spiritualism is now changing its form, veiling some of its more objectionable and immoral features, and assuming a Christian guise*. Formerly it denounced Christ and the Bible; now it professes to accept both. *The Bible is interpreted in a manner that is attractive to the unrenewed heart, while its solemn and vital truths are made of no effect. A God of love is presented; but his justice, his denunciations of sin, the requirements of his holy law, are all kept out of sight*. Pleasing, bewitching fables captivate the senses of those who do not make God's word the foundation of their faith. Christ is as verily rejected as before; but Satan has so blinded the eyes of the people that the deception is not discerned."[106]

Compare and contrast that statement with this one provided by a National Spiritualist Teacher (NST):

---

105   Ellen G. White, *Manuscript Releases*, vol. 18 (Silver Spring, MD: Ellen G. White Estate, 1990), 130, 131.
106   Ellen G. White, *The Spirit of Prophecy*, vol. 4 (Battle Creek, MI: Seventh-day Adventist Publishing Association, 1884), 405, emphasis added.

Those that come to a Spiritualist church do not come out of fear, they come to enjoy the peaceful vibration of love, communication with those that are on the spirit side of life and the opportunity to share their belief with friends. *It is a philosophy of unconditional love, understanding, healing, positive thinking and living.*

We accept that there is a universal creative, loving, energy force, or power, called God by many. We, as Spiritualists, call this creative force Infinite Intelligence. It is not power that we can ever understand, it is far beyond our mental ability to comprehend. A philosophy teacher once said, "The human being cannot completely understand another human or even an animal, so how can we expect to understand or comprehend a universal power?"...

Spiritualism does not accept that this life comes to an abrupt end with the grave. *It does not accept that we will eventually rise from the grave and be judged* and either sent to eternal Hell, or if we have earned a good life, be sent to a blissful Heaven, where one floats on a cloud, or some such useless form of existence.

Spiritualists know that through verifiable spirit messages from mediums and their own personal experiences from loved ones that once lived on Earth, that there is a continuity of life beyond the grave without any question.

As a Spiritualist, we can accept that each person is a living part of Infinite Intelligence and that we are all on this Earth for a purpose. Whatever role we find ourselves experiencing we should do the best we can with what we have....[107]

> *Even though we have this admission as to the origin of unconditional love, spiritualists attempt to mask its true meaning.*

The purpose for sharing these claims is not to promulgate their beliefs but to show how their sentiments have crept into the expressions of our ministers and teachers in the church today—if not deliberately, then unawares. Reader, beware. Spiritualism seeks to ensnare all those who will listen to these sentiments:

Unconditional love comes from the Spirit World. It's to be used in many ways. It is to be used in your actions, in your manners. It is to be used in the love that you should share, that you must share with others. That is the way of the Spirit World and that is the way that we would like to see in your world; Love one another, it's very rewarding....

Learn to be positive, to go forth with love. Practice love, share love, and use love in the

---

107   Rev. Rupert Sigurdsson, NST, "Spiritualism! What It Is! What It Is Not!" *The National Spiritualist Summit,* November 2002, 7.

way it is meant to be shared, to be shown and to be unconditional....[108]

Even though we have this admission as to the origin of unconditional love, spiritualists attempt to mask its true meaning. They seek to define the essence of love as unconditional so that every time one hears or sees the word love they automatically, almost hypnotically, draw the conclusion that the message is one of unconditional love. This approach is documented in the following statement by a spiritualist:

> Do you know what unconditional love is? We often hear you try to explain what unconditional love is. You do not understand. It is pure, it is simple, it is honest. It is simply love. Do not try to attach things to it. Do not try to qualify it. Do not try to quantify it. It is simply love. When you say unconditional you try to separate it, change its meaning. Do not do this. There is simply love.
>
> You do not have to say unconditional love. There are no conditions where love is given. There are no conditions when love is given. There are no conditions how love is given. Love is pure, love is everlasting, love is simple. Treat it that way. Accept it that way. Give it that way.
>
> As you give so you shall receive. The pure love that exists within is easily found. The hard part is the search for it. Do not make the simple things in your life difficult. That is a human trait, the spiritual way is found in its simplicity, love.
>
> Listen to the heart, listen to the mind, listen to the spirit. It is easy, it is simple, it is the easiest choice you will ever make. Shut out the noise of the outside world. Find peace, find happiness, find love.
>
> We wait, we watch, we lead. In your time each will find that which they seek, that which they need, that which they want, the simplicity of the pure love of God and Spirit. It is within each.[109]

Other National Spiritualist Teachers have made similar statements in *The National Spiritualist Summit* magazine:

> In Spiritualism we speak of the Oneness of ALL life, which is called by many names and in various ways, but we know that it is the substance of all that is good. This Oneness, or Infinite Intelligence, is a loving Source of Life which knows only goodness, abundance, wholeness, peace, joy, health and harmony, desiring the same qualities for ALL creation. Each of us, as we grow in our understanding, recognize and accept these truths and try to

---

108   Bradley E. Gosselin, "Source of Love: An inspired trance message, from a Spirit Helper," *The National Spiritualist Summit*, February 2002, 24, emphasis added.

109   Bradley E. Gosselin, "Love and Light: Trance messages from One Feather," *The National Spiritualist Summit*, August 2001, 12.

live in an attitude of continual gratitude. We know that every day and every moment, the natural good is there for us as we open ourselves to receive it. We understand the beautiful Natural Law, that as we express our appreciation to the Creator of ALL so more abundance and blessings flow to us in order that we may unleash our hidden potentials—like attracting like. The universe as created needs ALL life, so let us be grateful for every aspect of being that enters our existence.

Religion, politics, color, creeds, countries each tend to separate people, but we must remember we are all a part of the whole and be thankful for our differences. Rather than alienation, we desire unity, peace, with no wars, no hunger. *Our understanding that God is love, love for ALL, love that never stops, no matter what we do.* Spirit is always blessing us and sharing the abundance of life with us.[110]

Spirit is love and Spirit's Love is ours: unconditionally, eternally. *As improbable and as wildly fantastic as it sounds, there is absolutely nothing we can do to lose God's love.* Think about that for a moment. Feel it and know it in your hearts. God's Love is always there, for all of us, at all times.[111]

No exceptions. God is love, unconditional, impartial, perpetual, unsolicited... There is nothing we can do to increase or earn the Love of God for it is always available to all in a steady energy flow, a healing flow to accept.[112]

The Bible doesn't teach these doctrines. So why are Adventist pastors writing and preaching these very sentiments? Whether they realize it or not, it is clear that the idea of unconditional love is of spiritualistic origin.

All of the following quotes on the next few pages are from Seventh-day Adventist ministers as published in Adventist magazines or books. Because of the reach and influence of the denomination, their statements have tremendous global influence upon members of the Seventh-day Adventist Church.[113] Not all the ministers or authors cited have experienced a moral fall as did the early Adventist members and leaders—Billings, Bennett, Moses Hull, J. H. Waggoner, and E. J. Waggoner—who promoted the idea of unconditional love; however, the danger exists because of the historical origins and connotations associated with the term.

---

110   Rev. Sandra Pfortmiller, NST, "Thanksgiving—Gratitude Day!" *The National Spiritualist Summit*, November 1995, 3, emphasis added.

111   Edmund Bujalski, "Relationship Boxes," *The National Spiritualist Summit*, June 2001, 25, emphasis added.

112   Rev. Sandra Pfortmiller, NST, "Body=Mind=Health!" *The National Spiritualist Summit*, April 1998, 3.

113   There is not enough time or space to include a sampling from every minister that presents these sentiments. Only a sampling could be provided for comparison so that you might come to recognize the importance of the connection between spiritualism, the doctrine of unconditional love, and how pervasive this doctrine has become within the church.

Many believe that God has long been angry with the human race, most reluctant to forgive and bless His erring creatures. For thousands of years men have offered sacrifice—sometimes their own children—to win the favor of their offended God. Even in the Christian world, some teach that were it not for constant intercession, God could not find it in His heart to love and save us sinners.

But need we do anything to make God love us?

Nothing is more emphatic in Scripture than that God has always loved even His most wayward child....

"God so loved the world." *He is not angry with us, even though we are sinners.*[114]

God's unconditional love is certainly unexplainable. Unconditional love is a love that perseveres no matter what. It is love that is not dependent on the one being loved. *Here is an almost unbelievable thought.*

There is nothing you can do to get God to love you any less. Our actions do not determine His love—His heart does. When we turn our backs on Him, He loves us still. When we reject His invitation to follow Him, He loves us still. When we violate His will, He loves us still. Our actions may bring Him pain. Our wrong choices may break His heart. Our bad decisions may give Him deep grief, but nothing we do can change His stedfast love.

I can't turn away from that love. All I can do is fall at His feet and thank Him forever for loving me so.[115]

He does not love us more when we do right, nor does He love us less when we do wrong. Such is the amazing nature of the love which continually pulsates in the heart of the infinite

---

114 A. Graham Maxwell, "The Sacrifice of Christ, Our Victory," *Review and Herald*, September 30, 1965, 7, 8.

It is apparent that Maxwell is ignoring Psalm 7:11, which says, "God judgeth the righteous, and God is angry with the wicked every day." This appears to be the commencement of Maxwell's departure from penal substitution theory of atonement, although it is not fully expressed in this article, toward the moral influence model. He doesn't use "unconditional love" in this article, but the implied meaning is consistent with the term's definition.

From this point on, Maxwell preached and taught his conclusion that God does not kill or destroy, as is evident in the following quotes. "God had told the truth when He warned that the wages of sin is death. In His Son He was dying that death. But God was not executing His Son. He only 'gave Him up,' as He will give up the wicked at the end" (A. Graham Maxwell, "God's Law and My Freedom," *Signs of the Times*, April 1971, 21).

"Death is not an arbitrary punishment meted out by an angry God but a natural consequence of our separating ourselves from the source of life....

"Even as the wicked die, God will not be angry with his unsavable children. As He watches them perish, we shall hear His cry, 'How can I give you up! How can I let you go!' " (A. Graham Maxwell, "Why Did Jesus Have to Die?" *Signs of the Times*, July 1978, 19, 20).

"God will miss us if we're lost. He will miss us if we don't come home" (A. Graham Maxwell, "God's Respect for Us Sinners," *Signs of the Times*, August 1978, 23).

"Nowhere, absolutely nowhere, does the Bible say that our loving heavenly Father needs to be pleaded with to be reconciled to His children" (A. Graham Maxwell, "What the Father Means to Me," *Adventist Review*, September 18, 1986, 16).

115 Mark Finley, *Solid Ground* (Hagerstown, MD: Review and Herald Publishing Association, 2003), 97, emphasis added.

One.[116]

Our sin does not alter, lessen or put off His love. It is a changeless, undying love that cannot be quenched by sin's ugliness....

There is no cutoff point to God's love, no stopping place beyond which He will not go....

Everlasting love is love without end. Love that always *is* and never *is not*. Perpetual love. Unaffected love. Love that is not turned on or shut off by what we do or fail to do. It cannot be increased by our good performance or diminished by our bad performance. It simply, profoundly *is*. "God *is* love" (1 John 4:8). Always has been. Always will be. We can't earn it. We can't destroy it.[117]

If you are looking for victory and longing for true obedience, the very first prerequisite is that you *understand the unconditional love and acceptance of God for you*. We don't get peace by getting victory, we get victory by getting peace. The only person who can ever obey is the one who already has the peace of acceptance with God.[118]

Only when her new family finally communicated *unconditional acceptance* to her was she able to begin to heal....

But she was not allowed to misbehave "for free." At the same time, she slowly came to understand that the consequence of disobeying was *not* to be rejected and sent away. For as long as she was willing to remain in the household, her place was secure....

Jesus loves to have us come to Him just as we are, for that is the only way we *can* come. *He sets no limits on the number of times we can come and still be accepted*. He loves us because we are His children, not because of any good in us. And when we finally come to understand that we are loved and accepted by Him, we will begin to heal. Accepting His acceptance makes the difference.[119]

There is a close connection between stewardship, offerings, and worship. Worship is essentially the wholehearted response of the creature to the Creator; stewardship is the faithful administration by the servant of the Lord's property. Worship, like stewardship, involves the element of offering. This sense of offering in the mature Christian is not based

116   Ty Gibson, *Shades of Grace* (Nampa, ID: Pacific Press Publishing Association, 2001), 70.

117   Ty Gibson, *See with New Eyes: The True Beauty of God's Character* (Nampa, ID: Pacific Press Publishing Association, 2000), 31, 113, 114.

118   Morris L. Venden, *Faith That Works* (Hagerstown, MD: Review and Herald Publishing Association, 1980 and 1999), 167, emphasis added.

119   Morris L. Venden, *95 Theses on Righteousness by Faith: Apologies to Martin Luther* (Pacific Press Publishing Association, 2003), 145, 146, emphasis added.

on fear or the desire to earn God's pleasure, but on unconditional love and consecration of life.[120]

I am living in the never-ending grace of God's unconditional love.[121]

There is no characteristic so natural to God and so foreign to human beings as unconditional love and its byproduct, forgiveness without reservation.... Divine forgiveness is unconditionally offered, before it has been requested. It takes the initiative.[122]

Healthy boundaries include accepting other people as they are. This is unconditional love, which I define as follows: "I love you as you are. You need not change to receive my love, and if you change, you will not forfeit my love." This is at the heart of the gospel and at the heart of every healthy relationship, as well. Attempting to change people is manipulation, the antithesis of acceptance. The flip side of acceptance is confrontation. Without this aspect, acceptance becomes mere indulgence. Our outreach to secular people must be rooted in acceptance, a passionate love for the lost—a love that is not conditioned on whether the other person responds to our outreach.[123]

It requires tremendous strength of character to look the past in the eye. This is rarely possible outside a relationship in which you know that you are fully accepted no matter what. The gospel teaches us that the most valuable Person in the universe knows all about us, yet loves us with unconditional love. God accepts us as we are. The Cross demonstrates our value to God. We are worth the infinite life of the precious Son of God. And because Jesus will never die again, we can know that He will never abandon us. When we grasp the value we have in God's eyes, we can begin to have the courage to face the past and deal with it.[124]

You see, it is not enough for me to love Jesus completely and fully without reservation. This kind of love is rare enough, and it is pleasing to God, but it is hardly complete. If we were to look at it as reflected in the Ten Commandments, this love for God is epitomized in the first four commandments, but what about the other six? God has shared with me that I must learn to love others, not just those who are my friends, the ones who are easy to love, but also those who disagree with me, those who are my enemies!

---

120   B. B. Beach, "I Believe... in the Principle of Stewardship," *Review and Herald*, March 2, 1972, 7.

121   Sharon Montgomery (a pseudonym), "Alone!" *Review and Herald*, June 12, 1975, 13.

122   Brenda Friesen, "Love One Another," *Review and Herald*, March 30, 1978, 10. This goes blatantly contrary to 1 John 1:9, which says, "If we confess our sins, he is faithful and just to forgive us *our* sins, and to cleanse us from all unrighteousness."

123   Jon Paulien, *Everlasting Gospel Ever-Changing World: Introducing Jesus to a Skeptical Generation* (Nampa, ID: Pacific Press Publishing Association, 2008), 110.

124   Jon Paulien, *John: The Beloved Gospel* (Nampa, ID: Pacific Press Publishing Association, 2003), 57, 58.

"You must learn to love others unconditionally, whether they disagree with you or not. I want to bring you into this experience, Jim. Will you let Me?"

I said, "Lord, how far does this gospel of Yours have to go?"[125]

In light of these statements, it would be well to consider two warnings Ellen White raised when she wrote against the sophistries found in Kellogg's book *The Living Temple*. The first tells us that not every impulse is of the Holy Spirit. And the second tells how we open a door for the enemy to talk to us in a manner to deceive us.

I appeal to our ministers to be sure that their feet are placed on the platform of eternal truth. *Beware how you follow impulse, calling it the Holy Spirit.* Some are in danger in this respect. I call upon them to be sound in the faith, able to give to everyone who asks a reason of the hope that is in them.[126]

> *Beware how you follow impulse, calling it the Holy Spirit. Some are in danger in this respect.*

One and another come to me, asking me to explain the positions taken in *Living Temple*. I reply, "They are unexplainable." The sentiments expressed do not give a true knowledge of God. All through the book are passages of Scripture. These scriptures are brought in in such a way that error is made to appear as truth. Erroneous theories are presented in so pleasing a way that unless care is taken, many will be misled.

We need not the mysticism that is in this book. *Those who entertain these sophistries will soon find themselves in a position where the enemy can talk with them, and lead them away from God.* It is represented to me that the writer of this book is on a false track. He has lost sight of the distinguishing truths for this time. He knows not whither his steps are tending. The track of truth lies close beside the track of error, and both tracks may seem to be one to minds which are not worked by the Holy Spirit, and which, therefore, are not quick to discern the difference between truth and error.[127]

Adding to the confusion are those who recognize that unconditional acceptance is unbiblical but still desire to cling to the concept of unconditional love, as does an Adventist theologian who wrote: "Where in the Bible do we find that God 'accepts' us unconditionally? It's true that He *loves* us unconditionally, but we are

---

125   Jim Hohnberger, *It's About People: How to Treat Others, Especially Those We Disagree With, The Way Jesus Treats Us* (Nampa, ID: Pacific Press Publishing Association, 2003), 110.

126   White, *Testimonies for the Church*, vol. 8, 296, emphasis added.

127   White, *Selected Messages*, book 1, 202, emphasis added; A similar quote is used by Lewis Walton in *Omega II – God's Church at the Brink* on page 152.

unacceptable to God in our natural state. However, we are *made* acceptable 'in Christ,' with all that Paul means by that phrase."[128]

How can unconditional love process acceptance conditionally? How can unconditional love reject what it loves unconditionally? There is no condition by which unconditional love may reject anyone or anything! Therefore, the only logical conclusion of this devious doctrine is that all are accepted because all are acceptable! And this is precisely what Satan would desire, for then God must readmit all the rebellious angels and people to heaven and unspoiled Eden to live for their own selfish pleasure.

Or consider what one minister, who thinks conditional promises and warnings are consistent with unconditional love, says:

> God's promises and God's warnings alike have always been conditional. But just like my parents' love, His love never has been and never will be conditional. "No matter how you behave, I will love you to the end."
>
> But that's just it—it is precisely because God's love is *unconditional* that His promises and warnings are *always conditional.*[129]

Yet it would be out of character for unconditional love to formulate conditional promises and warnings (aka "threats").

More dangerous still are those who teach that we must be obedient to unconditional love as though it is a concept taught and believed by our pioneering church leaders, as one former General Conference president has done. "True obedience springs from a repentant, humble response to God's unconditional love."[130] To title a book *We Still Believe* misdirects the reader into thinking and believing that unconditional love is a historical belief held dear by our pioneers when in fact the opposite is quite true.

> *Thousands have a false conception of God and his attributes. They are as verily serving a false god as were the servants of Baal.*

The simple fact is that God's word condemns those who claim to represent Him, yet misrepresent Him by word or deed.[131] If the prophet Malachi were alive today, would he not give the same message he proclaimed to apostatizing priests and prophets of his time? "Ye have wearied the Lord with your words. Yet

---

128   Herbert E. Douglass, *Truth Matters: An Analysis of the* Purpose Driven Life *Movement* (Nampa, ID: Pacific Press Publishing Association, 2006), 89.

129   Dwight K. Nelson, *What "Left Behind" Left Behind: What the Bible Really Says About the End of Time* (Fallbrook, CA: Hart Research Center, 2001), 56.

130   Folkenberg, *We Still Believe*, 75.

131   Deuteronomy 13:1–5; Exodus 20:7. "It is as easy to make an idol of cherished ideas or objects as to fashion gods of wood or stone. Thousands have a false conception of God and his attributes. They are as verily serving a false god as were the servants of Baal" (Ellen G. White, "The Privileges and Duties of the Followers of Christ," *Review and Herald*, December 3, 1908).

ye say, Wherein have we wearied him? When ye say, Every one that doeth evil is good in the sight of the Lord, and he delighteth in them; or, Where *is* the God of judgment?"[132]

If the prophet Jeremiah heard what church leaders are saying today, would he not proclaim the same message he gave to leadership of his day? "And I have seen folly in the prophets of Samaria; they prophesied in Baal, and caused my people Israel to err. I have seen also in the prophets of Jerusalem an horrible thing: they commit adultery, and walk in lies: they strengthen also the hands of evildoers, that none doth return from his wickedness; they are all of them unto me as Sodom, and the inhabitants thereof as Gomorrah."[133]

Of such a class of professing Christians, Ellen White wrote:

> Do not these who claim sanctification while violating the commands of God, become a false and fatal sign to the world? Do they not say to the sinner, "It shall be well with thee"? The Lord has defined sin as the transgression of his law, but they say they are saved in sin, and thus make Christ the minister of sin. These professed Christians are doing the very work that Satan did in Paradise, they are leading souls astray by precept and example. They say to the sinner, to the transgressor, It shall be well with thee; you will rise to a higher, holier state by violating the law of God. The lesson that is heard throughout the land is, "Disobey and live." But how different is this teaching from the lessons of Christ.[134]

But, you may say, there is a difference between being saved in sin and being loved in sin! God hates the sin and loves the sinner! The Bible plainly says, "The foolish shall not stand in thy sight: thou hatest all workers of iniquity. Thou shalt destroy them that speak leasing: the Lord will abhor the bloody and deceitful man."[135] We shall deal more with this concept in a future chapter.

We have received warning upon warning concerning our need to build upon a firm foundation of truth as it is in Jesus:

> Those who follow their own mind and walk in their own way will form crooked characters. Vain doctrines and subtle sentiments will be introduced with plausible presentations, to deceive, if possible, the very elect. Are church members building upon the Rock? The storm is coming, the storm that will try every man's faith, of what sort it is. Believers must now be firmly rooted in Christ, or else they will be led astray by some phase of error. Let your faith be substantiated by the Word of God. Grasp firmly the living testimony of truth. Have faith in Christ as a personal Saviour. He has been and ever will be our Rock of Ages. The testimony of the Spirit of God is true. Change not your faith for any phase of doctrine, however pleasing it may appear, that will seduce the soul.

---

132   Malachi 2:17
133   Jeremiah 23:13, 14
134   White, "The Words and Works of Satan Repeated in the World."
135   Psalm 5:5, 6

The fallacies of Satan are now being multiplied, and those who swerve from the path of truth will lose their bearings. Having nothing to which to anchor, they will drift from one delusion to another, blown about by the winds of strange doctrines. Satan has come down with great power. Many will be deceived by his miracles.[136]

If there is one in a position to have a controlling influence over others, Satan works in a masterly manner to confuse that man's mind, and make right appear wrong, and wrong right. His suggestions are always designed to lessen the importance of God's requirements, and to set the mind at rest while the daily walk is contrary to the divine law, until finally the victim of his delusions flatters himself that he is walking with God, while he is all the time going contrary to his law.

Such persons think they have faith; but it is presumption. The great adversary has woven a snare for their feet; and when once they become entangled, he has no lack of agencies to involve them still more deeply in his toils. Thus the deception grows stronger and stronger until souls are involved in irretrievable ruin.[137]

Every soul will be tested. Oh, that we would, as a people, be wise for ourselves, and by precept and example impart that wisdom to our children! Every position of our faith will be searched into; and if we are not thorough Bible students, established, strengthened, and settled, the wisdom of the world's great men will lead us astray.[138]

The warnings of the word of God regarding the perils surrounding the Christian church belong to us today. As in the days of the apostles men tried by tradition and philosophy to destroy faith in the Scriptures, so today, by the pleasing sentiments of higher criticism, evolution, spiritualism, theosophy, and pantheism, the enemy of righteousness is seeking to lead souls into forbidden paths. To many the Bible is as a lamp without oil, because they have turned their minds into channels of speculative belief that bring misunderstanding and confusion. The work of higher criticism, in dissecting, conjecturing, reconstructing, is destroying faith in the Bible as a divine revelation. It is robbing God's word of power to control, uplift, and inspire human lives. By spiritualism, multitudes are taught to believe that desire is the highest law, that license is liberty, and that man is accountable only to himself.[139]

Those who endeavor to obey all the commandments of God will be opposed and derided.

---

136 Ellen G. White, *Evangelism* (Washington, D.C.: Review and Herald Publishing Association, 1946), 361, 362.
137 Ellen G. White, "The Law in the Christian Age," *The Signs of the Times*, August 5, 1886.
138 White, *Testimonies for the Church*, vol. 5, 546.
139 White, *The Acts of the Apostles*, 474.

They can stand only in God. In order to endure the trial before them, they must understand the will of God as revealed in His word; they can honor Him only as they have a right conception of His character, government, and purposes, and act in accordance with them. None but those who have fortified the mind with the truths of the Bible will stand through the last great conflict.[140]

The people must not be left to stumble their way along in darkness, not knowing what is before them, and unprepared for the great issues that are coming. There is a work to be done for this time in fitting a people to stand in the day of trouble, and all must act their part in this work. They must be clothed with the righteousness of Christ, and be so fortified by the truth, that the delusions of Satan shall not be accepted by them as genuine manifestations of the power of God.... Much upon these things has been shown to me, but I can only present a few ideas to you. Go to God for yourselves, pray for divine enlightenment, that you may know that you do know what is truth, that when the wonderful miracle-working power of Satan shall be displayed, and the enemy shall come as an angel of light, you may distinguish between the genuine work of God and the imitative work of the powers of darkness.[141]

With all these warnings, should we be careless and neglectful as the close of earth's history approaches—at a time when we should be at the highest level of alertness? Because we do not zealously strive to obtain for ourselves the faith once delivered to the saints, we are in danger of being deceived on any number of important issues: the immutable character of God's law, the revealed character of grace, the exposed nature of sin, and the real essence of God's love. Yet we are told that a proper understanding of God's character will be preached at the end of time—during the darkest hour.

The coming of the bridegroom was at midnight—the darkest hour. So the coming of Christ will take place in the darkest period of this earth's history. The days of Noah and Lot pictured the condition of the world just before the coming of the Son of man. The Scriptures pointing forward to this time declare that Satan will work with all power and "with all deceivableness of unrighteousness." 2 Thessalonians 2:9, 10. His working is plainly revealed by the rapidly increasing darkness, the multitudinous errors, heresies, and delusions of these last days. Not only is Satan leading the world captive, but his deceptions are leavening the professed churches of our Lord Jesus Christ. The great apostasy will develop into darkness deep as midnight, impenetrable as sackcloth of hair. To God's people it will be a night of trial, a night of weeping, a night of persecution for the truth's sake. But out of that night of darkness God's light will shine....

It is the darkness of misapprehension of God that is enshrouding the world. Men are losing their knowledge of His character. It has been misunderstood and misinterpreted. At

---

140   White, *The Great Controversy*, 593.
141   Ellen G. White, "An Address in Regard to the Sunday Movement," *Review and Herald*, December 24, 1889.

this time a message from God is to be proclaimed, a message illuminating in its influence and saving in its power. His character is to be made known. Into the darkness of the world is to be shed the light of His glory, the light of His goodness, mercy, and truth....

The last rays of merciful light, the last message of mercy to be given to the world, is a revelation of His character of love. The children of God are to manifest His glory. In their own life and character they are to reveal what the grace of God has done for them.[142]

In the kingdom of God, there is perfect order. To maintain blissful governance in that kingdom, law has been established for the purpose of affecting every aspect of life—moral, natural or physical, social, etc.—and keeping everything in its proper spheres of order. " 'God is love.' 1 John 4:16. His nature, His law, is love. It ever has been; it ever will be."[143] Yet in this world of sin we often see the work of misguided love, or the miscarriage of justice. It is immensely important for us to remember, as we live in relationship with God and others, that "there must be firmness in preserving order, but compassion, mercy, and forbearance should be mingled with the firmness. Justice has a twin sister, Love. These should stand side by side."[144]

We all have a responsibility to study for ourselves the truth as it is in Jesus Christ. We will fail in the quest of obtaining our best reward if we demurely accept whatever is spoken or written by our favorite minister without searching the Scriptures to see if it is so. We all ought to be Bereans and diligently search the Scriptures and Spirit of Prophecy to determine for ourselves the truth. Without the Holy Spirit abiding in us, and working through us, we will never attain the condition of fruitful Christians or the perfection of character that fits us for heaven. Ellen White again warns us of our spiritual danger when we fail to obtain for ourselves that knowledge of God of which He approves:

> Look to God. Trust in his infallible wisdom. *Regard as a sin, the practice so common, even among Seventh-day Adventists, of becoming the echo of any man, however lofty his position.* Listen to the voice of the great Shepherd, and you will never be led astray. Search the Scriptures for yourself, and be braced for duty and for trial by the truth of God's word. Let no friendship, no influence, no entreaty let not the smiles, the confidence, or the rewards of any man, induce you to swerve from the path in which the Lord would lead you. Let Christlike integrity and consistency control the actions of your life. The man who sits most at the feet of Jesus, and is taught by the Saviour's spirit, will be ready to cry out, "I am weak and unworthy, But Christ is my strength and my righteousness."[145]

True, we must all start somewhere—typically right where grace finds us, if we are willing to heed mercy's call—but we must never be satisfied with status quo. God loves us enough to change us. He loves

---

142   White, *Christ's Object Lessons*, 414, 415.
143   White, *Patriarchs and Prophets*, 33.
144   White, *Testimonies for the Church*, vol. 5, 559.
145   Ellen G. White, *The Paulson Collection of Ellen G. White Letters* (Payson, AZ: Leaves-Of-Autumn Books, 1985), 53.

us enough to correct us by chastising and rebuking us. We must remember that love can be painful because it disciplines.

When Christ walked on this earth, He asked His disciples, "Nevertheless when the Son of man cometh, shall he find faith on the earth?"[146] Will we, the body of Christ, His church, heed the rebuke from the True Witness and be ready for the second coming? John the Revelator warns us: "I know thy works, that thou art neither cold nor hot: I would thou wert cold or hot. So then because thou art lukewarm, and neither cold nor hot, I will spue thee out of my mouth"[147]

Truly we can see the conditions of love expressed in the promises of Revelation 3: "As many as I love, I rebuke and chasten: be zealous therefore, and repent. Behold, I stand at the door, and knock: if any man hear my voice, and open the door, I will come in to him, and will sup with him, and he with me. To him that overcometh will I grant to sit with me in my throne, even as I also overcame, and am set down with my Father in his throne. "[148]

True love will rebuke and chasten because conditions are not being met. Character is not being transformed and recreated into the express image of Christ. Therefore, true love must spare not in warning against sin and its sure results—separation and death. If only more ministers were faithful in preaching the truth as it is in Jesus!

> Thousands more might have been saved if men had preached the word, instead of the maxims, philosophies, and doctrines of men. If from every pulpit had sounded the faithful truth of God, men would have been left with a better knowledge of the Bible, with a deeper conviction of the truth of its principles, and the reality of its promises; and far more might have come to an understanding of what is truth. The world is full of unsound doctrines, of the traditions and opinions of men, of seducing theories of evil spirits; but let every one who has a knowledge of the present truth, study to show himself approved unto God; and by word and action let him proclaim the word of God that "liveth and abideth forever."[149]

Let us resolve to submit ourselves unconditionally to God, and wholeheartedly seek His face so that we might truly know His will. Let us continue to faithfully, perseveringly wrestle with the difficult passages of Scripture that give us a complete picture of the love of God and not rest upon (or wrest, as in misapply) those passages that would lead us to dangerous complacency in an incomplete understanding of love, justice, righteousness, and truth.

---

146   Luke 18:8
147   Revelation 3:15, 16
148   Revelation 3:15, 16, 19-21
149   Ellen G. White, "Preach the Word," *Review and Herald*, April 24, 1888.

Chapter 4

To Everything Is a Season

When I first met Kaoru Koyama, I was enthralled by her smile. The way her eyes literally danced with joy and shone with energy thrilled my heart. When I saw her smile, I was convinced she must smile the way Jesus does. I was compelled to get to know her better, so we began to spend more time together. A few days later, I fought to keep my emotions afloat while going through a stressful experience. Kaoru was so kind and supportive throughout my ordeal. I loved her more for her empathy. We had only known each other for little more than a week, but when she left Osaka to return to Tokyo, we were engaged.

All these years later, I don't think that either one of us could prove who loved whom first—we still disagree on who initiated holding hands. For the first five months of our marriage, we were separated because of the circumstances of our work. But that didn't keep us from talking over the phone every day we were apart.

However, when it comes to our children, we can prove that we loved them first. When we found out we were expecting, we were overjoyed, and we went to great lengths to choose names that we liked because of their rich meaning. We wanted those particular names to bring them honor and to bless them throughout their lives. We dreamed about the happy and joyous times we would share together. We thought about their well being and how we would meet their needs. We dedicated ourselves to raising them to accept the set of values established and modeled in the Bible. We both sacrificed of ourselves—in some cases our dreams—to provide our children with every advantage we could possibly afford. At times this meant being physically separated by great distances to financially support my family.

We didn't dwell much upon the likelihood that one of our children would rebel against our love for them. Nor did we consider the conflict between what we knew was best for our children and what they wanted. We simply did what we believed was right, while hoping and praying for the best.

Our love for our children is similar to God's love for us, and vice versa. The Bible tells us that we love God because He loved us first.[1] God chose to create us. He knew before He created the world that by making us free moral agents the possibility existed for us to rebel against Him. But He was confident that as He demonstrated His love, goodness, and righteousness we would ultimately receive greater joy and happiness by voluntarily

---

[1]   1 John 4:19

submitting to His set of values established by the justice of His law and the declaration of His loving character. In His infinite wisdom, He determined to reveal His love by willingly sacrificing Himself without abolishing His moral law—His integrity and righteousness—thereby revealing a love as strong as death.[2] Indeed, "it is a love stronger than death; for he died for us."[3] Yet, in dying, He magnified the law of love and, therefore, holds claim to our unceasing loyalty.

The wisest man recorded in the Old Testament is Solomon.[4] Inspired by the Holy Spirit, he wrote about the complexity of certain states of being or doing. Based upon observation, we can conclude with him that we either are alive or dead; speaking or silent; sleeping or waking; planting or harvesting; mourning or dancing; weeping or laughing; and warring or making peace. While you and I may experience, or exist in, one state or the other, we simply cannot be completely, fully engaged in both states at the same time. When trying to describe such contradictory states of being as we experience them, we do so in descriptive terms such as conflicting emotions—not so much as a peaceful coexistence, but the contention brought upon us by sharp competition where one state of being or emotion can and must master the other.

Before listing his poetic paradoxes, Solomon wrote, "To every *thing there is* a season, and a time to every purpose under the heaven."[5] Perhaps the most challenging statement of his list is "a time to love, and a time to hate."[6] Yet if we are to discuss love and understand it, we must also explore the other emotion of hatred or detestation. After mentioning all of the varying emotions that we can experience in life, Solomon concludes by giving glory to God.

> He hath made every *thing* beautiful in his time: also he hath set the world in their heart, so that no man can find out the work that God maketh from the beginning to the end.... I know that, whatsoever God doeth, it shall be for ever: nothing can be put to it, nor any thing taken from it: and God doeth *it*, that *men* should fear before him. That which hath been is now; and that which is to be hath already been; and God requireth that which is past. And moreover I saw under the sun the place of judgment, *that* wickedness *was* there; and the place of righteousness, *that* iniquity *was* there. I said in mine heart, God shall judge the righteous and the wicked: for *there is* a time there for every purpose and for every work.... Let us hear the conclusion of the whole matter: Fear God, and keep his commandments: for this *is* the whole *duty* of man. For God shall bring every work into judgment, with every secret thing, whether *it be* good, or whether *it be* evil.[7]

The Bible is quite straightforward on this matter of love and hate, justice and mercy—we are acquitted for satisfactorily meeting certain established conditions and condemned for not meeting them. As we consider the

---

2   Song of Solomon 8:6
3   Ellen G. White, "The Trial of Your Faith," *The Review and Herald,* June 20, 1907.
4   1 Kings 10:23, 24
5   Ecclesiastes 3:1
6   Ecclesiastes 3:8
7   Ecclesiastes 3:11, 14–17; 12:13, 14

contrast of love and hate, we must not overlook other words that help us understand biblical hate from God's perspective. The Bible uses synonyms of hate as a means of conveying the hatred God has for sin—defined as the transgression of His law or knowing what is good and refusing or neglecting to do that good.[8]

Following are examples of other words synonymous with hatred and their meanings. Hate implies an emotional aversion often coupled with enmity or malice (hated the enemy with a passion). Enmity is a positive hatred. Detest suggests violent antipathy (detests cowards). Abhor implies a deep, often shuddering repugnance (a crime abhorred by all). Abominate, or abomination, suggests strong detestation and often moral condemnation (abominates all forms of violence). Loathe implies utter disgust and intolerance (loathed the mere sight of them). Despise may suggest an emotional response ranging from strong dislike to loathing. Contemn is a vehement condemnation of a person or thing as low, vile, feeble, or ignominious. Scorn implies a ready or indignant contempt. Disdain is an arrogant or supercilious aversion to what is regarded as unworthy. These are words that denote powerful meaning to us. Yet we overlook them and their usage in conveying a message that God would have us rightly understand.

The Bible plainly states, "And ye shall not walk in the manners of the nation, which I cast out before you: for they committed all these things, and therefore I abhorred them."[9] "And if ye shall despise my statutes, or if your soul abhor my judgments, so that ye will not do all my commandments, *but* that ye break my covenant ... I will destroy your high places, and cut down your images, and cast your carcases upon the carcases of your idols, and my soul shall abhor you."[10]

These verses clearly show a progression from God abhorring the action—the sin committed—to abhorring the one committing the abomination. The progressions has to do with the results of righteousness or of sin upon the character. The relationship described is not merely an interaction of tit for tat, or equivalent retaliation, but a cause-to-effect delineation explaining what God must do to protect those who love Him and give Him acceptable service. It is a means by which He actively shelters the righteous from eternal evil when His rebellious creation tests Him on the point of His love of righteousness and His hate for wickedness. It reflects the type of justice God exercises, as taught by Jesus in the New and Old Testaments:

- "But if ye do not forgive, neither will your Father which is in heaven forgive your trespasses."[11]
- "Thou shalt destroy them that speak leasing [falsehoods]: the Lord will abhor the bloody and deceitful man."[12]
- "For the wicked boasteth of his heart's desire, and blesseth the covetous, *whom* the Lord abhorreth."[13]
- "Neither shalt thou bring an abomination into thine house, lest thou be a cursed thing like it: *but* thou shalt utterly detest it, and thou shalt utterly abhor it; for it *is* a cursed thing."[14]

Therefore, we must understand that God's love and hate is based upon the relationship we have to God's

---

8   1 John 3:4; James 4:17
9   Leviticus 20:23
10   Leviticus 26:15, 30
11   Mark 11:26
12   Psalm 5:6
13   Psalm 10:3
14   Deuteronomy 7:26

law. God tests His creation to discover if they will adhere to the embodiment of His character by their demonstrated cheerful and voluntary obedience to His law. Jesus reminded His disciples of this fact when He said, "If ye love me, keep my commandments."[15] Also, we must conclude that by harboring, or beholding, the abomination, we are in danger of being cursed by becoming the accursed thing.

The Bible and Spirit of Prophecy further reveal the nature of God's love and hate by addressing the relational workings of God's repentance. "And it repented the Lord that he had made man on the earth, and it grieved him at his heart. And the Lord said, I will destroy man whom I have created from the face of the earth; both man, and beast, and the creeping thing, and the fowls of the air; for it repenteth me that I have made them."[16]

The following verses demonstrate God's authority over humanity, even though we may be tempted to consider God's choices as arbitrary.

- "God *is* not a man, that he should lie; neither the son of man, that he should repent: hath he said, and shall he not do *it*? or hath he spoken, and shall he not make it good?"[17]
- "For the Lord shall judge his people, and repent himself for his servants, when he seeth that *their* power is gone, and *there is* none shut up, or left."[18]
- "It repenteth me that I have set up Saul *to be* king: for he is turned back from following me, and hath not performed my commandments.... And also the Strength of Israel will not lie nor repent: for he *is* not a man, that he should repent."[19]

If we are confused by the above verses, we have this clarifying remark by Ellen White to help us:

> God's repentance is not like man's repentance.... Man's repentance implies a change of mind. God's repentance implies a change of circumstances and relations. Man may change his relation to God by complying with the conditions upon which he may be brought into the divine favor, or he may, by his own action, place himself outside the favoring condition; but the Lord is the same "yesterday, and today, and forever." Hebrews 13:8. Saul's disobedience changed his relation to God; but the conditions of acceptance with God were unaltered—God's requirements were still the same, for with Him there "is no variableness, neither shadow of turning." James 1:17.[20]

Another quote further aids us in understanding this change in relationship.

> God will have a people separate and distinct from the world. And as soon as any have a desire to imitate the fashions of the world, that they do not immediately subdue, just so soon

---

15   John 14:15; compare to Exodus 20:5, 6
16   Genesis 6:6, 7
17   Numbers 23:19
18   Deuteronomy 32:36
19   1 Samuel 15:11, 29
20   White, *Patriarchs and Prophets*, 630.

God ceases to acknowledge them as His children. They are the children of the world and of darkness. They lust for the leeks and onions of Egypt, that is, desire to be as much like the world as possible; by so doing, those that profess to have put on Christ virtually put Him off, and show that they are strangers to grace and strangers to the meek and lowly Jesus. If they had acquainted themselves with Him, they would walk worthy of Him.[21]

Just how does this progression affect us as we resist the unselfish, unchanging love of God? Jesus preached, "The light of the body is the eye: therefore when thine eye is single, thy whole body also is full of light; but when *thine eye* is evil, thy body also *is* full of darkness. Take heed therefore that the light which is in thee be not darkness. If thy whole body therefore *be* full of light, having no part dark, the whole shall be full of light, as when the bright shining of a candle doth give thee light."[22]

Jesus gave us the principle by which God reveals the light of His love to expel sin from the soul. Ellen White gives us further clarification as to exactly how this principle works.

No soul is ever finally deserted of God, given up to his own ways, so long as there is any hope of his salvation. "Man turns from God, not God from him." Our heavenly Father follows us with appeals and warnings and assurances of compassion, until further opportunities and privileges would be wholly in vain. The responsibility rests with the sinner. By resisting the Spirit of God today, he prepares the way for a second resistance of light when it comes with mightier power. Thus he passes on from one stage of resistance to another, until at last the light will fail to impress, and he will cease to respond in any measure to the Spirit of God. Then even "the light that is in thee" has become darkness. The very truth we do know has become so perverted as to increase the blindness of the soul.[23]

There should be no more confusion as to how our relationship with God is affected by our response to His conditions.

Since God is unchanging and He has conditions that are unalterable, we must know how to identify what those conditions are. Furthermore, if we are to rightly understand this relationship of love and hate in the context of God's law, we must have the right timeframe for our reference.

Time is so very important because many believe that God's love is unconditional but that salvation is conditional—overlooking that time itself is a condition. How unconditional love can formulate conditional salvation becomes a sticking point when one considers that salvation is so closely associated with acceptance, which in turn is connected to love. The process of acceptance or rejection is defined by judgment. Yet judgment is a prominently missing part of unconditional love, for it loves no matter what you do, or what you become. In the process of understanding the distinction between unconditional love and conditional salvation, we must

---

21   White, *Testimonies for the Church*, vol. 1, 137.
22   Luke 11:34–36
23   White, *Thoughts from the Mount of Blessing*, 93.

acknowledge that a conditional salvation is contrary to the very nature of unconditional love. If God's love is unconditional and He does not change, then how can we explain a plan of salvation that has conditions, for that would indicate that God has changed! However, we know for a fact that the Bible tells us that God does not change.[24]

A perfect illustration of how inconsistent it is to proclaim something unconditional when there are indeed notable conditions is provided by commercial advertising. LensCrafters declares an unconditional guarantee on their eyeglasses, stating that customers can exchange or receive a full refund for their eyeglasses or prescription sunglasses if they are not completely happy with their purchase. In order to take advantage of this offer, the glasses must be in their original condition and the return must be made within thirty days of purchase. Did you notice the two conditions embedded in their guarantee? The first one is to return the eyeglasses in their original condition, and the second is to make the return within thirty days. If these two conditions are not met, the guarantee is null and void!

So then why did they include the phrase "unconditional guarantee"? It is obvious that this phrase is used for marketing purposes and to strike a pleasurable chord in the human heart. Most people do not think that time is a condition, but I have personally participated in a phone survey where the primary objective was to determine if most people considered thirty days a reasonable amount of time to establish customer satisfaction with a product.

> *Since God is unchanging and He has conditions that are unalterable, we must know how to identify what those conditions are.*

The matter of timeframe becomes much more important as one sees past the conditions arising from merely selfish convenience to the conditions that allow consideration for the conveniences of all without impinging upon the happiness of any. Consider this. Let's say that your spouse returns from a month-long business trip and says, "Wow, those glasses are hideous. What were you thinking? Why didn't you wait for my input on this significant purchase?" What recourse does a thirty-day condition give the purchaser who suddenly discovers unhappiness with the glasses on day thirty-one? Time is an important condition when contemplating LensCrafters' unconditional guarantee.

Time is also an important factor when determining the veracity of the claim that God's love is unconditional—given the element of probation that God places upon all free moral agents. To that effect one must accept that time itself is a condition of God's love as we consider the breadth of a timeframe, which embraces the concept of probation. The timeframe begins with the creation of Lucifer and the angelic host, with the continuum concluding at the destruction of sin, death, and the unrepentant rebels.

Within the timeframe of probation we must see the proper setting of love and law as rudimentary to the government of God.

---

24   Malachi 3:6

The law of love being the foundation of the government of God, the happiness of all intelligent beings depends upon their perfect accord with its great principles of righteousness. God desires from all His creatures the service of love—service that springs from an appreciation of His character. He takes no pleasure in a forced obedience; and to all He grants freedom of will, that they may render Him voluntary service.

So long as all created beings acknowledged the allegiance of love, there was perfect harmony throughout the universe of God.[25]

God does not force the will or judgment of any. He takes no pleasure in a slavish obedience. He desires that the creatures of His hands shall love Him because He is worthy of love. He would have them obey Him because they have an intelligent appreciation of His wisdom, justice, and benevolence. And all who have a just conception of these qualities will love Him because they are drawn toward Him in admiration of His attributes.[26]

The law of love is the foundation of God's government, and the service of love the only service acceptable to Heaven. God has granted freedom of will to all, endowed men with capacity to appreciate His character, and therefore with ability to love Him and to choose His service. So long as created beings worshiped God they were in harmony throughout the universe. While love to God was supreme, love to others abounded. As there was no transgression of the law, which is the transcript of God's character, no note of discord jarred the celestial harmonies.[27]

In other words, God created all sentient, free moral agents without the taint of sin and with a willingness to be unconditionally surrendered to Him. They were created happy with their situation because God created them to have only that knowledge of good. In the very act of creating, God embedded in every sentient mind—those categorically called free moral agents—knowledge of His law and a desire to learn of Him. We see, then, that "in order to keep the law it is necessary to have a knowledge of God; for the law is a transcript of his character, and his character is love."[28]

The apostle John confirms this truth when he penned, "He that saith, I know him, and keepeth not his commandments, is a liar, and the truth is not in him.... We know that whosoever is born of God sinneth not; but he that is begotten of God keepeth himself, and that wicked one toucheth him not.... And we know that the Son of God is come, and hath given us an understanding, that we may know him that is true, and we are in him that is true, *even* in his Son Jesus Christ. This is the true God, and eternal life."[29]

25   White, *Patriarchs and Prophets*, 34, 35.
26   White, *The Great Controversy*, 541.
27   Ellen G. White, *That I May Know Him* (Washington, D.C.: Review and Herald Publishing Association, 1964), 366.
28   Ellen G. White, "Love Toward God and Man," *Review and Herald*, September 13, 1906.
29   1 John 2:4; 5:18, 20

So, from their creation, unfallen beings have God's law of love written upon their hearts. And, initially, all obeyed that law with joyous harmony until the time when Lucifer chose to rebel against God's law and government because he was envious of Michael the Prince–Christ. When his purpose was further revealed by his discontent, the loyal angels tried to reason with him and bring him into harmony with God. In spite of the unrest and the trouble that Lucifer was stirring up, God was patient with his errant creation. Ellen White provides us with valuable insight into this conflict:

> They [the loyal angels] clearly set forth [to Lucifer] that Christ was the Son of God, existing with Him before the angels were created; and that He had ever stood at the right hand of God, and His mild, loving authority had not heretofore been questioned; and that He had given no commands but what it was joy for the heavenly host to execute.[30]

> God in His great mercy bore long with Lucifer. He was not immediately degraded from his exalted station when he first indulged the spirit of discontent, not even when he began to present his false claims before the loyal angels. Long was he retained in heaven. Again and again he was offered pardon on condition of repentance and submission.[31]

> Such efforts as infinite love and wisdom only could devise, were made to convince him of his error. His disaffection was proved to be without cause, and he was made to see what would be the result of persisting in revolt. Lucifer was convinced that he was in the wrong. He saw that ... the divine statutes are just, and that he ought to acknowledge them as such before all heaven.[32]

Sadly, Lucifer did not heed the pleadings of Christ and the loyal angels.

It is only because God's love is forgiving, merciful, and patient that He does not instantly destroy those who rebel against His justice. God bore long with Lucifer and revealed His love for Lucifer by His patient labors to lead him to repentance. But when Lucifer chose to remain a rebel, and became sin, as well as the originator of sin, then God revealed His love for the rest of His creation by banning Lucifer from heaven and limiting Lucifer's access to others by restricting his movements to the tree of knowledge of good and evil.

While God has graciously given Lucifer time to attempt to prove his false accusations, when God destroys the unrepentant wicked, He will show His wrath and His hatred against sin and those who chose to become sin by their unrighteous thoughts and deeds. In the case of Lucifer and the fallen angels, we see how the timeframe of probation concluded with their refusal to repent until they became sin–unredeemable–having passed that boundary established by God.

What then of the probation of men? "God, in counsel with his Son, formed the plan of creating man in

---

30   Ellen G. White, *The Story of Redemption* (Hagerstown, MD: Review and Herald Publishing Association, 1947), 15.

31   White, *The Great Controversy*, 495, 496.

32   White, *Patriarchs and Prophets*, 39.

their own image. He was placed upon probation. Man was to be tested and proved, and if he should bear the test of God, and remain loyal and true after the first trial, he was not to be beset with continual temptations; but was to be exalted equal with the angels, and henceforth immortal."[33] At their creation, God warned Adam and Eve that, should they eat of the tree of knowledge of good and evil, they would fall under the irrevocable sentence of death. "Immortality was promised them on condition of obedience; by transgression they would forfeit eternal life. That very day they would be doomed to death."[34]

> God placed man under law, as an indispensable condition of his very existence. He was a subject of the divine government, and there can be no government without law. God might have created man without the power to transgress His law; He might have withheld the hand of Adam from touching the forbidden fruit; but in that case man would have been, not a free moral agent, but a mere automaton. Without freedom of choice, his obedience would not have been voluntary, but forced. There could have been no development of character. Such a course would have been contrary to God's plan in dealing with the inhabitants of other worlds. It would have been unworthy of man as an intelligent being, and would have sustained Satan's charge of God's arbitrary rule.[35]

If Adam and Eve had exercised faith in God's word so as to work out obedience to His command not to eat from the tree of knowledge of good and evil, they would have acquitted God's character, as well as themselves since they were created in God's image. Their characters would have been further developed in righteousness

> *God placed man under law, as an indispensable condition of his very existence.*

to the point where no further test would be necessary. Eventually, they would have shown a degree of loyalty that would have resulted in the removal of the prohibited tree. But they corrupted faith by their doubt and disobeyed the express command of God, presuming upon Him to extract them from their sinful condition by the power of His love. Even so, Jesus interposed Himself between the living and the dead from the moment Adam and Eve fell from their perfect state.[36] The resulting consequences are grounded in two laws mentioned by the apostle Paul in his epistle to the Romans: the law of faith and the law of sin.[37] But these two are subordinate to another law—the law of beholding and changing.

Paul explained to the brethren in Corinth how the law of beholding and changing works for our good. "But

---

33   Ellen G. White, "Redemption—No. 1," *Second Advent Review and Sabbath Herald*, February 24, 1874.
34   White, *Patriarchs and Prophets*, 60.
35   Ibid., 49.
36   Ellen G. White, *SDA Bible Commentary*, vol. 1 (Washington, D.C.: Review and Herald Publishing Association, 1953), 1085.
37   Romans 3:27; 7:23

we all, with open face beholding as in a glass the glory of the Lord, are changed into the same image from glory to glory, *even* as by the Spirit of the Lord."[38] Ellen White expands our understanding on the importance of this principle.

> It is a law of the human mind that by beholding we become changed. Man will rise no higher than his conceptions of truth, purity, and holiness. If the mind is never exalted above the level of humanity, if it is not uplifted by faith to contemplate infinite wisdom and love, the man will be constantly sinking lower and lower. The worshipers of false gods clothed their deities with human attributes and passions, and thus their standard of character was degraded to the likeness of sinful humanity. They were defiled in consequence.[39]

> It is a law both of the intellectual and the spiritual nature that by beholding we become changed. The mind gradually adapts itself to the subjects upon which it is allowed to dwell. It becomes assimilated to that which it is accustomed to love and reverence.[40]

Both Paul and Ellen White are restating what Moses had already recorded after speaking to the children of Israel: "Neither shalt thou bring an abomination into thine house, *lest thou be a cursed thing like it: but* thou shalt utterly detest it, and thou shalt utterly abhor it; for it *is* a cursed thing."[41] Joshua strictly warned the Israelites before the conquest of Canaan: "And ye, in any wise keep *yourselves* from the accursed thing, *lest ye make yourselves accursed*, when ye take of the accursed thing, and make the camp of Israel a curse, and trouble it."[42] And David reinforces our understanding of this law of beholding when he penned his observations regarding idol worship: "They that make them are like unto them; *so is* every one that trusteth in them."[43]

The beholding of God's righteousness, love, and faith changes us into His righteousness, love, and faith.

> Looking unto Jesus we obtain brighter and more distinct views of God, and by beholding we become changed. Goodness, love for our fellow men, becomes our natural instinct. We develop a character which is the counterpart of the divine character. Growing into His likeness, we enlarge our capacity for knowing God. More and more we enter into fellowship with the heavenly world, and we have continually increasing power to receive the riches of the knowledge and wisdom of eternity.[44]

Therefore, beholding Jesus strengthens the law of faith in our hearts and minds, empowering us to be

---

38   2 Corinthians 3:18
39   White, *Patriarchs and Prophets*, 91.
40   White, *The Great Controversy*, 555.
41   Deuteronomy 7:26
42   Joshua 6:18
43   Psalm 115:8
44   White, *Christ's Object Lesson*, 355.

changed from glory to glory into Christ's image.

On the other hand, the beholding of the specious attractions presented to us by Satan changes us into sinful and wicked creatures over time until we cross the boundary beyond which the love of Christ can no longer draw the unrepentant sinner to Him.

> By beholding we become changed. Though formed in the image of his Maker, man can so educate his mind that sin which he once loathed will become pleasant to him. As he ceases to watch and pray, he ceases to guard the citadel, the heart, and engages in sin and crime. The mind is debased, and it is impossible to elevate it from corruption while it is being educated to enslave the moral and intellectual powers, and bring them in subjection to grosser passions. Constant war against the carnal mind must be maintained; and we must be aided by the refining influence of the grace of God, which will attract the mind upward and habituate it to meditate upon pure and holy things.[45]

> It is thus that Satan still seeks to compass the ruin of the soul. A long preparatory process, unknown to the world, goes on in the heart before the Christian commits open sin. The mind does not come down at once from purity and holiness to depravity, corruption, and crime. It takes time to degrade those formed in the image of God to the brutal or the satanic. By beholding we become changed. By the indulgence of impure thoughts man can so educate his mind that sin which he once loathed will become pleasant to him.[46]

It was by this process that the antediluvians eventually became sin. "And God saw that the wickedness of man *was* great in the earth, and *that* every imagination of the thoughts of his heart *was* only evil continually."[47] The Hebrew word here translated as imagination actually encompasses the desires and purposes of the unrepentant antediluvians. They became sin by their continuous evil thoughts, purposes, and desires until they no longer were inclined to behold righteousness at all. "By beholding evil, men became changed into its image, until God could bear with their wickedness no longer, and they were swept away by the flood."[48] The time came when God's hate of sin was aimed at the sinner who so cherished sin that he had become sin itself, and "God was forced to destroy its inhabitants for their heaven-defying wickedness."[49]

For 120 years, wicked men abused mercy and grace. Did they want what they had abused when the waters came in the deluge?

From the highest peaks men looked abroad upon a shoreless ocean. The solemn warnings

---

45   Ellen G. White, *Testimonies for the Church*, vol. 2 (Mountain View, CA: Pacific Press Publishing Association, 1871), 479.
46   White, *Patriarchs and Prophets*, 459.
47   Genesis 6:5
48   Ellen G. White, *Fundamentals of Christian Education* (Nashville, TN: Southern Publishing Association, 1923), 422
49   Ellen G. White, "The Privilege of God's People," *The Review and Herald*, October 23, 1888.

of God's servant no longer seemed a subject for ridicule and scorning. How those doomed sinners longed for the opportunities which they had slighted! How they pleaded for one hour's probation, one more privilege of mercy, one call from the lips of Noah! But the sweet voice of mercy was no more to be heard by them. Love, no less than justice, demanded that God's judgments should put a check on sin. The avenging waters swept over the last retreat, and the despisers of God perished in the black depths.[50]

If God's love is unconditional, then how can it demand executed judgment? Such a love has no conditions by which one could make a distinction between justice and injustice.

Fortunately, the Bible makes the distinction by providing us with a record establishing God's Ten Commandments as the moral law of love. Then it tells us that there is a time to love and a time to hate—everything in its season. What else does the Bible have to say about hate as it relates to God?

Remember, in all these passages, we are learning about a God who is Omniscient. We are seeking to know a God who already knows us. He said to Jeremiah, "Before I formed thee in the belly I knew thee; and before thou camest forth out of the womb I sanctified thee, *and* I ordained thee a prophet unto the nations."[51] He already knows the outcome of our life choices before we are even faced with the challenges presented to us. How else could He have foretold the actions of Judas Iscariot, of which the prophesy states, "Yea, mine own familiar friend, in whom I trusted, which did eat of my bread, hath lifted up *his* heel against me."[52]

How well did the psalmist prophesy of Judas when he wrote Psalm 109:2–14:

> For the mouth of the wicked and the mouth of the deceitful are opened against me: they have spoken against me with a lying tongue. They compassed me about also with words of hatred; and fought against me without a cause. For my love they are my adversaries: but I *give myself unto* prayer. And they have rewarded me evil for good, and hatred for my love. Set thou a wicked man over him: and let Satan stand at his right hand. When he shall be judged, let him be condemned: and let his prayer become sin. Let his days be few; *and* let another take his office. Let his children be fatherless, and his wife a widow. Let his children be continually vagabonds, and beg: let them seek *their bread* also out of their desolate places. Let the extortioner catch all that he hath; and let the strangers spoil his labour. Let there be none to extend mercy unto him: neither let there be any to favour his fatherless children. Let his posterity be cut off; *and* in the generation following let their name be blotted out. Let the iniquity of his fathers be remembered with the Lord; and let not the sin of his mother be blotted out.

---

50   White, *Patriarchs and Prophets*, 100, 101.
51   Jeremiah 1:5
52   Psalm 41:9

Judas fulfilled prophecy—not because God forced him to the prophesied destiny—but because Judas made the choice to hold on to his greed and selfish ambition until it overpowered him and he became sin. If Judas had perceived the warning given to Cain—"If thou doest well, shalt thou not be accepted? and if thou doest not well, sin lieth at the door. And unto thee *shall be* his desire, and thou shalt rule over him"[53]—as applicable to himself, perhaps he would have heeded the call of unselfish love to repentance from selfishness.

Throughout the Psalms we see a pattern as it relates to what the end shall be of the unrepentant wicked. "The foolish shall not stand in thy sight: thou hatest all workers of iniquity."[54] "The Lord trieth the righteous: but the wicked and him that loveth violence his soul hateth."[55] "I hate them with perfect hatred: I count them mine enemies."[56] "The Lord preserveth all them that love him: but all the wicked will he destroy."[57]

Such distinctions are the product of a love that judges with a far-reaching, righteous discernment. "God will not be trifled with.... God is a sin-hating God. And those who encourage the sinner, saying, It is well with thee, God will curse."[58] "Though God is strict to mark iniquity and to punish transgression, He takes no delight in vengeance. The work of destruction is a 'strange work' to Him who is infinite in love."[59] Ellen White also wrote:

> The Lord does not delight in vengeance, though he executes judgment upon the transgressors of his law. He is forced to do this, to preserve the inhabitants of the earth from utter depravity and ruin. In order to save some, he must cut off those who have become hardened in sin....
>
> The very fact of God's unwillingness to punish sinners shows the enormity of the sins that call forth his judgments.[60]

Yet His unwillingness to punish sinners will not interfere with His purpose, for Moses spoke to the people the truth when he proclaimed, after warning them of the curses which should follow them if they departed from God's law, "And it shall come to pass, *that* as the Lord rejoiced over you to do you good, and to multiply you; so the Lord will rejoice over you to destroy you, and to bring you to nought; and ye shall be plucked from off the land whither thou goest to possess it."[61]

Can we then conclude that from the moment an unfallen free moral agent chooses to sin that God then immediately hates this new sinner? Not at all! Although Satan would tempt us to believe that we must somehow do something to change God's hate to love and that Christ was given for that purpose, we are told that:

---

53   Genesis 4:7
54   Psalm 5:5
55   Psalm 11:5
56   Psalm 139:22
57   Psalm 145:20
58   White, *Testimonies for the Church*, vol. 3, 272.
59   White, *Patriarchs and Prophets*, 139.
60   Ellen G. White, "A Doomed People," *The Signs of the Times*, August 24, 1882.
61   Deuteronomy 28:63.

The atonement of Christ was not made in order to induce God to love those whom he otherwise hated; it was not made to produce a love that was not in existence; but it was made as a manifestation of the love that was already in God's heart, an exponent of the divine favor in the sight of heavenly intelligences, in the sight of worlds unfallen, and in the sight of a fallen race.... We are not to entertain the idea that God loves us because Christ has died for us, but that he so loved us that he gave his only-begotten Son to die for us. The death of Christ was expedient in order that mercy might reach us with its full pardoning power, and at the same time that justice might be satisfied in the righteous substitute. The glory of God was revealed in the rich mercy that he poured out upon a race of rebels, who through repentance and faith might be pardoned through the merits of Christ, for God will by no means clear the guilty who refuse to acknowledge the merit of a crucified and risen Saviour.[62]

When we clearly understand what is meant by the simple fact that God will not clear the unrepentant guilty then we can begin to comprehend that God is consistent with His character and the law, which reflects that character.

God executes justice upon the wicked, for the good of the universe, and even for the good of those upon whom His judgments are visited. He would make them happy if He could do so in accordance with the laws of His government and the justice of His character. He surrounds them with the tokens of His love, He grants them a knowledge of His law, and follows them with the offers of His mercy; but they despise His love, make void His law, and reject His mercy. While constantly receiving His gifts, they dishonor the Giver; they hate God because they know that He abhors their sins. The Lord bears long with their perversity; but the decisive hour will come at last, when their destiny is to be decided. Will He then chain these rebels to His side? Will He force them to do His will?[63]

We get a more complete understanding of what the Bible teaches about God's hatred of sin and those who become sin as we read what the prophet Hosea wrote: "All their wickedness is in Gilgal: for there I hated them: for the wickedness of their doings I will drive them out of mine house, I will love them no more: all their princes are revolters."[64] Those who continue to war against God and His law will suffer the very same fate as the devil and his fallen cohorts, for only to the unfallen beings and to the repentant sinner is infinite love immeasurable. "But if men continue to resist light and evidence, they will cut themselves off from God's mercy, and then will come the ministry of wrath. God can not save the sinner in his sin. The love of God is immeasurable to those

---

62   Ellen G. White, "Christ Our Complete Salvation," *The Signs of the Times*, May 30, 1895.
63   White, *The Great Controversy*, 542.
64   Hosea 9:15

who repent, but His justice is firm and uncompromising to those who abuse his long-suffering love."[65]

God does not arbitrarily love some and hate others. No one is predestined to be hated by God while He bestows love upon others. In Malachi 1:2, 3, we read, "I have loved you, saith the Lord. Yet ye say, Wherein hast thou loved us? Was not Esau Jacob's brother? saith the Lord: yet I loved Jacob, And I hated Esau, and laid his mountains and his heritage waste for the dragons of the wilderness." And Paul referred to Malachi when he wrote Romans 9:13, 14: "As it is written, Jacob have I loved, but Esau have I hated. What shall we say then? Is there unrighteousness with God? God forbid."

> *The love of God is immeasurable to those who repent, but His justice is firm and uncompromising to those who abuse his long-suffering love.*

True, Esau despised the responsibilities of the birthright while desiring the wealth derived from the double portion granted to the firstborn. But that did not cut him off from the hope of salvation. "Esau was not shut out from the privilege of seeking God's favor by repentance, but he could find no means of recovering the birthright. His grief did not spring from conviction of sin; he did not desire to be reconciled to God. He sorrowed because of the results of his sin, but not for the sin itself."[66] Not willing to be reconciled with God, he did not obtain from God the only power by which he might be transformed and renewed.

Jacob had no advantage over Esau by reason of his birth. He had inherited no more a natural propensity to goodness than Esau. So, why would God love Jacob and hate Esau?

> Esau and Jacob had alike been instructed in the knowledge of God, and both were free to walk in His commandments and to receive His favor; but they had not both chosen to do this. The two brothers had walked in different ways, and their paths would continue to diverge more and more widely.
>
> There was no arbitrary choice on the part of God by which Esau was shut out from the blessings of salvation. The gifts of His grace through Christ are free to all. There is no election but one's own by which any may perish. God has set forth in His word the conditions upon which every soul will be elected to eternal life—obedience to His commandments, through faith in Christ. God has elected a character in harmony with His law, and anyone who shall reach the standard of His requirement will have an entrance into the kingdom of glory.[67]

And so it is with us as we make decisions throughout our lives. We may have made poor choices in the past, as did Jacob, but God is merciful and gracious to those who desire to sincerely repent. Always remember:

---

65   Ellen G. White, "The Law Revealed in Christ," *The Signs of the Times*, November 15, 1899.
66   White, *Patriarchs and Prophets*, 181.
67   Ibid., 207.

No soul is ever finally deserted of God, given up to his own ways, so long as there is any hope of his salvation. "Man turns from God, not God from him." Our heavenly Father follows us with appeals and warnings and assurances of compassion, until further opportunities and privileges would be wholly in vain. The responsibility rests with the sinner. By resisting the Spirit of God today, he prepares the way for a second resistance of light when it comes with mightier power. Thus he passes on from one stage of resistance to another, until at last the light will fail to impress, and he will cease to respond in any measure to the Spirit of God. Then even "the light that is in thee" has become darkness. [Matthew 6:23; Luke 11:35] The very truth we do know has become so perverted as to increase the blindness of the soul.[68]

Just as it is important to distinguish between the wrath of God and the wrath of Satan, we must understand the difference between God's hatred and Satan's hatred. God hates sin. However, He loves sinners to the extent that He gave His only begotten Son. But He will never abolish His law to save the sinner.

It is not by abolishing one jot or tittle of the law of God that salvation is brought to the fallen race. If God were a changeable being, no confidence could be placed in His government. If He retracted what He said, we could not then take His Word as the foundation of our faith. Had He changed His law to meet fallen men, Satan's claim that man could not keep the law would have been proved true. But God did not alter His law. The death of Christ testifies to the heavenly universe, to the worlds unfallen, and to all the sons and daughters of Adam, that the law of God is immutable, and that in the judgment it will condemn every one who has persisted in transgression. The God who rules the world in love and wisdom testifies in the death of His Son to His changeless character. He could not change His character as expressed in His law, but He could give His Son, one with Himself, possessing His attributes, to a fallen world. By so doing, He magnified His name and glory as a God above all gods.[69]

While God certainly doesn't take pleasure in the death of the wicked, Satan delights in the destruction of anyone and anything that was created in the image of God. There is definitely a righteous hatred and an unrighteous hatred as is demonstrated in the following statements:

- "Satan had worked long to efface the true impression of God, and to represent Him as a God having no love. This is Satan's character. He is destitute of mercy and compassion. Overbearing and revengeful, he delights in the misery that he brings on the human family. With these attributes he attempted to clothe the God of heaven."[70]
- "Satan has ascribed to God all the evils to which flesh is heir. He has represented him as a God who

---

68   White, *Thoughts from the Mount of Blessing*, 93.
69   White, "The Sabbath of the Lord—No. 2."
70   Ellen G. White, "The Way, the Truth, and the Life—No. 3," *The Signs of the Times*, January 20, 1898.

delights in the sufferings of his creatures, who is revengeful and implacable. It was Satan who origi-nated the doctrine of eternal torment as a punishment for sin, because in this way he could lead men into infidelity and rebellion, distract souls, and dethrone the human reason."[71]

- "Christ came to represent the Father. We behold in him the image of the invisible God. He clothed his divinity with humanity, and came to the world that the erroneous ideas Satan had been the means of creating in the minds of men, in regard to the character of God, might be removed."[72]

Within Ellen White's writings we find a couple of bothersome expressions that many have sought to rec-oncile to their own ideas.[73] One is found in a letter dated March 14, 1860, to her son Willie White when he was about six years old:

> The Lord loves those little children who try to do right, and he has promised that they shall be in his kingdom. But wicked children God does not love. He will not take them to the beautiful City, for he only admits the good, obedient, and patient children there. One fretful, disobedient child, would spoil all the harmony of heaven. When you feel tempted to speak impatient and fretful, remember the Lord sees you, and will not love you if you do wrong. When you do right and overcome wrong feelings, the Lord smiles upon you.[74]

When contrasted with other statements, apparent contradictions rankle in the minds of unconditional love proponents. For example, "The glory of the Lord is his goodness and love. Then do not teach your children that God frowns upon them, but that when they sin they grieve the Spirit of God who always loves them."[75] The usual argument is that Ellen White wrote to a six-year-old child concerning a theology that that age group cannot possibly understand. Also argued is the concept that the timing of the letter was early in Ellen White's ministry, resulting in the unwarranted conclusion that her own understanding of God's love lacked matura-tion. The later point is problematic as we see in the next quote.

Published multiple times throughout Ellen White's ministry in an appeal to indulgent parents who dis-honor God by their overindulgent practices, she wrote:

> Parents stand in the place of God to their children and they will have to render an account, whether they have been faithful to the little few committed to their care. Parents, some of you are rearing children to be cut down by the destroying angel, unless you speedily change your course, and be faithful to them. God cannot cover iniquity, even in children. He cannot love unruly children who manifest passion, and he cannot save them in the time

71   Ellen G. White, *Christian Education* (Battle Creek, MI: International Tract Society, 1894), 73.
72   *The Signs of the Times*, January 20, 1890.
73   Herbert E. Douglass, *Messenger of the Lord: The Prophetic Ministry of Ellen G. White* (Nampa, ID: Pacific Press Publishing Association, 1998), 59, 60. This view is the most balanced of the several ideas I have come across. However, it does not have a time condition approach, nor does it incorporate the law of beholding, both of which better reconcile the apparent contradiction.
74   Ellen G. White, *An Appeal to the Youth* (Battle Creek, MI: Seventh-day Adventist Publishing Association, 1864), 62, 63.
75   Ellen G. White, "Ye Are Complete in Him," *The Signs of the Times*, February 22, 1892.

of trouble. Will you suffer your children to be lost through your neglect? Unfaithful parents, their blood will be upon you, and is not your salvation doubtful with the blood of your children upon you?[76]

Since this quote was published as early as 1854 and as late as 1913, no change in Ellen White's view on love can be attributed to a maturation process, or she would have corrected or adjusted the statement when published at later times.

The apparent contradiction that makes these statements bothersome is reconciled with the understanding that God loves until He is forced to respond with an inflexible, uncompromised justice. Time is a condition. The law of beholding must have time to unfold and reveal the true nature and character of the person. God, as Creator, is "the Rock, his work *is* perfect: for all his ways *are* judgment: a God of truth and without iniquity, just and right *is* he."[77] The following is true of Lucifer, his angels, and Adam and Eve: "Thou *wast* perfect in thy ways from the day that thou wast created, till iniquity was found in thee."[78]

God would not hate that which is perfect. Nor would He hate that which is redeemable. But neither can God, who is love, continue to love that which is rejected. And those who teach that God's love is unconditional cannot accept any statement of Scripture or the Spirit of Prophecy that contradicts their view. The only alternative is to diminish God by attributing to Him a love that they themselves desire in place of the truth, or diminishing what the Bible and Ellen White have written in regards to God's hate and His wrath.

One way by which they attempt to diminish the concept of hate in the Bible is by misapplying a statement made by Ellen White that pertains to Luke 14:26 to many other Bible passages. Not only do they misapply it, but they also only focus on the first part of the quote.

> Hate referred to in Luke 14:26, means a less degree of love. We are to have supreme love to God, and our friends are to be loved secondarily. Our love for husband, wife, brother, sisters, father, or mother, must be inferior to our love to God. Our love for these dear relatives must not be blind and selfish, and cause us to forget God. When these ties of relationship lead us to prefer their favor by disregarding the truth, we love them more than we love Jesus, and are not worthy of him. In that fearful time when we need an arm to protect and shield us, stronger than any human arm, stronger than the arm of father, brother, or husband, and shall call upon him that is mighty to save, he will not hear us. He will bid us to lean upon those whom we preferred before him, whom we loved above him, whom we would not forsake for him. He will say, Let them deliver you, let them save you. I gave you proof of my love. I left the glory of my Father, and all my majesty and splendor, and came

---

76   Ellen G. White, "Duty of Parents to Their Children," *The Review and Herald*, September 19, 1854. See also the same quote in "Duty of Parents to Their Children," *The Review and Herald*, October 14, 1875; "Obedience the Path to Life," *The Review and Herald*, March 28, 1893; and "Need of Church Schools," *Gospel Medical Messenger*, November 19, 1913.

77   Deuteronomy 32:4

78   Ezekiel 28:15

into a world cursed with sin and pollution. For your sakes I became poor, that you through my poverty might be made rich. I bore insult and mockery, and died a shameful death upon the cross, to save you from hopeless misery and death. Yet this did not excite your love enough to obey me, and lead you to prefer my favor above the favor of earthly friends, who have given you but feeble proofs of their love. I know you not; depart from me.[79]

If Ellen White intended for us to define every biblical use of the word hate in relationship to God and workers of iniquity, why then did she specifically tell us the appropriate meaning as applied specifically to Luke 14:26?

Closer examination of the whole quote shows that love is to be hierarchical, which implies a condition of place in relationship to one another and God. Unconditional love has no such hierarchy because it is condition-less—all are loved with equal intimacy; no one is preferred above another. God's demonstration of love—Christ's perfect obedience to the commandments of the Father and substituted death on our behalf for our disobedience—perfectly requires an excited love on our part, which motivates us to follow Christ's example of perfect obedience to the Father. Coupled with the simple fact that we are given a probationary time in which we are sanctified by the Holy Spirit dwelling in us, we can only see conditions righteously associated with God's love—not for His selfish convenience, but for the happiness of all who will obey out of genuine appreciation for God's wisdom and justice.

We cannot deny that "the Saviour regards with infinite tenderness the souls whom He has purchased with His own blood. They are the claim of His love. He looks upon them with unutterable longing. His heart is drawn out, not only to the best-behaved children, but to those who have by inheritance objectionable traits of character. Many parents do not understand how much they are responsible for these traits in their children. They have not the tenderness and wisdom to deal with the erring ones whom they have made what they are. But Jesus looks upon these children with pity. He traces from cause to effect."[80]

So, in context of time, this quote indicates that probation has not yet closed for these children. We are not to hate our brothers, or our enemies, or children with objectionable traits of character while their probation remains open. To do so would contradict the commands of Christ to not judge others, instead we are to be His ambassadors and try to reconcile others to Christ.[81] Although God calls us not to judge others, we can rest assured that He will give us wisdom and discernment to make a distinction between the righteous and the wicked—those who serve Him and those who disobey Him.[82]

"While we cannot love and fellowship those who are the bitter enemies of Christ, we should cultivate that spirit of meekness and love that characterized our Master,—a love that thinketh no evil and is not easily provoked."[83] Still, we ought not to accept the vain philosophies and teachings of individuals. We should always

---

79   Ellen G. White, "An Extract from a Letter Written to a Distance Female Friend," *The Review and Herald*, September 16, 1862.
80   White, *The Desire of Ages*, 517.
81   1 Corinthians 4:5; 2 Corinthians 5:20
82   Malachi 3:18
83   Ellen G. White, "Love Among Brethren," *The Review and Herald*, June 3, 1884.

remember that "spiritual things are spiritually discerned. Those who have no vital union with God are swayed one way and another; they put men's opinions in the front, and God's word in the background. They grasp human assertions, that judgment against sin is contrary to God's benevolent character, and, while dwelling upon infinite benevolence, try to forget that there is such a thing as infinite justice."[84]

Another quote upheld by those who teach unconditional love needs to be seen in its context.

> It is not Christ's follower that, with averted eyes, turns from the erring, leaving them unhindered to pursue their downward course. Those who are forward in accusing others, and zealous in bringing them to justice, are often in their own lives more guilty than they. Men hate the sinner, while they love the sin. Christ hates the sin, but loves the sinner. This will be the spirit of all who follow Him. Christian love is slow to censure, quick to discern penitence, ready to forgive, to encourage, to set the wanderer in the path of holiness, and to stay his feet therein.[85]

In cultivating that spirit of meekness and love that characterized Christ's life and deportment, we will go out and seek the lost. In the context of probation, we are to hate the sin and love the sinner. We show our love by seeking them out, pointing them to the love and obedience of Christ accomplished on their behalf, and showing them how to repent of their sins.

However, there will be a time when judgment must be rendered. When Christ returns at the second coming, He will take the righteous to heaven where they will live for one thousand years. During the millennium the redeemed righteous are to judge the unrepentant wicked and assign to them the length of punishment. Judgment will reflect the justice of God and His hatred of sin as well as those who have become sin by reason of the law of beholding.[86]

Throughout Scripture and Spirit of Prophecy, we see that God's love (as mercy) is in close relationship with justice. Unconditional love has no relationship with justice because it does away with the bi-products of justice—judgment and accountability. Those who choose to believe that God's love is unconditional will find out too late that they are mistaken.

> The truth as it is in Jesus will teach most important lessons. It will show that the love of God is broad and deep; that it is infinite; and that in awarding the penalty to the disobedient, those who have made void God's law, it will be uncompromising. This is the love and the justice of God combined. It reaches to the very depth of human woe and degradation, to lift up the fallen and oppressed who lay hold of the truth by repentance and faith in Jesus. And

---

84   Ellen G. White, "Science and Revelation," *The Signs of the Times*, March 13, 1884.

85   White, *The Desire of Ages*, 462.

86   See Daniel 7:22; Psalm 58:10, 11; 1 Corinthians 6:3; Revelation 20:4; "In union with Christ they judge the wicked, comparing their acts with the statute book, the Bible, and deciding every case according to the deeds done in the body. Then the portion which the wicked must suffer is meted out, according to their works; and it is recorded against their names in the book of death" (White, *The Great Controversy*, 661). "Some are destroyed as in a moment, while others suffer many days" (Ibid., 673).

God works for the good of the universe, for the good of the rebellious sinner, by causing the sinner to suffer the penalty of his sin.[87]

The time for long-suffering mercy is nearly fulfilled. Soon the destinies of all will be eternally sealed. Satan knows that his time is short, and he is working with cunning deceptiveness and great wrath to cause as many people as possible to join his ranks.[88] Therefore, we should heed the warning of the Spirit of Prophecy:

> The great controversy between Christ and Satan, that has been carried forward for nearly six thousand years, is soon to close; and the wicked one redoubles his efforts to defeat the work of Christ in man's behalf and to fasten souls in his snares. To hold the people in darkness and impenitence till the Saviour's mediation is ended, and there is no longer a sacrifice for sin, is the object which he seeks to accomplish.[89]

Knowing Satan's purpose, we should be diligent in seeking God with all our hearts so that we may find Him.

---

87   Ellen G. White, "The Truth Revealed in Jesus," *The Review and Herald*, February 8, 1898.
88   Revelation 12:12
89   White, *The Great Controversy*, 518.

Chapter 5

Shades of Provocation

Throughout history the eventuality of war is directly linked to provocations—both real and imagined. Tracing those circumstances, and identifying them for what they truly are, can be very rewarding because the truth allows us freedom to judge whether the cause was truly righteous or not. Depending upon the development of any given situation, we can determine whether further attempts at diplomacy would indeed have been beneficial or if the wronged party was actually forced to arms to protect their sphere of influence as well as vital interests. Unfortunately, the task of tracing the circumstances is always arduous because of the tendency of certain scoundrels to camouflage their true intent.

Debate still continues to flourish over whether or not the Twin Towers of the World Trade center were brought down by either commercial or military airliners on September 11, 2001, at great cost of innocent lives. But the provocation by the accused militants of fanatic Muslims was enough to justify a "crusade" against terrorist extremists while denying a war against any one religion despite the accumulating evidences that the whole world may have been set up to accept this inevitability.[1]

Because of the scope of the attacks on September 11, many drew references to the Japanese attacks on Pearl Harbor, Hawaii, that infamous day, December 7, 1941. But some contend that the real reason for Japan's attack was because of unbearable strain upon that government's resources because of the sanctions embargo, known as the 1940 Export Control Act, imposed by the United States.

> Under that act, licenses were refused for the export to Japan of aviation gasoline and most types of machine tools, beginning in August 1940. After it was announced in September that the export of iron and steel scrap would be prohibited, Japanese Ambassador Horinouchi protested to Secretary Hull on October 8, 1940 that this might be considered an "unfriendly act". The Secretary told the Ambassador that it was really "amazing" for the Japanese Government, which had been violating in the most aggravating manner American rights and interests throughout most of China, to question the fullest right of

---

1   President George W. Bush made the remark, "This crusade, this war on terrorism, is going to take awhile," in a speech to the American people on Sunday, September 16, 2001. The next day, from an Islamic center in Washington, DC, he told Americans, "The face of terror is not the true faith of Islam. That's not what Islam is all about." Calling the attacks on New York City and Washington, DC, acts of war, President Bush moved Congress to authorize him with the power to use force in punishing those responsible for the acts of terror committed against the American people. For detailed evidence that it may have been a setup, see the DVD "In Plane Sight" produced by The Power Hour radio talk show host Dave vonKleist.

this Government to impose such an embargo. To go further and call it an "unfriendly act", the Secretary said, was still more amazing in the light of Japan's conduct in disregarding all law, treaty obligations, and other rights and privileges and the safety of Americans, while proceeding to an ever-increasing extent to seize territory by force....

The effect of United States policy in regard to exports to Japan was that by the winter of 1940–41 shipment had ceased of many strategic commodities including arms, ammunition, and implements of war, aviation gasoline and many other petroleum products, machine tools, scrap iron, pig iron, iron and steel manufactures, copper, lead, zinc, aluminum, and a variety of other commodities important to war effort.[2]

So, in the opinion of the Japanese, America was the provocateur, thereby justifying their preemptive strike against Pearl Harbor.

Hitler declared war against Poland on September 1, 1939, on the pretext of what turned out to be a staged attack against a German radio station by Nazis fitted in Polish uniforms the day before—now known as the Gleiwitz incident. In order to make the guilt of Poland more convincing, the Germans set up Franciszek Honiok, a German-speaking Polish Silesian who was known for sympathizing with the Poles. He had been arrested the previous day by the Gestapo. To carry out their plan, the SS troopers dressed Honiok up as a saboteur. They then lethally injected him, shot him, and left him for dead at the scene. They attempted to make it look as if Honiok was killed while attacking the station. With Honiok's body as proof of the attack, Hitler proclaimed Polish provocation and justified Germany's invasion. Not until the Nuremburg trials at the close of the war did the truth come out.[3]

Many other examples of provocations to war could be used to embellish the need for illustrating the non-existence of unconditional love wherever provocation is realized. After all, if unconditional love has no conditions by which tolerance or intolerance may be determined, then one can certainly conclude that no act would be a provocative one!

However, one such example from the Bible depicts the willingness of a king to submit to another monarch—to a point. The story is found in 1 Kings 2:1–11, and we enter the story with King Ahab being surrounded by the Syrian army. King Benhadad gave him the conditions of peace: "Thy silver and thy gold *is* mine; thy wives also and thy children, *even* the goodliest, *are* mine." Wanting to keep the peace, Ahab replied, "My lord, O king, according to thy saying, I *am* thine, and all that I have."

Benhadad must have thought Ahab a weak, frightened leader, so he pushed his luck and demanded more. "Although I have sent unto thee, saying, Thou shalt deliver me thy silver, and thy gold, and thy wives, and thy children; Yet I will send my servants unto thee to morrow about this time, and they shall search thine house, and the houses of thy servants; and it shall be, *that* whatsoever is pleasant in thine eyes, they shall put *it* in their hand, and take *it* away."

2   *Peace and War, United States Foreign Policy 1931–1941* (Washington, D.C.: U.S. Government Printing Office, 1943), 96, 97.

3   Museum on Radio History and Visual Arts, Gliwice Radio Station, http://1ref.us/l.

This proved to be too much for Ahab. He said to his counselors, "Mark, I pray you, and see how this *man* seeketh mischief: for he sent unto me for my wives, and for my children, and for my silver, and for my gold; and I denied him not." So they approved Ahab's use of force to repel the invaders. Upon receiving this news, Benhadad angrily exclaimed, "The gods do so unto me, and more also, if the dust of Samaria shall suffice for handfuls for all the people that follow me."

Here is where Ahab gets a bit sassy and a little jocular in his response to Benhadad's threat. He told the messengers sent by Benhadad to say to the king, "Let not him that girdeth on *his harness* boast himself as he that putteth it off."[4]

Fighting words indeed! God chose to fight for Israel that day, and Ahab won a great victory. Still, it only provoked another war the next year, which God, through His prophet, told Ahab he would have the victory. However, the conquest was tarnished because Ahab did not kill Benhadad. Instead he allowed him to live and escape. This sin on Ahab's part brought about a death sentence. "Thus saith the Lord, Because thou hast let go out of *thy* hand a man whom I appointed to utter destruction, therefore thy life shall go for his life, and thy people for his people."[5]

In most instances, provocation leads to an expected, if not forced, response. When one provokes another, it is usually to incite to anger. It is a deliberate act prompted by intentions to frustrate, exasperate, aggravate, inflame, or otherwise rile.

When we turn to the Bible, we see evidence to debunk the false claim that love cannot be provoked. Despite the proclamation of many proponents of unconditional love that there are no prerequisites, condemnation, or judgment, the Bible proves otherwise. Their contention only proves that unconditional love has no moral boundaries, thereby limiting one's behaviors to a confined absolute. So, the logical conclusion is that unconditional love cannot be provoked—therefore judgments will not be executed. Unconditional love has an expected consequence whereby otherwise known acts of provocation are ignored, and evil is not resisted. Proponents proudly cite Jesus' command to turn the other cheek. Never mind that God said vengeance belongs to Him or that He will exercise judgment in the last day by sending fire from heaven to consume and cleanse the earth.[6]

> *Unconditional love and jealousy are mutually exclusive. How can jealousy be identified except there be some condition by which it can exist?*

When considering the revealed properties of love, we turn to Paul's first letter to the Corinthians. "Charity suffereth long, *and* is kind; charity envieth not; charity vaunteth not itself, is not puffed up, Doth not behave itself unseemly, seeketh not her own, is not easily provoked, thinketh no evil; Rejoiceth not in iniquity, but rejoiceth in the truth; Beareth all things, believeth all things, hopeth all things, endureth all things. Charity

---

4   1 Kings 20:1–11
5   1 Kings 20:42
6   Matthew 5:39; Deuteronomy 32:35; Psalm 94:1; Romans 3:5; 2 Thessalonians 1:8; Hebrews 10:30

never faileth."[7]

Regarding love's response to provocation, the King James Version definitely tells us that love, or charity, is not easily provoked. Yet several modern translations tell us that love "is not provoked."[8] Regarding love, the King James Version states that it "thinketh no evil." Yet many modern translations state that love doesn't keep a record of wrongs.[9] These versions, adhering more to the Latin Vulgate than to the Reformers' Bibles, based upon the received text compiled by Erasmus, are definitely trying to give support for the concept of unconditional love that the rest of the Bible simply does not supply.

We know that God is love.[10] Yet, can God be jealous? Does God keep a record of transgressions? Can God be provoked? What does the Bible say about the only true God that reflects upon the nature of His love and character?

The second commandment states, "Thou shalt not make unto thee any graven image, or any likeness of any thing that is in heaven above, or that is in the earth beneath, or that is in the water under the earth. Thou shalt not bow down thyself to them, nor serve them: for I the Lord thy God am a jealous God, visiting the iniquity of the fathers upon the children unto the third and fourth generation of them who hate me; and shewing mercy unto thousands of them that love me, and keep my commandments."[11]

Later, Moses reminded the Israelites of God's character, saying, "For thou shalt worship no other god: for the Lord, whose name is Jealous, is a jealous God."[12] Before he made his last journey up Mount Pisgah, Moses again reminded the people that "the Lord thy God is a consuming fire, even a jealous God."[13]

These statements indicate the degree of intimacy God desires to have with all who profess to be His people. The relationship was to be exclusive in that God's people were to cleave to no other one who attempts to assert a higher claim than His—that they would be included as those who loved Him if they kept His commandments, or they would be excluded as those who hated Him by rebelling against His law. "The close and sacred relation of God to His people is represented under the figure of marriage. Idolatry being spiritual adultery, the displeasure of God against it is fitly called jealousy."[14] To the polyamourist, unconditional love allows for inclusiveness and intimacy that God, being a jealous God, prohibits—judging it adultery, which carries with it a penalty of death. Unconditional love and jealousy are mutually exclusive. How can jealousy be identified except there be some condition by which it can exist?

Because God is a jealous God, it is possible to provoke Him to jealousy and to anger. In communing with Moses before calling him up into the mount for the first forty days of instruction, God told him, "Behold, I send an Angel before thee, to keep thee in the way, and to bring thee into the place which I have prepared. Beware of him, and obey his voice, provoke him not; for he will not pardon your transgressions: for my name [Jealous]

---

7   1 Corinthians 13:4–8
8   NKJV, NASB, ASV, Young, Douay-Rheims
9   CEV, TEV, BBE, ASV, Darby, Young, NIV, NLT, NCV, NIRV, TNIV
10   1 John 4:8
11   Exodus 20:4–6
12   Exodus 34:14
13   Deuteronomy 4:24
14   White, *Patriarchs and Prophets*, 306.

is in him. But if thou shalt indeed obey his voice, and do all that I speak; then I will be an enemy unto thine enemies, and an adversary unto thine adversaries."[15]

Furthermore, God keeps a record of all our thoughts and acts. Psalms 109:14, predicting the betrayal of Jesus by Judas Iscariot, reads, "Let the iniquity of his fathers be remembered with the Lord; and let not the sin of his mother be blotted out." The act of blotting, in this case, is making a mark that obscures what is written or marked on a page. Referring to his own sins, David wrote, "Blot out my transgressions.... Hide thy face from my sins, and blot all mine iniquities."[16] So, blotting out sins would entail obscuring what is already written down.

Regarding the omniscience of God, the psalmist wrote, "Thine eyes did see my substance, yet being unperfect; and in they book all my members were written, which in continuance were fashioned, when as yet there was none of them."[17] We are taught that "God knows [us] all by name; and [our] every transaction, [our] every word, is written in His books. This record [we] must meet in the Day of Judgment."[18]

We have this warning and promise revealed to us: "During the time of trouble, the position of God's people will be similar to the position of Joshua [the high priest]. They will not be ignorant of the work going on in heaven in their behalf. They will realize that sin is recorded against their names, but they will also know that the sins of all who repent and lay hold of the merits of Christ will be canceled."[19]

After the children of Israel accepted the evil report from the ten spies sent to search out Canaan, ignoring the good report of Caleb and Joshua, God said to Moses, "How long will this people provoke me? and how long will it be ere they believe me, for all the signs which I have shewed among them?... Because all those men which have seen my glory, and my miracles, which I did in Egypt and in the wilderness, and have tempted me now these ten times, and have not hearkened to my voice; Surely they shall not see the land which I sware unto their fathers, neither shall any of them that provoked me see it: But my servant Caleb, because he had another spirit with him, and hath followed me fully, him will I bring into the land whereinto he went; and his seed shall possess it."[20]

God did not exaggerate their case. Ten times they had provoked Him by their unbelief. From the crossing of the Red Sea to the borders of Canaan, they had murmured and complained against God and His chosen leaders. They had apostatized at Sinai with their idolatry, complained about the manna, and spoken against Moses. And now they refused to believe that God was willing or able to bring them into the land of promise as their Champion and Defender. And for that they suffered the consequences of their own choice, being banished from seeing the Promised Land.

> *Wicked men are generally pleased with a form without true godliness, and they will aid and support such a religion.*

---

15 Exodus 23:20–22
16 Psalm 51:1, 9
17 Psalm 139:16
18 Ellen G. White, *The Kress Collection* (Payson, AZ: Leaves-Of-Autumn Books, 1985), 96.
19 Ellen G. White, "Is Not This a Brand Plucked Out of the Fire?" *The Signs of the Times*, June 2, 1890.
20 Numbers 14:11, 22–24

Centuries after their refusal to enter Canaan, the litany of their poor choices was recited upon the completion of rebuilding Jerusalem's walls in Nehemiah's day. The people had just finished the feast of booths, and on the eighth day they called for a solemn assembly according to their custom. After reading from the book of the Law one fourth of the day, and confessing their sins and worshipping the Lord another fourth of the day, the Levites closed the assembly with a prayer. In addition to listing the wonderful blessings God had bestowed upon Israel throughout their history, they confessed their forefathers' sins:

> But they and our fathers dealt proudly, and hardened their necks, and hearkened not to thy commandments, And refused to obey, neither were mindful of thy wonders that thou didst among them; but hardened their necks, and in their rebellion appointed a captain to return to their bondage ...
>
> Yea, when they had made them a molten calf, and said, This is thy God that brought thee up out of Egypt, and had wrought great provocations; Yet thou in thy manifold mercies forsookest them not in the wilderness: the pillar of the cloud departed not from them by day, to lead them in the way; neither the pillar of fire by night, to shew them light, and the way wherein they should go. Thou gavest also thy good spirit to instruct them, and withheldest not thy manna from their mouth, and gavest them water for their thirst. Yea, forty years didst thou sustain them in the wilderness, so that they lacked nothing; their clothes waxed not old, and their feet swelled not....
>
> Nevertheless they were disobedient, and rebelled against thee, and cast thy law behind their backs, and slew thy prophets which testified against them to turn them to thee, and they wrought great provocations....
>
> And testifiedst against them, that thou mightest bring them again unto thy law: yet they dealt proudly, and hearkened not unto thy commandments, but sinned against thy judgments, (which if a man do, he shall live in them;) and withdrew the shoulder, and hardened their neck, and would not hear....
>
> Howbeit thou art just in all that is brought upon us; for thou hast done right, but we have done wickedly: Neither have our kings, our princes, our priests, nor our fathers, kept thy law, nor hearkened unto thy commandments and thy testimonies, wherewith thou didst testify against them. For they have not served thee in their kingdom, and in thy great goodness that thou gavest them, and in the large and fat land which thou gavest before them, neither turned they from their wicked works.[21]

So, as the Jews acknowledged their guilt for provoking God in their past history on that day of worship, so the psalmist calls us to worship God with hearts lifted up with gratitude for the wonderful things God has done for us—keeping in mind that God judges those who rebel against Him.

---

21   Nehemiah 9:16–21, 26, 29, 33–35

O come, let us worship and bow down: let us kneel before the Lord our maker. For he is our God; and we are the people of his pasture, and the sheep of his hand. To day if ye will hear his voice, harden not your heart, as in the provocation, and as in the day of temptation in the wilderness: When your fathers tempted me, proved me, and saw my work. Forty years long was I grieved with this generation, and said, It is a people that do err in their heart, and they have not known my ways: Unto whom I sware in my wrath that they should not enter into my rest.[22]

God, in His mercy and love, is slow to anger. In our guilty state, we are vulnerable to His judgments, which in this time of probation are mingled with mercy. As forgiven, penitent sinners we should be grateful that God is slow to anger, as Ellen White so aptly points out:

How grateful we should be that the Lord is slow to anger! What a wonderful thought it is, that Omnipotence puts a restraint upon His mighty power! But because the Lord is forbearing and long-suffering, the human heart often manifests a tendency to venture presumptuously to add sin to sin! ... "Because sentence against an evil work is not executed speedily, therefore the heart of the sons of men is fully set in them to do evil" (Ecclesiastes 8:11). Instead of God's patience hardening the sinner to continual transgression, it should lead him to determine to seek God's forgiveness, in order that the figures standing against his account in the heavenly record may be canceled.[23]

Had not the Lord been slow to anger, and mercifully considerate of the ignorance and weakness of the children of Israel, he would have destroyed them in his wrath. He exercises the same pitying tenderness toward modern Israel. But we are less excusable than was ancient Israel. We have had every opportunity to elevate and ennoble our characters, which they did not have. We also have their history, recorded that we may shun their example of unbelief and impatient murmuring and rebellion.[24]

To the unrepentant wicked, there is only a fearful day of reckoning.[25] Yet the carnal heart refuses to accept this biblical fact. Instead, we see an increase in provocation as the deceived and deluded embrace a form of godliness while rejecting the power of God.

They have been growing more and more corrupt; yet they bear the name of being Christ's followers. It is impossible to distinguish them from the world. Their ministers take their

---

22   Psalm 95:6–11
23   White, *The Upward Look*, 41.
24   Ellen G. White, "Journeyings of the Israelites," *The Signs of the Times*, April 15, 1880.
25   Hebrews 10:26, 27

text from the Word, but preach smooth things. The natural heart feels no objection to this. It is only the spirit and power of the truth, and the salvation of Christ, that is hateful to the carnal heart. There is nothing in the popular ministry that stirs the wrath of Satan, makes the sinner tremble, or applies to the heart and conscience the fearful realities of a judgment soon to come. Wicked men are generally pleased with a form without true godliness, and they will aid and support such a religion. Said the angel, Nothing less than the whole armor of righteousness can overcome, and retain the victory over the powers of darkness. Satan has taken full possession of the churches as a body. The sayings and doings of men are dwelt upon instead of the plain cutting truths of the word of God. Said the angel, The friendship and spirit of the world are at enmity with God. When truth in its simplicity and strength, as it is in Jesus, is brought to bear against the spirit of the world, it awakens the spirit of persecution at once. Many, very many, who profess to be Christians, have not known God. The character of the natural heart has not been changed, and the carnal mind remains at enmity with God. They are Satan's own faithful servants, notwithstanding they have assumed another name.[26]

This dangerous condition is further cemented by the attractive doctrine that it matters not what one believes, as many proponents and adherents argue. May we listen to the counsel and warnings of Ellen White regarding this perilous situation:

The great deceiver has many agents ready to present any and every kind of error to ensnare souls—heresies prepared to suit the varied tastes and capacities of those whom he would ruin. It is his plan to bring into the church insincere, unregenerate elements that will encourage doubt and unbelief, and hinder all who desire to see the work of God advance and to advance with it. Many who have no real faith in God or in His word assent to some principles of truth and pass as Christians, and thus they are enabled to introduce their errors as Scriptural doctrines.

The position that it is of no consequence what men believe is one of Satan's most successful deceptions. He knows that the truth, received in the love of it, sanctifies the soul of the receiver; therefore he is constantly seeking to substitute false theories, fables, another gospel. From the beginning the servants of God have contended against false teachers, not merely as vicious men, but as inculcators of falsehoods that were fatal to the soul. Elijah, Jeremiah, Paul, firmly and fearlessly opposed those who were turning men from the word of God. That liberality which regards a correct religious faith as unimportant found no favor with these holy defenders of the truth.[27]

---

26   Ellen G. White, *Spiritual Gifts*, vol. 1 (Battle Creek, MI: Seventh-day Adventist Publishing Association, 1858), 189, 190.
27   White, *The Great Controversy*, 520.

Probationary time will not continue much longer. Now God is withdrawing his restraining hand from the earth. Long has he been speaking to men and women through the agency of his Holy Spirit; but they have not heeded the call. Now he is speaking to his people, and to the world, by his judgments. The time of these judgments is a time of mercy for those who have not yet had opportunity to learn what is truth. Tenderly will the Lord look upon them. His heart of mercy is touched; his hand is still stretched out to save.

The day of Christ's coming will be a day of judgment upon the world. When the multitude of the lost—those whom God has favored with great light, but who rejected the light; those who might have been saved, had they obeyed God's law, but who refused to obey—when these see the Son of man coming in the clouds of heaven, they will understand the great sacrifice made in their behalf; they will understand the unmeasured love of the Redeemer, his incarnation, the sweat-drops of blood, the marks of the nails in his hands and feet, the pierced side; and they will ask to be hidden from the face of him that sitteth on the throne, and from the wrath of the Lamb.[28]

The death of Christ brings to the rejecter of His mercy the wrath and judgments of God, unmixed with mercy. This is the wrath of the Lamb. But the death of Christ is hope and eternal life to all who receive Him and believe in Him.

God will most assuredly call the world to judgment to avenge the death of His only-begotten Son, the One who stood at the bar of Pilate and Herod. That One is now in the heavenly courts making intercession for the people who refused Him. Shall we choose the stamp of the world, or shall we choose to be God's separate, peculiar people?[29]

---

28 Ellen G. White, "'Even at the Door,'" *Southern Watchman*, December 1, 1909.
29 Ellen G. White, *Testimonies to Ministers and Gospel Workers* (Mountain View, CA: Pacific Press Publishing Association, 1923), 139.

Chapter 6

Unconditional Love Versus Unconditional Surrender

Throughout the course of military histories recorded amongst the various countries of the world, we repeatedly see a concept that should be universally understood—unconditional surrender. Fundamentally, belligerent parties involved in the horrors of warfare have three options to end hostilities: a conditional surrender where all parties involved contribute to the terms of peace much like the Middle East peace process ongoing today, or like the 1973 Paris Peace Accords at the close of the Vietnam War; an unconditional surrender where only the perceived superior force makes demands that must be met by the perceived weaker force in order for peace to commence; or the "no quarter" version of total annihilation, also known as "take no prisoners," which usually results from a "fight-to-the-death" sense of honor by those about to make the ultimate sacrifice and results in the victors showing no mercy.

History records several instances where no quarter occurred such as the Massacre of Tripolitsa, April 1821, or the Battle of the Alamo, March 1836. In the first mentioned event, about 30,000 Turks were killed—men, women, and children—including the entire Jewish population. In the second mentioned instance, women, children, and those slaves inclined to forsake their soldier-masters were allowed safe passage before the remaining officers, enlisted men, and volunteers were overwhelmed. Since the Hague Conventions of 1907, it is internationally accepted that the call for no quarter by a commander of arms, including acts of genocide, will be deemed either a war crime or a crime against humanity.

The armistice signed on November 11, 1918, was not a document of unconditional surrender of German forces to the Allies since it merely ended hostilities without dealing with the details of peace and reparations. German troops were allowed to pull back from the trenches to go home peacefully, while the allies remained on the field. But the Treaty of Versailles, signed on June 28, 1919, most certainly marked the end of World War I with a formal surrender in which Germany was not allowed to negotiate terms and Germany was declared the sole nation responsible for the war. Simply put, the treaty managed to foment a generation of resentful Germans who, understandably, would eventually strive to overthrow that yoke of bondage. With this context of surrender, it is small wonder that we observe the general apprehension amongst Japanese military leaders upon hearing an interpretation of President Truman's speech from Potsdam requiring Japan to unconditionally surrender to the allies.

The reality of unconditional surrender is that the superior force is the only one in the position to determine what the terms or conditions will be. The weaker, surrendering force simply has to yield to the demands of the default victor while trusting that the troops surrendered will be treated humanely as stipulated by recognized "international law."

Unconditional surrender is often compared to another, quite synonymous, concept of surrender at discretion. Both require that the defeated make no terms of their own accord but that they capitulate to the discretion of, and with no further assurances or guarantees, the superior force. Any time a conditional surrender takes place one can rest assured that terms have been supplied by the vanquished, as well as accepted by the victor.

In his biography on General Ulysses Simpson Grant and regarding Grant's note to General Buckner during the battle for Fort Donelson, John Mosier appears to conclude that unconditional surrender involves a capitulation where not even the obviously victorious commander may stipulate terms, or conditions, in negotiations of surrender with the weaker, nearly defeated opponent.[1] But in Grant's memoires, the context of the letters exchanged between the two generals indicates that Buckner wanted to negotiate terms—conditions put forth by both parties—to which Grant responded, "Yours of this date, proposing armistice and appointment of Commissioners to settle terms of capitulation, is just received. No terms except an unconditional and immediate surrender can be accepted. I propose to move immediately upon your works."[2]

This demand resulted in his new moniker: General "Unconditional Surrender" Grant. But Grant's call for unconditional surrender didn't at all help General Buckner's attitude as indicated by his somewhat surly response: "The distribution of the forces under my command, incident to an unexpected change of commanders, and the overwhelming force under your command, compel me, notwithstanding the brilliant success of the Confederate arms yesterday, to accept the ungenerous and unchivalrous terms which you propose."[3]

In actuality, Grant was quite generous to the defeated, permitting a burial detail made up of Confederates to go outside battle lines to bury their dead comrades, and he even allowed men to go to their respective homes on the promise that they would never again join the ranks of the Confederacy.[4] He suspected that some took advantage of his leniency by using the opportunity to escape without making such promises of submission, but his intent was to make the soldiers so sick of war that they would sooner surrender unconditionally and go home than fight on.

Contrary to some historians' conclusions, Vicksburg surrendered unconditionally to Union forces. Grant wrote to General Pemberton:

> Your note of this date is just received, proposing an armistice for several hours, for the
> purpose of arranging terms of capitulation through commissioners, to be appointed, etc.

---

1   John Mosier, *Grant* (New York: Palgrave Macmillan, 2006).
2   Ulysses S. Grant, *Personal Memoirs of U. S. Grant* (New York: Charles L. Webster & Company, 1894), 183, 184.
3   Ibid., 184.
4   Ibid., 185.

The useless effusion of blood you propose stopping by this course can be ended at any time you may choose, by the unconditional surrender of the city and garrison. Men who have shown so much endurance and courage as those now in Vicksburg, will always challenge the respect of an adversary, and I can assure you will be treated with all the respect due to prisoners of war. I do not favor the proposition of appointing commissioners to arrange the terms of capitulation, because I have no terms other than those indicated above.[5]

Later, Grant indicated that he would formalize his terms. But under no circumstances were the Confederates party to negotiate on any point. They had the choice to accept the call to surrender or be destroyed by famine and onslaught. So they surrendered and remained at Vicksburg until the whole could be paroled.

Even before Appomattox Courthouse, both Grant and Lee recognized that any surrender would be unconditional. Lee simply was not in a position to demand or enforce any terms before submitting to surrender. The sole purpose of meeting with Grant was to discover what specific terms would be imposed by a vastly superior force. After conversing at length about matters having nothing to do with an immediate surrender, General Lee reminded Grant of their purpose for meeting and the Union general proceeded to write out formalized conditions. Grant recalled, "No conversation, not one word, passed between General Lee and myself, either about private property, side arms, or kindred subjects. He appeared to have no objections to the terms first proposed; or if he had a point to make against them he wished to wait until they were in writing to make it."[6]

General Lee read the conditions, made a comment with obvious feelings about how the conditions would "have a happy effect upon his army," and then asked a point of clarification regarding the differences between their respective armies, stating that the horses and mules used by cavalrymen and artillerists were owned by them and were not the property of the Confederacy as such. Recognizing that only unnecessary hardship would result from leaving the terms unchanged, Grant acceded to the clarification by assuring Lee that he would order the officers overseeing the parole process to allow cavalrymen and artillerists to keep their horses and mules.

> *We see that unconditional surrender occurs when the weaker party submits to the demands of the stronger party without making demands of their own.*

With this assurance, General Lee wrote a letter accepting the terms: "I received your letter of this date containing the terms of the surrender of the Army of Northern Virginia as proposed by you. As they are substantially the same as those expressed in your letter of the 8th inst., they are accepted. I will

---

5   Ibid., 328.
6   Ibid., 631.

proceed to designate the proper officers to carry the stipulations into effect."[7]

In the letter referenced by Lee, Grant had written the following: "...there is but one condition I would insist upon, namely: that the men and officers surrendered shall be disqualified for taking up arms again against the Government of the United States until properly exchanged."[8] But in formalizing generous terms, Grant was instrumental in making a difficult reconciliation that much easier.

When General Robert E. Lee surrendered unconditionally to General Grant, he submitted to the judgment processes of the Federal government. He signed an oath of amnesty in 1865, which his political enemies apparently "lost" or gave away. From that time until his death, Lee was a man without a nation. (Not until August 5, 1975, did a resolution of Congress signed into law by President Gerald Ford restore posthumously all rights of citizenship to General Lee.) Yet he wrote of healing the wounds of the nation so recently at war with itself:

> I believe it to be the duty of every one to unite in the restoration of the country, and the reestablishment of peace and harmony.... It should be the object of all to avoid controversy, to allay passion, give full scope to reason and every kindly feeling. By doing this and encouraging our citizens to engage in the duties of life with all their heart and mind, with a determination not to be turned aside by thoughts of the past and fears of the future, our country will not only be restored in material prosperity, but will be advanced in science, in virtue, and in religion.[9]

One might conclude that General Lee was fully surrendered.

In all these exchanges, we see that unconditional surrender occurs when the weaker party submits to the demands of the stronger party without making demands of their own. Again, unconditional surrender is not a modern concept, nor is it confined to Western culture. Only the terminology is different.

The story of Jabesh-gilead is a tremendous biblical example of the fine art of surrender negotiations. Only in that day, one would recognize it as breaking one covenant relationship in order to form another.

Jabesh-gilead, located within the portion assigned to the eastern half-tribe of Manasseh beyond the Jordan River, was a large, powerful metropolis. Nahash, as a general practice, "put out the right eyes of those that either delivered themselves to him upon terms, or were taken by him in war; and this he did, that when their left eyes were covered by their shields, they might be wholly useless in war.... And having pitched his camp at the metropolis of his enemies, which was the city of Jabesh, he ... gave them their choice, whether they would cut off a small member of their body, or universally perish."[10]

The Bible tells the same story, in a different way. "Then Nahash the Ammonite came up, and encamped

---

7   Ibid., 632.
8   Ibid., 624.
9   Elizabeth Brown Pryor, *Reading the Man: A Portrait of Robert E. Lee Through His Private Letters* (New York: Penguin Group, 2007), 434.
10   Josephus, *Jewish Antiquities*, book six (Ware, Hertfordshire: Wordsworth Editions Limited, 2006), 227. See also Numbers 32:29, 40.

against Jabeshgilead: and all the men of Jabesh said unto Nahash, Make a covenant with us, and we will serve thee. And Nahash the Ammonite answered them, On this *condition* will I make *a covenant* with you, that I may thrust out all your right eyes, and lay it *for* a reproach upon all Israel. And the elders of Jabesh said unto him, Give us seven days' respite, that we may send messengers unto all the coasts of Israel: and then, if *there be* no man to save us, we will come out to thee."[11] "To this the Ammonites consented, thinking thus to heighten the honor of their expected triumph."[12]

However, Saul, the anointed king of Israel and general of the army, responded to their plea for help, and God delivered the Ammonites into the hands of King Saul and his army. Nahash and Saul would remain bitter enemies for life. The men of Jabesh-gilead chose not to surrender, and they were spared.

The military examples of the Bible and recent history demonstrate that surrendering to a more powerful force means giving up all rights and accepting the terms that the stronger party sets out. From a spiritual viewpoint, God is supreme as our Creator and Redeemer. All creation should cheerfully submit to His wise, benevolent rule. Yet rebellion against His government and laws pervades this woeful planet. Despite our sinful condition, which naturally separates us from God, He implemented the work of redemption and salvation planned before the creation of this world. Therefore, He has every right to demand from us an unconditional surrender. It is the work of merciful love to warn of consequences, announce acceptable conditions intended to restore peace and happiness, and execute judgments that will protect those loyal to His government from eternal harassment and discord.

> *If God loved with an unconditional love, we would not be His subjects, but rather, His equals.*

Now we must ask, how can unconditional love ever demand unconditional surrender? After all, there would be no condition by which surrender would be necessary. As one author put it, "Unconditional love is all-inclusive. It does not demand, but accepts."[13] If God loved with an unconditional love, we would not be His subjects, but rather, His equals. If such were the case, we would not be accountable to anyone but our own singular selves. Such is the logical conclusion with unconditional love.

However, Satan has a knowledge of what appeals to the carnal heart.

Satan studies every indication of the frailty of human nature, he marks the sins which each individual is inclined to commit, and then he takes care that opportunities shall not be wanting to gratify the tendency to evil. He tempts men to excess in that which is in itself lawful, causing them, through intemperance, to weaken physical, mental, and moral power. He has destroyed and is destroying thousands through the indulgence of the passions,

---

11   1 Samuel 11:1–3
12   White, *Patriarchs and Prophets*, 612.
13   Llewellyn Vaughan-Lee, *Catching the Thread: Sufism, Dreamwork, and Jungian Psychology* (Inverness, CA: The Golden Sufi Center, 1998), 154.

thus brutalizing the entire nature of man. And to complete his work, he declares, through the spirits that "true knowledge places man above all law;" that "whatever is, is right;" that "God doth not condemn;" and that "*all* sins which are committed are innocent." When the people are thus led to believe that desire is the highest law, that liberty is license, and that man is accountable only to himself, who can wonder that corruption and depravity teem on every hand? Multitudes eagerly accept teachings that leave them at liberty to obey the promptings of the carnal heart. The reins of self-control are laid upon the neck of lust, the powers of mind and soul are made subject to the animal propensities, and Satan exultingly sweeps into his net thousands who profess to be followers of Christ.[14]

Because God is supreme and ruler of us all,

God has sacred claims upon us all. He claims the whole heart, the whole soul, the whole affections. The answer which is sometimes made to this statement is, "Oh I do not profess to be a Christian!" What if you do not? Has not God the same claims upon you that He has upon the one who professes to be His child? Because you are bold in your careless disregard of sacred things, is your sin of neglect and rebellion passed over by the Lord? Every day that you disregard the claims of God, every opportunity of offered mercy that you slight, is charged to your account, and will swell the list of sins against you in the day when the accounts of every soul will be investigated.... God calls for your affections, for your cheerful obedience and devotion to Him. You now have a short time of probation, and you may improve this opportunity to make an unconditional surrender to God.[15]

Acknowledgement of our condition and a desire for a better state is merely the beginning of the Christian's warfare God calls us to enjoin. We should recognize that love of the world will only squeeze out a love for Jesus, and that our only hope for rest and peace is found in a full, unconditional surrender of our lives to Him. "The requirements of God's word are positive. 'Thou shalt love the Lord thy God with all thy heart, and with all thy mind, and with all thy strength, and thy neighbor as thyself.' This is the only condition laid down in the word of God upon which we can claim eternal life. The promises of God are ample. The gospel was not given to awaken desires it could not satisfy."[16]

King David realized his great need, which is summed up in his song of thanksgiving:

Blessed is he whose transgression is forgiven, whose sin is covered. Blessed is the man unto whom the Lord imputeth not iniquity, and in whose spirit there is no guile. When I kept silence, my bones waxed old through my roaring all the day long. For day and night thy hand

---

14　White, *The Great Controversy*, 555, 556.
15　Ellen G. White, "God's Claims Equally Binding on All," *Bible Echo*, September 19, 1898.
16　Ellen G. White, "Notes of Travel," *The Review and Herald*, December 11, 1883.

was heavy upon me: my moisture is turned into the drought of summer. Selah. I acknowledge my sin unto thee, and mine iniquity have I not hid. I said, I will confess my transgressions unto the Lord; and thou forgavest the iniquity of my sin. Selah. For this shall every one that is godly pray unto thee in a time when thou mayest be found: surely in the floods of great waters they shall not come nigh unto him. Thou art my hiding place; thou shalt preserve me from trouble; thou shalt compass me about with songs of deliverance. Selah. I will instruct thee and teach thee in the way which thou shalt go: I will guide thee with mine eye. Be ye not as the horse, or as the mule, which have no understanding: whose mouth must be held in with bit and bridle, lest they come near unto thee. Many sorrows shall be to the wicked: but he that trusteth in the Lord, mercy shall compass him about. Be glad in the Lord, and rejoice, ye righteous: and shout for joy, all ye that are upright in heart.[17]

As scary as unconditional surrender may be, it was David's experience that blessings and true happiness were the result of turning his life over completely to God. His experience can be ours.

Throughout history God has sent His prophets to notify His wayward people of His conditions. Isaiah proclaimed:

Hear, ye that are far off, what I have done; and, ye that are near, acknowledge my might. The sinners in Zion are afraid; fearfulness hath surprised the hypocrites. Who among us shall dwell with the devouring fire? who among us shall dwell with everlasting burnings? He that walketh righteously, and speaketh uprightly; he that despiseth the gain of oppressions, that shaketh his hands from holding of bribes, that stoppeth his ears from hearing of blood, and shutteth his eyes from seeing evil; He shall dwell on high: his place of defence shall be the munitions of rocks: bread shall be given him; his waters shall be sure. Thine eyes shall see the king in his beauty: they shall behold the land that is very far off.[18]

Jeremiah announced:

Return, thou backsliding Israel, saith the Lord; and I will not cause mine anger to fall upon you: for I am merciful, saith the Lord, and I will not keep anger for ever. Only acknowledge thine iniquity, that thou hast transgressed against the Lord thy God, and hast scattered thy ways to the strangers under every green tree, and ye have not obeyed my voice, saith the Lord. Turn, O backsliding children, saith the Lord; for I am married unto you: and I will take you one of a city, and two of a family, and I will bring you to Zion: And I will give you pastors according to mine heart, which shall feed you with knowledge and understanding.[19]

---

17   Psalm 32:1–11
18   Isaiah 33:13–17
19   Jeremiah 3:12–15

Hosea informs us that God will not defend us when we deliberately separate ourselves from Him: "I will go and return to my place, till they acknowledge their offence, and seek my face: in their affliction they will seek me early."[20] Then he encourages us with the course we ought to follow, and its sure results: "Come, and let us return unto the Lord: for he hath torn, and he will heal us; he hath smitten, and he will bind us up. After two days will he revive us: in the third day he will raise us up, and we shall live in his sight. Then shall we know, if we follow on to know the Lord: his going forth is prepared as the morning; and he shall come unto us as the rain, as the latter and former rain unto the earth."[21]

These verses are consistent with the words of the psalmist.[22]

Because of the shortness of time remaining to us probationers, God would not leave us ignorant of His will to liberate us from sin or of Satan's plans to ensnare us as his captives forever. Peter issues this warning: "But there were false prophets also among the people, even as there shall be false teachers among you, who privily shall bring in damnable heresies, even denying the Lord that bought them, and bring upon themselves swift destruction. And many shall follow their pernicious ways; by reason of whom the way of truth shall be evil spoken of. And through covetousness shall they with feigned words make merchandise of you: whose judgment now of a long time lingereth not, and their damnation slumbereth not."[23]

We are to obtain from God the knowledge necessary for an intelligent, informed decision.

> We are not to rush into the acceptance of the gospel without any fixed stability of purpose. If we receive Jesus Christ, we must receive all the conditions, all the requirements, and make it our life business in everything to make the kingdom of God our first consideration. Difficulties will present themselves as obstructions. *But the greatest difficulties originate with self.* It will cost all there is of the man, for Christ demands the heart, the soul, the strength, and the mind of every human agent. "Ye are not your own for ye are bought with a price; therefore glorify God in your body and in your spirit which are God's." It will cost self-humiliation, self-denial, self-sacrifice, a constant conflict with human passions. *Our natural temperaments can not be carried along in the road, cast up for the ransomed of the Lord to walk in.* Shame and weakness and disgrace are the sure result of professedly following Christ while walking in the ways and practises of the unrenewed, unconverted men.[24]

God, in His infinite wisdom and love, will always accept the sincere penitent who seeks Him wholeheartedly. "Christ is the great remedy for sin. Our compassionate Redeemer has provided for us the help we need. He is waiting to impute his righteousness to the sincere penitent, and to kindle in his heart such divine love as

---

20   Hosea 5:15
21   Hosea 6:1–3
22   Psalm 32:5
23   2 Peter 2:1–3
24   White, "Christianity."

only our gracious Redeemer can inspire. Then let us who profess to be his witnesses on earth, his ambassadors from the court of Heaven, glorify Him whom we represent, by being faithful to our trust as light-bearers to the world."[25]

---

25   Ellen G. White, "The Christian Light-Bearer," *The Signs of the Times*, March 25, 1886.

Chapter 7

What Wondrous Love!

How can any person describe, or illustrate, the love of God? Any comparison of God's love to the imperfect relationships or the defective things of this world risks blighting God's reputation and bringing Him down to our level and making Him be like us, instead of the other way around.

Love is more than an emotion. It is principle. Love is more than emotions. It is duty cheerfully carried out. Love is more than theory. It is demonstrative. It is concrete in that it is absolute and consistent. More elusive than abstract (as a matter of definition), love is infinitely vast and comprehensive. Yet it is so closely linked to God's justice that Ellen White associates the two by identifying them as twin sisters. "Justice has a twin sister, which is love."[1] "Love has a twin sister, which is duty."[2] Justice denotes duty, which, when performed out of love for each other without sacrificing the moral standard that is foundational to God's government, promotes the happiness and welfare of all.

We tread upon dangerous ground when we romanticize God's love, degrading it to the level of mere sentimentalism. Because we are sinners, the truth hurts when it points out our glaring defects. So, when love presents the truth, love is perceived as hateful by the self-justified, guilty soul to the point that the rejecter of love and truth would denounce both as hate and falsehood. How many times has a naughty child, after being properly spanked, thanked the parent for so doing? The common response from the child would be a denunciation along the lines of, "You hate me!"

When we accept the Bible as it reads regarding the sinful condition of the fallen race and the righteous wisdom of God, we cannot help but exclaim, "What wondrous love! What marvelous grace!" One of my favorite hymns proclaims, "What wondrous love is this, O my soul, O my soul?"

When God created Adam and Eve, He established a relationship best described as a covenant of love with them.

> In the midst of the garden, near the tree of life, stood the tree of knowledge of good and evil. This tree was especially designed of God to be the pledge of their obedience, faith, and love to Him. Of this tree the Lord commanded our first parents not to eat, neither to touch it, lest they die. He told them that they might freely eat of all the trees in the garden except

---

1   Ellen G. White, *Child Guidance* (Washington, D.C.: Review and Herald Publishing Association, 1954), 262.
2   Ibid., 258.

one, but if they ate of that tree they should surely die.

> When Adam and Eve were placed in the beautiful garden they had everything for their happiness which they could desire. But God chose, in His all-wise arrangements, to test their loyalty before they could be rendered eternally secure. They were to have His favor, and He was to converse with them and they with Him. Yet He did not place evil out of their reach. Satan was permitted to tempt them. If they endured the trial they were to be in perpetual favor with God and the heavenly angels.[3]

The Bible is clear that Adam and Eve both transgressed against God's law when they took the forbidden fruit, thereby breaking the covenant of love. Just as clear is the simple fact that Jesus stepped forward to take the guilt and to suffer the penalty the broken law demanded. "The instant man accepted the temptations of Satan, and did the very things God had said he should not do, Christ, the Son of God, stood between the living and the dead, saying, 'Let the punishment fall on Me. I will stand in man's place. He shall have another chance.'"[4] "As soon as there was sin, there was a Saviour. Christ knew what He would have to suffer, yet He became man's substitute. As soon as Adam sinned, the Son of God presented himself as surety for the human race, with just as much power to avert the doom pronounced upon the guilty as when He died upon the cross of Calvary."[5]

What the law demanded of Adam and Eve in Eden, and what it demanded of Christ, the second Adam, it demands of every human being.

What we observe here is God providing instantaneous penal substitution through the immediate surety established by Jesus Christ's voluntary offering. This plan was formulated before our creation, and yet it was veiled until the moment it was needed to execute this mission of mercy and grace for our salvation. It was a difficult choice, but God the Father made it because of love. He sent Jesus, His only begotten Son, to meet the conditions we failed to meet because of our inherent inability—because of our sinful condition—to perform perfect obedience of our own selves. In so doing, God demonstrates His love while maintaining justice. It is a love that is as "strong as death," and yet as uncompromising as justice.

> The truth as it is in Jesus will teach most important lessons. It will show that the love of God is broad and deep; that it is infinite; and that in awarding the penalty to the disobedient, those who have made void God's law, it will be uncompromising. This is the love and the justice of God combined. It reaches to the very depth of human woe and degradation, to lift

---

3   White, *Story of Redemption*, 24.

4   Ellen G. White, *The Faith I Live By* (Washington, D.C.: Review and Herald Publishing Association, 1958), 75.

5   Ellen G. White, "Lessons from the Christ-Life," *The Review and Herald*, March 12, 1901.

up the fallen and oppressed who lay hold of the truth by repentance and faith in Jesus. And God works for the good of the universe, for the good of the rebellious sinner, by causing the sinner to suffer the penalty of his sin.[6]

The obedience demanded by the law was to be provided by Christ on behalf of fallen humanity—righteousness imputed. The power to obey the law as Jesus obeyed also was to be provided by faith, which works by love—righteousness imparted. The penalty for disobedience demanded by the law was to be remitted by Christ's life, death, and resurrection. This other chance provides us with an opportunity to once again be loyal subjects of God's kingdom. "What the law demanded of Adam and Eve in Eden, and what it demanded of Christ, the second Adam, it demands of every human being."[7] And yet this law is love, because the law reflects the character of God who is love.

> When the theory that the law of Jehovah is not binding upon the human family is adopted and taught, man is blinded to his terrible ruin. He cannot discern it. Then God has no moral standard by which to measure character, and to govern the heavenly universe, the worlds unfallen, and this fallen world. Could God have abolished the law in order to meet man in his fallen condition, and yet have maintained his honor as Governor of the universe, Christ need not have died. But the death of Christ is the convincing, everlasting argument that the law of God is as unchanging as his throne. In the place of the great sacrifice's abating one jot or one tittle of the Father's law, that sacrifice exalts the law; it proclaims to worlds unfallen and to the fallen race that God's law is changeless, and that he will maintain his authority and sustain his law.[8]

We have already seen in a previous chapter that Ellen White begins and ends the Conflict of the Ages series with "God is love," but I want to focus now on some statements made in the opening chapters of some of her other books regarding the nature of God's love:

> Nature and revelation alike testify of God's love. Our Father in heaven is the source of life, of wisdom, and of joy. Look at the wonderful and beautiful things of nature. Think of their marvelous adaptation to the needs and happiness, not only of man, but of all living creatures. The sunshine and the rain, that gladden and refresh the earth, the hills and seas and plains, all speak to us of the Creator's love....
>
> "God is love" is written upon every opening bud, upon every spire of springing grass. The lovely birds making the air vocal with their happy songs, the delicately tinted flowers in their perfection perfuming the air, the lofty trees of the forest with their rich foliage of

---

6   White, "The Truth Revealed in Jesus." See also Song of Solomon 8:6.
7   Ellen G. White, "The Influence of the Truth," *The Review and Herald*, February 26, 1901.
8   White, "The Truth Revealed in Jesus."

living green—all testify to the tender, fatherly care of our God and to His desire to make His children happy.[9]

Christ came to this world to show that by receiving power from on high, man can live an unsullied life. With unwearying patience and sympathetic helpfulness He met men in their necessities. By the gentle touch of grace He banished from the soul unrest and doubt, changing enmity to love, and unbelief to confidence....

Christ recognized no distinction of nationality or rank or creed. The scribes and Pharisees desired to make a local and a national benefit of the gifts of heaven and to exclude the rest of God's family in the world. But Christ came to break down every wall of partition. He came to show that His gift of mercy and love is as unconfined as the air, the light, or the showers of rain that refresh the earth.

The life of Christ established a religion in which there is no caste, a religion by which Jew and Gentile, free and bond, are linked in a common brotherhood, equal before God. No question of policy influenced His movements. He made no difference between neighbors and strangers, friends and enemies. That which appealed to His heart was a soul thirsting for the waters of life.[10]

Some may try to read into these passages "unconditional love" as they read "gift of mercy and love ... as unconfined as the air, the light, or the showers of rain that refresh the earth." But they do not see the whole picture because their distinction has nothing to do with unselfishness as opposed to selfishness. The conditions within the context of self "disinterested love" will not be seen as similar to those conditions established by selfishness.[11]

Read again how the scribes and Pharisees made distinctions that exalted self: "I am a Jew, and you are a worthless Gentile"; "I am a Pharisee, and you are a publican"; "I am healthy, and you are a leper"; or, "I am wealthy, and you are a poor, wretched slave." These distinctions have nothing to do with the condition of the heart or the character. These distinctions are based upon conditions rooted in pride, self-ambition, and self-exaltation.

Imaginary boundaries determined by geological features established by the power of individuals can never prevent the air, sunshine, and rain from falling upon all. But go beyond the boundaries established by God, and these three elements will be lacking. Ask any astronaut or cosmonaut if survival is possible for long outside of the atmosphere of our globe without the benefit of sufficient tanks containing the necessities for life! Think of all the human effort and energy to overcome the challenges faced by the Apollo 13 crew after they lost an oxygen tank early into their mission. Recall how many climbers have died, or nearly died, on Mount Everest for lack of oxygen or improper acclimation while attempting to gain its summit. God would have to exert a power

9   White, *Steps to Christ*, 9, 10.
10   Ellen G. White, *The Ministry of Healing* (Mountain View, CA: Pacific Press Publishing Association, 1905), 25.
11   "The charity that seeketh not her own is the fruit of that disinterested love that characterized the life of our Redeemer" (Ellen G. White, "Business Principles in the Religious Life," *The Bible Echo*, December 9, 1895).

above and beyond natural law as it is demonstrated in this sinful world. Such an illustration only shows the grace of God to all who will accept the gift of mercy and repent from transgression of God's commandments.

I recently finished reading a book by Roger Oakland titled *Faith Undone*. Before reading this book, I was already completely convinced that faith and love are so closely knit together that one's faith could be destroyed if one has the wrong understanding of God's love, and one's love would be misguided if one's faith is perverted by erroneous beliefs. After reading this book, I better understood the need for acquiring knowledge about, and an understanding of, the concepts and rationale for those conclusions, which strike at the very nature of God's love, justice, and wisdom in demonstrating both love and justice.

It is not my goal or objective to merely intellectualize a theory, or pose a derivative of already established theories, regarding God's love as revealed by the atonement provided in Christ's birth, life, death, and resurrection. God's love is vital. It is a living principle that is directly imprinted, along with His natural and moral laws, in our very physiological and psychological being, though sin has marred that publication.

Yet one often cannot intellectually identify what one experiences, or desires to experience, on the emotional, kinesthetic level without developing a definitive, quantifiable, verbal expression—inadequate a medium as that is—best described as a theory. How can the finite mind fully grasp and communicate infinite love? Unfortunately, the very act of pursuing knowledge of the truth can become a chore, for one must sort through all the false conclusions drawn and taught by others. If we are not discerning regarding what we hear, we will fall prey to Satan's deceptive traps as the apostle Paul warned:

> But I fear, lest by any means, as the serpent beguiled Eve through his subtlety, so your minds should be corrupted from the simplicity that is in Christ. For if he that cometh preacheth another Jesus, whom we have not preached, or if ye receive another spirit, which ye have not received, or another gospel, which ye have not accepted, ye might well bear with him....
>
> For such are false apostles, deceitful workers, transforming themselves into the apostles of Christ. And no marvel; for Satan himself is transformed into an angel of light. Therefore it is no great thing if his ministers also be transformed as the ministers of righteousness; whose end shall be according to their works.[12]

Certain premises ought to be accepted without compromise from the onset, such as, "The heart and core of the Christian faith is based upon Jesus Christ's shed blood at Calvary as the only acceptable substitutionary atonement for mankind's sins."[13] Amazingly enough, not all professed Christians agree on this point. Much has been written on the various atonement theories presented over the centuries (as many as nine different teachings), some of which is called new theology, yet it is rooted in old mysticism.

The positions taken by those who teach unbiblical theories of atonement are also closely aligned with the concept of unconditional love as first promoted by the Universalist—such as the moral influence view of the atonement. Moral influence theology teaches us that a positive final judgment is achieved by a moral change of

---

12   2 Corinthians 11:3, 4, 13–15
13   Roger Oakland, *Faith Undone* (Silverton, OR: Lighthouse Trails Publishing, 2008), 190.

people simply by the teachings of Jesus and spiritual exercises including such disciplines as prayer labyrinths. Proponents of the moral influence theology will tell others that God didn't need Jesus to die on the cross in order to remove sin from us—it can happen by believing that His teachings and spiritual exercises will accomplish that separation from sin.

The Bible warns us about teachers who seek to abolish the doctrine of blood atonement. The apostle John wrote:

> Whosoever believeth that Jesus is the Christ is born of God: and every one that loveth him that begat loveth him also that is begotten of him. By this we know that we love the children of God, when we love God, and keep his commandments. For this is the love of God, that we keep his commandments: and his commandments are not grievous. For whatsoever is born of God overcometh the world: and this is the victory that overcometh the world, even our faith.
>
> Who is he that overcometh the world, but he that believeth that Jesus is the Son of God? This is he that came by water and blood, even Jesus Christ; not by water only, but by water and blood. And it is the Spirit that beareth witness, because the Spirit is truth. For there are three that bear record in heaven, the Father, the Word, and the Holy Ghost: and these three are one. And there are three that bear witness in earth, the Spirit, and the water, and the blood: and these three agree in one.
>
> If we receive the witness of men, the witness of God is greater: for this is the witness of God which he hath testified of his Son. He that believeth on the Son of God hath the witness in himself: he that believeth not God hath made him a liar; because he believeth not the record that God gave of his Son. And this is the record, that God hath given to us eternal life, and this life is in his Son. He that hath the Son hath life; and he that hath not the Son of God hath not life. These things have I written unto you that believe on the name of the Son of God; that ye may know that ye have eternal life, and that ye may believe on the name of the Son of God.[14]

Ellen White penned a warning to those who trifle with the expression "God is love" by misconstruing its true meaning and importance in connection with the blood atonement remitted on the cross of Calvary.

> In giving his only begotten Son to die for sinners, God has manifested to fallen man love that is without a parallel. We have full faith in the scripture that says, "God is love;" and yet many have shamefully perverted this word, and have fallen into dangerous error because of a false interpretation of its meaning. God's holy law is the only standard by which we can estimate divine affection. If we do not accept the law of God as our standard, we set up a standard of our own. God has given us precious promises of his love, but we are not to

---

14   1 John 5:1–13

ascribe to Jehovah a tenderness that will lead him to pass over guilt and wink at iniquity.[15]

She also warns about setting up our own standards when she wrote:

> It is not the greatness of the act of disobedience that constitutes sin, but the fact of variance from God's expressed will in the least particular; for this shows that there is yet communion between the soul and sin. The heart is divided in its service. There is a virtual denial of God, a rebellion against the laws of His government.
>
> Were men free to depart from the Lord's requirements and to set up a standard of duty for themselves, there would be a variety of standards to suit different minds and the government would be taken out of the Lord's hands. The will of man would be made supreme, and the high and holy will of God—His purpose of love toward His creatures—would be dishonored, disrespected.
>
> Whenever men choose their own way, they place themselves in controversy with God. They will have no place in the kingdom of heaven, for they are at war with the very principles of heaven. In disregarding the will of God, they are placing themselves on the side of Satan, the enemy of God and man. Not by one word, not by many words, but by every word that God has spoken, shall man live. We cannot disregard one word, however trifling it may seem to us, and be safe.[16]

Even though we are warned about false theories and doctrines regarding salvation, and the nature of a love that would plan for salvation before it was even necessary to implement that very plan, we often are oblivious to the efforts of those who rationalize away blood atonement, penal substitution, and an unselfish love that has conditions for the good of the whole universe. Many go so far as to defend the concept of unconditional love without fully comprehending the deception or appreciating the danger of their position. So, let us take time to understand the positions held by many from their own writings.

> *"God is love," and yet many have shamefully perverted this word, ... because of a false interpretation of its meaning.*

Brian McLaren is a well-known emergent church leader, trumpeted by *Time* magazine as an elder statesman in the emerging church movement, as well as one of the twenty-five most influential evangelicals in America. "If his movement can survive in the politicized world of conservative Christianity, McLaren could find a way for young Evangelicals and more liberal Christians to march into the future together despite their

---

15   Ellen G. White, "The Truth as It Is in Jesus," *The Review and Herald*, June 17, 1890.
16   White, *Thoughts from the Mount of Blessing*, 51, 52.

theological differences."[17] What he teaches about the atonement and unconditional love will provide insight to the heart of the matter.

In an interview on the subject of atonement, McLaren stated:

> One of the huge problems is the traditional understanding of hell. Because if the cross is in line with Jesus' teaching then—I won't say, the only, and I certainly won't say even the primary—but a primary meaning of the cross is that the kingdom of God doesn't come like the kingdoms of this world, by inflicting violence and coercing people. But that the kingdom of God comes through suffering and willing, voluntary sacrifice, right? But in an ironic way, the doctrine of hell basically says, no, that's not really true. That in the end, God gets His way through coercion and violence and intimidation and domination, just like every other kingdom does. The cross isn't the center then. The cross is almost a distraction and false advertising for God....
>
> I heard one well-known Christian leader, who—I won't mention his name, just to protect his reputation, 'cause some people would use this against him. But I heard him say it like this: The traditional understanding says that God asks of us something that God is incapable of Himself. God asks us to forgive people. But God is incapable of forgiving. God can't forgive unless He punishes somebody in place of the person He was going to forgive. God doesn't say things to you—Forgive your wife, and then go kick the dog to vent your anger. God asks you to actually forgive.... And there's a certain sense that, a common understanding of the atonement presents a God who is incapable of forgiving. Unless He kicks somebody else.[18]

We could dwell upon the misunderstandings contributing to this conclusion, but we must move on to the consequences resulting from the misunderstandings.

The idea of unconditional love is noticeably prevalent in the emerging church when speaking about the gay community:

> From a straight Christian perspective, the ideal life is to get married and have a family. From a gay perspective the ideal is to come out and live a happy, sexually reconciled faith as a gay man or lesbian woman. And for those believers with a same-sex attraction who don't fit in the other two ideals, the third ideal is to be celibate. What each ideal has in common is that they focus on sex—or lack thereof—as the standard by which to judge a life....
>
> There's a fourth ideal that gets overlooked, an ideal that's not based on sex: It's OK to be yourself before God and not conform to any of the other three ways that seem ideal to the outside world.

---

17   TIME staff, "Brian McLaren: Paradigm Shifter," *Time*, February 7, 2005.

18   The Bleeding Purple Podcast, interview by Leif Hansen with Brian McLaren, January 8, 2006, as cited by Roger Oakland, *Faith Undone*, 192, 193.

The fourth ideal communicates God's acceptance, validation, affirmation and unconditional love in meeting people as they are, where they are.[19]

Essentially, McLaren and his contemporaries are rejecting the wisdom and love of God as revealed in the Bible because they don't agree with the justice of God revealed in the Bible, or at the very least they disagree with the traditional human interpretation of the justice of God regarding the destruction of the unrepentant wicked. Those who hold to these ideas are basically excusing behavior that God, through Scripture, says is abhorrent by erroneously concluding that God made people homosexual.[20] But these are not new ideas; theologians from eras past have held similar views regarding the cross and its role in revealing the love and justice of God.

Alan Jones, dean of the Episcopal Grace Cathedral in San Francisco, California, from 1985 until January 2009, wrote the following in his book *Reimagining Christianity*: "The Church's fixation on the death of Jesus as the universal saving act must end, and the place of the cross must be reimagined in Christian faith. Why? Because of the cult of suffering and the vindictive God behind it."[21] "The other thread of just criticism addresses the suggestion implicit in the cross that Jesus' sacrifice was to appease an angry God. Penal substitution [the Cross] was the name of this vile doctrine."[22]

Former Catholic priest Brennan Manning, a major influence in the emerging spirituality community, wrote, "The god whose moods alternate between graciousness and fierce anger ... the god who exacts the last drop of blood from his Son so that his just anger, evoked by sin, may be appeased, is not the God revealed by and in Jesus Christ. And if he is not the God of Jesus, he does not exist."[23]

Marcus J. Borg, one of the most widely known and influential voices in progressive Christianity today, wrote:

> I let go of the notion that the Bible is a divine product. I learned that it is a human cultural product, the product of two ancient communities, biblical Israel and early Christianity. As such, it contained their understandings and affirmations, not statements coming directly or somewhat directly from God.... I realized that whatever 'divine revelation' and the 'inspiration of the Bible' meant (if they meant anything), they did not mean that the Bible was a divine product with divine authority.... Jesus almost certainly was not born of a virgin, did not think of himself as the Son of God, and did not see his purpose as dying for the sins of the world.[24]

---

19   Andrew Marin, *Love Is an Orientation: Elevating the Conversation with the Gay Community* (Downers Grover, IL: InterVaristy Press, 2009), 102, 103.

20   Leviticus 18:22, 23; 20:11–22; Romans 1:21–32

21   Alan Jones, *Reimagining Christianity* (Hoboken, NJ: John Wiley & Sons, Inc., 2005), 132.

22   Ibid., 168.

23   Brennan Manning, *Above All* (Brentwood, TN: Integrity Publishers, 2003), 58, 59.

24   Marcus Borg, *The God We Never Knew* (New York: HarperCollins Publishers Inc., 1998), 25.

Yet his conclusion on God's unconditional acceptance appears full of authoritative assurance, when in reality he is attempting a paradigm shift while using the revisionist's perspective. He attempts to accomplish this by admitting that the God of love and the God of justice are related, but then stating we have the wrong perspective if we think that that relationship translates into a requirements and rewards emphasis. The correct emphasis, according to Borg, ought to be on relationship and transformation. Then he concludes, "God as the lawgiver and judge is the God of 'works' that Paul and Luther and the Protestant Reformation in general rejected. Instead, they affirmed radical grace: God's acceptance of us is unconditional, not dependent upon what we believe or what we do."[25]

The response that we have for this so-called unconditional acceptance is this:

> But let none deceive themselves with the thought that God, in His great love and mercy, will yet save even the rejecters of His grace. The exceeding sinfulness of sin can be estimated only in the light of the cross. When men urge that God is too good to cast off the sinner, let them look to Calvary. *It was because there was no other way in which man could be saved, because without this sacrifice it was impossible for the human race to escape from the defiling power of sin, and be restored to communion with holy beings,—impossible for them again to become partakers of spiritual life,—it was because of this that Christ took upon Himself the guilt of the disobedient and suffered in the sinner's stead.* The love and suffering and death of the Son of God all testify to the terrible enormity of sin and declare that there is no escape from its power, no hope of the higher life, but through the submission of the soul to Christ.[26]

Borg addresses the need for transformation and relationship, but what governs the relationship? What measures the transformation? Borg has rejected that the law requires anything, so where is the need to transform? If God is love, and His law is love, we then correctly understand that love is a vital power governing relationships and transforming lives ruined by the transgression of the law. Therefore, love demonstrates itself to be the undeserved grace by which we are saved through faith. We are saved to do the works that God has ordained for us to do from the beginning when He created Adam and Eve.[27] That transformation is possible only because of the shedding of Christ's blood upon the cross.

The God of Sinai is the God of Calvary. To reject the one (because we don't like or appreciate the

> *Those who flatter themselves that He is too merciful to execute justice upon the sinner, have only to look to the cross of Calvary.*

---

25   Marcus Borg, *The Heart of Christianity: Rediscovering a Life of Faith* (New York: HarperCollins Publishers, Inc., 2003), 76.
26   White, *Steps to Christ*, 31, 32, emphasis added.
27   Ephesians 2:6–10

condemnation Christ took upon Himself in order to provide for us a way of escape from hopeless, eternal doom) is to reject the other.

> God has given in His word decisive evidence that He will punish the transgressors of His law. Those who flatter themselves that He is too merciful to execute justice upon the sinner, have only to look to the cross of Calvary. The death of the spotless Son of God testifies that "the wages of sin is death," that every violation of God's law must receive its just retribution. Christ the sinless became sin for man. He bore the guilt of transgression, and the hiding of His Father's face, until His heart was broken and His life crushed out. All this sacrifice was made that sinners might be redeemed. *In no other way could man be freed from the penalty of sin.* And every soul that refuses to become a partaker of the atonement provided at such a cost must bear in his own person the guilt and punishment of transgression.[28]

In light of these ministers' claims—their rejection of both God's law and the blood of Christ shed upon the cross—one can only wonder in amazement, along with Ellen White, that they still believe they will be fitted to live in heaven. "It is astonishing to see upon what flimsy foundations very many build their hopes of heaven! They rail at the law of the Infinite One as though they would defy Him and make His word null. Even Satan with his knowledge of the divine law would not dare to make the speeches which some law-hating ministers make from the pulpit, yet he exults in their blasphemy."[29]

Elsewhere she explains why the rejection of the law and the cross will not be an excuse to those who would lay claim to heaven without either:

> Those who are unacquainted with the laws of God's government as expounded upon the mount, are unacquainted with the truth as it is in Jesus. Christ revealed the far-reaching principles of the law; he expounded every precept, and exhibited every demand in his example. He that knows the truth as it is in the law, knows the truth as it is in Jesus; and if through faith in Christ he renders obedience to the commandments of God, his life is hid with Christ in God. The knowledge of the claims of the law would crush out the last ray of hope from the soul if there were no Saviour provided for man; but the truth as it is in Jesus, is a savor of life unto life. God's dear Son died that he might impute unto man his own righteousness, and not that he might be at liberty to break God's holy law, as Satan tries to make men believe. Through faith in Christ, man may be in possession of moral power to resist evil.[30]

We have many examples granted us to explain why the ceremonial rites of animal sacrifice were given to

---

28   White, *The Great Controversy*, 539, 540, emphasis added.
29   Ellen G. White, *Testimonies for the Church*, vol. 4 (Mountain View, CA: Pacific Press Publishing Association, 1881), 14.
30   White, "The Truth as It Is in Jesus."

Adam and Eve at the fall. Sin, with its guilt and shame, separates the fallen race from a holy God who hates sin.

> Fallen man, because of his guilt, could no longer come directly before God with his sup-
> plications; for his transgression of the divine law had placed an impassable barrier between
> the holy God and the transgressor. But a plan was devised that the sentence of death should
> rest upon a Substitute. In the plan of redemption there must be the shedding of blood, for
> death must come in consequence of man's sin. The beasts for sacrificial offerings were to
> prefigure Christ. In the slain victim, man was to see the fulfillment for the time being of
> God's word, 'Thou shalt surely die.' And the flowing of the blood from the victim would
> also signify an atonement. There was no virtue in the blood of animals; but the shedding
> of the blood of beasts was to point forward to a Redeemer who would one day come to the
> world and die for the sins of men. And thus Christ would fully vindicate His Father's law.[31]

Aiden Wilson Tozer, a Christian and Missionary Alliance minister who became concerned about the direction contemporary Christian living was headed with its compromising worldly concerns, makes important points as he refutes this rejection of penal substitution by those teaching doctrines similar to emerging church theologians:

> A lot of people are interested in religion, but are far from God, nevertheless. Maybe they
> are practicing religion. Maybe they are practicing heathen rites of various kinds. Maybe
> they are praying their beads with unconsciously moving lips on the bus or the airplane....
>
> They say, "We don't believe in 'slaughterhouse religion.' We don't believe that God
> Almighty was pleased because Aaron and his sons cut a heifer, cut her throat, and bled her
> out in a basin. Then they sprinkled things with blood, and offered her ... burnt body on that
> altar. We don't believe that. We think that it must have been an unpleasant and terrible
> thing."
>
> Well, there's one place that must be more unpleasant, and that's hell. The Scripture
> tells us that if a man is not redeemed by the blood of an acceptable sacrifice, he is most cer-
> tainly going to spend his eternity in hell. When we spruce it up, and sugarcoat it, and take
> away the slaughterhouse element from it, we've taken away the cross....
>
> Why was the man on a cross? Because there was one thing worse than that, and that
> was hell, where men were going. So God sent His only begotten Son so that man might
> go to the cross and stop the gates of hell, and shut them up so those who believed in Him
> should not perish, but have everlasting life. Of course, there was a slaughterhouse there,
> and, of course, that was a slaughter hill there where a man died, but a man died in terror
> because sin is a terrible thing, and a man died in pain because sin is a painful thing. A man
> died ostracized and forsaken, because sin brings ostracism and rejection. God turned His

---

31   Ellen G. White, *Confrontation* (Washington, D.C.: Review and Herald Publishing Association, 1971), 21, 22.

back on that hill while that man died there, because He will turn His back on every man who doesn't die with Him or every man that does not take advantage of the blood Jesus shed.[32]

While we might differ with Tozer on the concept of an eternally burning hell, because Malachi 4:3 tells us the wicked will be ashes under the feet of the righteous, we do agree on the simple fact that only by the shedding of blood can there be any remission of sin.[33] All throughout the New Testament, the apostles teach that blood is an important part of the gospel. Peter wrote that we are, "Elect according to the foreknowledge of God the Father, through sanctification of the Spirit, unto obedience and sprinkling of the blood of Jesus Christ."[34] John penned that it is "the blood of Jesus Christ his Son [that] cleanseth us from all sin."[35]

Paul repeatedly taught, "Whom God hath set forth to be a propitiation through faith in his blood, to declare his righteousness for the remission of sins that are past, through the forbearance of God."[36] "In whom we have redemption through his blood, even the forgiveness of sins:... And, having made peace through the blood of his cross, by him to reconcile all things unto himself; by him, I say, whether they be things in earth, or things in heaven."[37] "How much more shall the blood of Christ, who through the eternal Spirit offered himself without spot to God, purge your conscience from dead works to serve the living God?... And almost all things are by the law purged with blood; and without shedding of blood is no remission."[38]

Especially strong is the warning Paul gives to those who count the blood of the covenant as of no importance: "Of how much sorer punishment, suppose ye, shall he be thought worthy, who hath trodden under foot the Son of God, and hath counted the blood of the covenant, wherewith he was sanctified, an unholy thing, and hath done despite unto the Spirit of grace?"[39]

Those that reject the Bible truth regarding the atoning sacrifice of Jesus are creating a fantasy for their religion. Ellen White wrote the truth about their spiritual condition when she penned:

> Many have a fanciful religion. They talk of God's love, claiming that he is not severe and exacting, but long-suffering and lenient; at the same time, they echo the suggestion of Satan, "Hath God said, Ye shall not eat of every tree of the garden? ... Ye shall not surely die: for God doth know that in the day ye eat thereof, then your eyes shall be opened, and ye shall be as gods, knowing good and evil." It was though he had declared that God's threatening was all a pretense, and man need not be alarmed, for God would not be so severe and exacting. The very same reasoning is employed today in the Christian world. When the claims of the law are presented, men begin to frame excuses for continuing in disobedience, stating that God

---

32   A. W. Tozer, *Tozer: Fellowship of the Burning Heart* (Alachua, FL: Bridge-Logos, 2006), 149–152.
33   Hebrews 9:22
34   1 Peter 1:2
35   1 John 1:7
36   Romans 3:25
37   Colossian 1:14, 20
38   Hebrews 9:14, 22
39   Hebrews 10:29

will not punish them for the breaking of his precepts. But let us think of it soberly. Will God change his holy law to suit my convenience? Will he sanction sin, and countenance disobedience? If God had a character of this kind, we could not reverence him. His authority could not be respected. Every transgression of God's law will be visited with its penalty upon the transgressor. The wages of sin is death. God is jealous for the honor of his law; it is the foundation of his government in heaven and earth, and it will stand throughout eternal ages. The prophet declares, "The soul that sinneth, it shall die." Sin is the transgression of the law. But, again, it is written for the comfort and salvation of the penitent: "If we confess our sins, he is faithful and just to forgive us our sins, and to cleanse us from all unrighteousness."[40]

The fatal deception of the religious world is the old disregard for the claims of the law of God. The desire for an easy religion that requires no striving, no self-denial, no divorce from the follies of the world, has made the doctrine of faith, and faith only, a popular doctrine; but we must sound a note of warning. What saith the word of God? Says the apostle James, "What doth it profit, my brethren, though a man say he hath faith, and have not works? can faith save him? ... Thou believest that there is one God; thou doest well; the devils also believe, and tremble. But wilt thou know, O vain man, that faith without works is dead? Was not Abraham our father justified by works, when he had offered Isaac his son upon the altar? Seest thou how faith wrought with his works, and by works was faith made perfect? And the Scripture was fulfilled which saith, Abraham believed God, and it was imputed unto him for righteousness; and he was called the Friend of God. Ye see then how that by works a man is justified, and not by faith only."

The testimony of the word of God is against this ensnaring doctrine of faith without works. It is not faith that claims the favor of Heaven without complying with the conditions upon which mercy is to be granted; it is presumption; for genuine faith has its foundation in the promises and provisions of the Scriptures.[41]

Hope is not extinguished when we realize our true condition. It grows, unless presumptuous selfishness is allowed to poison it. As we acknowledge the horror of the cross as an expression of God's unselfish love to reconcile us to Him, we acknowledge the sinfulness of sin and approve of God's wisdom in uprooting and exterminating it from our lives, regardless of how painful a process that may be.

And as Christ draws them to look upon His cross, to behold Him whom their sins have pierced, the commandment comes home to the conscience. The wickedness of their life, the deep-seated sin of the soul, is revealed to them. They begin to comprehend something of the righteousness of Christ, and exclaim, "What is sin, that it should require such a

---

40   Ellen G. White, "A Peculiar People," *The Review and Herald*, November 18, 1890.
41   White, "Faith and Works."

sacrifice for the redemption of its victim? Was all this love, all this suffering, all this humiliation, demanded, that we might not perish, but have everlasting life?"

The sinner may resist this love, may refuse to be drawn to Christ; but if he does not resist he will be drawn to Jesus; a knowledge of the plan of salvation will lead him to the foot of the cross in repentance for his sins, which have caused the sufferings of God's dear Son.[42]

So then, how does selfishness and sin poison the hope and faith that God gives to everyone through the sacrificial death of His Son? To someone locked in sin, the very facts of the gospel are repugnant to those who have no desire to follow after Christ. They refuse to overcome sin in their flesh in the same manner by which Jesus overcame sinful flesh by perfectly submitting to God's law. So they reject the possibility of complete victory over sin, as well as the possibility to perfect the character, this side of heaven. However,

Christ took human nature upon him, and became a debtor to do the whole law in behalf of those whom he represented. Had he failed in one jot or tittle, he would have been a transgressor of the law, and we would have had in him a sinful, unavailing offering. But he fulfilled every specification of the law, and condemned sin in the flesh; yet many ministers repeat the falsehoods of the scribes, priests, and Pharisees, and follow their example in turning the people away from the truth.

God was manifested in the flesh to condemn sin in the flesh, by manifesting perfect obedience to all the law of God. Christ did no sin, neither was guile found in his mouth. He corrupted not human nature, and, tho in the flesh, he transgressed not the law of God in any particular. More than this, he removed every excuse from fallen man that he could urge for a reason for not keeping the law of God. Christ was compassed with the infirmities of humanity, he was beset with the fiercest temptations, tempted on all points like as men, yet he developed a perfectly upright character. No taint of sin was found upon him.[43]

We must be very careful on this matter, because a distinction must be made in order to understand the dangers involved in a half-hearted commitment to the gospel.

We are not to rush into the acceptance of the gospel without any fixed stability of purpose. If we receive Jesus Christ, we must receive all the conditions, all the requirements, and make it our life business in everything to make the kingdom of God our first consideration. Difficulties will present themselves as obstructions. *But the greatest difficulties originate with self.* It will cost all there is of the man, for Christ demands the heart, the soul, the strength, and the mind of every human agent. "Ye are not your own for ye are bought with a price; therefore glorify God in your body and in your spirit which are God's." It will cost

---

42   White, *Steps to Christ*, 27.
43   White, "Sin Condemned in the Flesh."

self-humiliation, self-denial, self-sacrifice, a constant conflict with human passions. *Our natural temperaments can not be carried along in the road, cast up for the ransomed of the Lord to walk in.* Shame and weakness and disgrace are the sure result of professedly following Christ while walking in the ways and practices of the unrenewed, unconverted men.

To be half for Christ and half unrenewed, having the mind of the enemy, means to be a stumbling-block to one's self and a stumbling-block to others, a reproach to Christ and a weakness in the church and in the ministry. If we do not propose to be wholly converted, to be doers of the word, then for Christ's sake let us not spoil the Christian experience of others, causing them to be led astray by our serving sin and the devil while professedly serving the Lord.[44]

Yet this is exactly what hundreds of ministers and theologians are teaching millions of professed Christians to do. If Christ's blood is unnecessary to cleanse us from all unrighteousnesss, then it stands to reason that we don't need to experience the suffering that comes from subjecting the body and the will to the same discipline to which Christ submitted in order to make His sacrifice perfectly viable. We will not be found loving God, because we will not be found connected to Christ—crucified with Christ—so that we can obey His commandments with acceptable levels of gratitude.

On the other hand, and the spiritual reality of the matter, is the simple fact that we are only acceptable to God when we follow Christ's example of perfect obedience and selfless sacrifice, having accepted His bloody death as the substitute for our own eternal separation from God because of sin. Only then does "the Christian becomes one with Christ in God, and God loves him as he loves his own Son. When the disciples of Christ become one with him, as he is one with the Father, they will be a power in the world in revealing God's mercy, forgiveness, and truth. Those who do the works of Christ are accepted in the Beloved. Union with Christ means the dispensing of his blessings. The bright beams from the Sun of Righteousness shine forth in mercy and love."[45]

We must accept God's love, justice, and wisdom for what it is. We are not to change it into something it is not. By contemplating upon the demonstration of God's love, we can discern its true nature.

In the light of divine revelation, through the atoning Sacrifice, we may see the glorious plan of redemption whereby our sins are pardoned, and we drawn near to the heart of infinite love. We see how God can retain all his justice, and yet pardon the transgressor of his law. And we are not simply forgiven, but we are accepted of God through the Beloved. The plan of redemption is not merely a way of escape from the penalty of transgression, but through it the sinner is forgiven his sins, and will be finally received into heaven,—not as a forgiven culprit pardoned and released from captivity, yet looked upon with suspicion and not admitted to friendship and trust; but welcomed as a child, and taken back into fullest

---

44   White, "Christianity," italics original.
45   Ellen G. White, "Exercise Compassion," *The Signs of the Times*, September 19, 1895.

confidence. The sacrifice of our Saviour has made ample provision for every repenting, believing soul. We are saved because God loves the purchase of the blood of Christ; and not only will he pardon the repentant sinner, not only will he permit him to enter heaven, but he, the Father of mercies, will wait at the very gates of heaven to welcome us, to give us an abundant entrance to the mansions of the blest. Oh what love, what wondrous love the Father has shown in the gift of his beloved Son for this fallen race! And this Sacrifice is a channel for the outflow of his infinite love, that all who believe on Jesus Christ may, like the prodigal son, receive full and free restoration to the favor of Heaven.[46]

While I was a college student at Union College in Lincoln, Nebraska, I experienced the reconciliation to God that forever changed my perspective on the beauty and power of God's love. I felt impressed to write a song about the experience. Here are the words to that song:

Life was so dull. Love had lost its sheen, when He came to me to set me free. But still I went on my own way to follow Him some other day. And the love that I hadn't seen followed me to Calvary.

Refrain: He gave His life, He died for me, He hung upon a cruel tree, so that I from sin might be set free—what wondrous love!

Well the worse things got, the worse I felt, the deceit of sin had boxed me in. But as I continued to fight, He gave me more light. And my heart began to melt as He came to me once again.

And the life He gave—so full and sweet—strife will cease with release as to my God I will always run, saying, Father, Thy will be done—to fall at my Savior's feet and to know His blissful peace!

This life to share, this love to extend to you right here, let Him draw near to touch your stony heart—He's promised you a brand new start—together joined to share our Friend who would come and take away our fear.

It is my sincere desire and prayer that you will see just how wonderful God's love is because it is unselfish and faithful. God's love is willing to sacrifice all but His law. In fact, it magnifies God's law. God's love is as much a part of His government as is His law. Its strength surpasses the intimidating force of death and the tomb. It has conditions that, after the fall of Adam and Eve, could only be met by the One who is equal with

---

46   Ellen G. White, "Christ Our Sacrifice," *The Review and Herald*, September 21, 1886.

God. And it was most eloquently demonstrated when Christ gave of Himself on our behalf:

> Christ consented to connect himself with the disloyal and sinful, to partake of the nature of man, to give his own blood, and to make his soul an offering for sin. In the counsels of heaven, the guilt of man was measured, the wrath for sin was estimated, and yet Christ announced his decision that he would take upon himself the responsibility of meeting the conditions whereby hope should be extended to a fallen race. He understood the possibility of the human soul, and united humanity to himself, even as the vine knits the grafted branches and twigs into its being, until, vein by vein, and fiber by fiber, the branches are united to the living Vine.[47]

So then, let us unite in the truth as it is in Jesus, and share this wondrous love to those we meet!

---

47   White, "Divinity in Humanity."

Chapter 8

From Here to Eternity

I am a fourth generation Seventh-day Adventist. I don't reveal this fact as a matter of pride but simply for what it is—a part of my testimony. As I recall my childhood, my formative years, I don't have any doubt that my parents loved me and provided me with everything that I needed. There were even times when they gave me things I wanted but weren't really in my best interest. Rather than judge them too harshly, I will confess that my obstinate persistence on those occasions most likely wore them down.

In one such instance, Christmas was approaching and my parents took us to a toy store to see what struck our fancy. I recall my sisters showing interest in dolls; however, I was bored with their enthusiasm, as any five- or six-year-old boy would be. But then I spotted something I wanted. In fact, I wanted it so badly that I thought life would end as I knew it if I could not have it. It was a plastic safari rifle that had spring-loaded plastic bullets capable of traveling approximately twenty feet or so. My mother definitely didn't want me to have it. I begged. I pleaded. I don't recall throwing a temper tantrum, but I was persistent.

Of course, my parents didn't buy anything that day since we were with them. However, sometime later I discovered a long box—reminiscent in size to the one containing the safari rifle I had seen in the store—hidden behind the sofa adjacent to the Christmas tree. I didn't have to guess at the contents of the wrapped box. It had no name tag taped to it, but I intuitively knew the present was for me. When Christmas arrived, I patiently waited for all the presents to be handed out. Then I asked my father if there was one more behind the sofa that should go to its rightful recipient. Much to my joy, and my mother's consternation, I received my desired gift.

I had fun with that toy, shooting at birds, rodents, and the dairy cows in the fields down the road

> *The delicacy is in presenting the correct response of love at the right time and in the right way.*

from us. Attempting to retrieve the plastic bullets got a little messy at times, especially in the dairy pasture, but it was sheer fun pulling the trigger.

Unfortunately, I let my temper get the best of me one day, and I deliberately shot a friend, Brian, in the throat at point-blank range. No skin was broken, no blood was spilt—just a painful welt in close proximity to the larynx. But in that instance I learned that parental love can change from gentleness to severity in a heartbeat when the conditions are right. My father not only took away my prized possession, he applied the unvarnished board of education to the un-upholstered seat of learning. The crime was punished without any penal substitution to illustrate biblical grace. But then again, it was not punished in a manner so as to illustrate biblical justice.

In many ways Christian parental love teaches us about the nature of God's love. "As the mother teaches her children to obey her because they love her, she is teaching them the first lessons in the Christian life. The mother's love represents to the child the love of Christ, and the little ones who trust and obey their mother are learning to trust and obey the Saviour."[1]

Unfortunately, because selfishness intrudes, parental love is often expressed with unnecessary severity, turning the hearts of the children away from the parents and from God, which is something Paul warns parents not to do.[2] Nevertheless, conditions do exist whereby love must be tough, and even severe, as is a parents' duty according to the wise counsel of Solomon.[3] The delicacy is in presenting the correct response of love at the right time and in the right way. This balance can only be achieved and successfully demonstrated when one is converted, receives a new heart with God's law written upon it, and is filled with the power of the indwelling Holy Spirit.

Jesus came to reveal the love of the Father and strip away the lies that Satan has told so that we might see the character of God.

> God has bound our hearts to Him by unnumbered tokens in heaven and in earth. Through the things of nature, and the deepest and tenderest earthly ties that human hearts can know, He has sought to reveal Himself to us. Yet these but imperfectly represent His love. Though all these evidences have been given, the enemy of good blinded the minds of men, so that they looked upon God with fear; they thought of Him as severe and unforgiving. Satan led men to conceive of God as a being whose chief attribute is stern justice,—one who is a severe judge, a harsh, exacting creditor. He pictured the Creator as a being who is watching with jealous eye to discern the errors and mistakes of men, that He may visit judgments upon them. It was to remove this dark shadow, by revealing to the world the infinite love of God, that Jesus came to live among men.[4]

But those who separate God's love from His law are presenting the opposite extreme from the severe, unforgiving judge.

God's love is embodied in His law. His law is a reflection of His character. His love and justice are revealed in His Word—the Bible—so we might begin to comprehend His respect for an order and harmony culminating in peace and joy, while at the same time perceiving the hatred He has for anything that disrupts that order

---

1   White, *The Desire of Ages*, 515.
2   Ephesians 6:4
3   Proverbs 10:13; 13:24; 22:15; 23:13, 14; 29:15
4   White, *Steps to Christ*, 10, 11.

and harmony. Sin—the transgression of God's law—is not only disruptive, it's deadly.[5] Sin and, consequently, those who cherish it are the cause of unnecessary sorrow and painful separation—the sure results of death and its process. So we must understand that the warnings given in the Bible about the results of sin are for our ultimate benefit. "The judgments of God pronounced against sin, the inevitable retribution, the degradation of our character, and the final destruction, are presented in God's word to warn us against the service of Satan."[6]

The Bible tells us that God does not treat those who repent as they deserve to be treated.[7] This principle was illustrated in an experience I had with a police officer when he pulled me over for speeding.

After seeing lights flashing in my mirror and looking around to find no other vehicles in sight, I pulled over and, with seat belt still fastened, got out my license, truck registration, medical card—all the documentation for which I knew he would be asking. When he arrived at my window, he asked me, "Do you know why I pulled you over?"

I believed I did. And knowing how this would go, I replied, "I know how fast I was going, officer. But I don't know what the speed limit was at the time you clocked me with your radar."

He proceeded to tell me I was doing 65 in a 45 mph zone. I grimaced. Twenty over would mean a reckless driving ticket, which is huge when driving is one's livelihood. Then he asked me, "What is your driving record like?"

I smiled and spoke confidently. "Clean as a whistle, sir." I didn't specify if the whistle was new or used.

He looked incredulous. "Do you mean to tell me that you have never been pulled over for speeding before?"

My smile got bigger. "No, sir. I mean that my record is as clean as a whistle." The truth was, after all, that some of my speeding tickets had been expunged by going to traffic school or had simply gone unrecorded in the state system because often small municipalities didn't record the infraction if the fine was paid before the established court dates—not to mention the times law enforcement officers simply let me off with a warning.

> *In taking our nature, the Saviour has bound Himself to humanity by a tie that is never to be broken.*

He shook his head and said, "We'll see about that." Then he pulled out his PDA, entered my license number, name, date of birth, and waited for a response. Nothing came up. The PDA was out of range of the cell tower, and he could not pull up my driving record. I was starting to get anxious, because I had a deadline to meet. Finally, he asked me, "Where did you get your trailer loaded?" I told him. Then he said, "I'll tell you what I am going to do. I am going to write you a ticket for not wearing your seat belt."

I objected that I had been wearing my seat belt and that he knew it. His hands came down to his hips, and he looked me right in the eye. "But a seat belt ticket won't go on your record." I nodded my head. Then he said, "So why weren't you wearing your seat belt?"

---

5   1 John 3:4; Romans 6:23
6   White, *Steps to Christ*, 21, 22.
7   Ezra 9:13; Job 11:6.

Again, I objected that I had been wearing my seat belt. After all, I hadn't lied about speeding, so why should I start by lying about wearing my seat belt?

Again the hands went to his hips. "Look, a seat belt ticket is only a $25 fine. Are you going to fight me on this?"

I shook my head, "Not over $25, sir. Not worth the expense to fight it." I wasn't going to get out of a ticket altogether, but it wasn't going to be what I deserved to get.

The same is true of the wages of our sin and the gift of salvation. As the psalmist wrote, "He [God] hath not dealt with us after our sins; nor rewarded us according to our iniquities."[8] This is not an act of unconditional love, instead it is an act of merciful love associated with uncompromising justice for which Christ's atoning and reconciliatory death paid the penalty for our transgressions. Note how Ellen White expresses this wonderful theme:

> Christ was treated as we deserve, that we might be treated as He deserves. He was condemned for our sins, in which He had no share, that we might be justified by His righteousness, in which we had no share. He suffered the death which was ours, that we might receive the life which was His. "With His stripes we are healed."
>
> By His life and His death, Christ has achieved even more than recovery from the ruin wrought through sin. It was Satan's purpose to bring about an eternal separation between God and man; but in Christ we become more closely united to God than if we had never fallen. In taking our nature, the Saviour has bound Himself to humanity by a tie that is never to be broken. Through the eternal ages He is linked with us.... Christ is our brother. Heaven is enshrined in humanity, and humanity is enfolded in the bosom of Infinite love.... By love's self-sacrifice, the inhabitants of earth and heaven are bound to their Creator in bonds of indissoluble union.
>
> The work of redemption will be complete. In the place where sin abounded, God's grace much more abounds. The earth itself, the very field that Satan claims as his, is to be not only ransomed but exalted. Our little world, under the curse of sin the one dark blot in His glorious creation, will be honored above all other worlds in the universe of God. Here, where the Son of God tabernacled in humanity; where the King of glory lived and suffered and died,—here, when He shall make all things new, the tabernacle of God shall be with men, "and He shall dwell with them, and they shall be His people, and God Himself, shall be with them, and be their God." And through endless ages as the redeemed walk in the light of the Lord, they will praise Him for His unspeakable Gift, Immanuel, "God with us."[9]

How is this even possible? Because "the Lord is known by the judgment which he executeth."[10] The Bible is filled with revelations of God's judgments. It is everywhere one looks, if one will take more than

---

8   Psalm 103:10
9   Ellen G. White, "Heaven's Unspeakable Gift," *The Review and Herald*, February 25, 1915.
10   Psalm 9:16

a casual glance. Let it be remembered that not all judgments conclude in the condemnation we deserve because of sin. We who believe on the Lord Jesus Christ and follow His example of obedience to God's commandments by faith will be acquitted because Christ's righteousness is imputed to our names, and so effectually imparted to our lives so that our thoughts, feelings, and works will be a reflection of God's character.

The truth about the biblical judgment is that it is unavoidable. "For we must all appear before the judgment seat of Christ; that every one may receive the things done in his body, according to that he hath done, whether it be good or bad."[11] Of course, controversy on this point exists because some theologians would have us conclude that believers aren't judged. They quote from certain modern versions that state that believers "shall not come into judgment" or "will not be judged."[12] This perverts the meaning of Christ's teaching, which says, "Verily, verily, I say unto you, He that heareth my word, and believeth on him that sent me, hath everlasting life, and shall not come into condemnation; but is passed from death unto life."[13]

We must distinguish between judgment and condemnation because not all judgment results in condemnation. The judicial process usually begins with an inquiry or investigation that concludes with the decision to prosecute or to release the one being detained without bail, or released on bail. Often this is done by a grand jury. Upon determining that one should stand trial, further investigation is needed to make one's case. Again, just because a case goes to trial doesn't necessarily mean that the result of condemnation is certain.

The certainty of a trial's outcome is, to a very large degree, dependent upon the preparedness of the advocate and prosecuting attorneys. Beyond this, all the preparation of a defense attorney is for nothing if the defendant doesn't appear at the courtroom when that appearance is required. In 2 Corinthians 5:10 Paul tells us that "we must all appear before the judgment seat of Christ." So, it benefits us to be prepared before we appear.

As an example of preparedness when appearing before a judge, I will share another story involving another speeding ticket. While driving my Mazda RX-7 through Tennessee on a February evening, I was pulled over for speeding. I admitted that I was speeding, and I even told the officer how fast I was going. He proceeded to tell me that he had clocked me at 72 mph (which was much faster than my speedometer had indicated), and then he wrote me a ticket for going 79 mph, which was 24 mph over the speed limit. He smiled really big and said he was giving me a July court date so I could budget the very expensive fine associated with this ticket. I was furious with this injustice. I determined that rather than mailing in the fine, I was going to fight the ticket in court.

A sympathetic neighbor loaned me a book on how to fight speeding tickets. I prepared. I learned that in some jurisdictions the state trooper issuing the ticket also prosecuted the infraction. Tennessee is one of those jurisdictions. I gathered data every time I drove through that part of the state. And finally, when the court date arrived, I dressed for success.

As soon as I entered the courtroom, I sought out other defendants who had tickets signed by the same officer. I had learned that Trooper Pears was on vacation and would not be appearing in court, so I told each

---

11   2 Corinthians 5:10
12   John 5:24, NKJV, NIV. Other translations that use similar language are NASB, RSV, and TEV.
13   John 5:24

defendant that the only thing they needed to say was, "Your Honor, Trooper Pears is not here." With that one phrase, the judge would have to dismiss the ticket written against them.

I suppose if I had gone first, my example might have been all the encouragement needed. But I ended up being the last case on the docket. I cringed every time a defendant started to say something other than what I had instructed them to say. As soon as they started talking, the judge immediately became the prosecutor, and each one was given a fine or traffic school.

When my turn came, I approached the bench and remained silent. After a moment or two, the judge looked up and asked, "Where is the trooper prosecuting this case?"

I responded, "Your Honor, Trooper Pears is not here."

She smiled broadly, and stated, "You would like for me to dismiss this ticket, wouldn't you." I nodded my head in agreement.

After the judge dismissed the ticket, I decided to make my complaint. I told her what had transpired that February evening, and then said, "Your Honor, I believe Trooper Pears lied about the speed, and that he gave me this court date knowing he would be on vacation. I believe he thought I would simply mail in the fine because I am from Georgia. In assigning this date, he deprived me of my right to a speedy trial." The judge wrote down my complaint. And from then unto this day I drive the speed limit through that part of Tennessee. I don't ever want to meet Trooper Pears again for fear he might remember me.

> *In this great controversy between God and Satan, no revelation of God's love and justice goes unopposed.*

In many ways biblical judgment is similar. We have only so much time to prepare. We must not only believe on the Lord Jesus Christ as our Savior, but we must behold and follow His example so that our characters will be changed into His righteousness and glory. We want to be found dressed for success—covered by the robe of His righteousness, without spot or wrinkle. This work He has promised to do in us through the abiding presence of the Holy Spirit.[14]

However, many misunderstand this process. In October 1879 Ellen White had a vision of the judgment that left her unable to express in any language the effect the sight had upon her. Yet she noted the signal distress of those who were careless of their preparation for the judgment during its investigative stage.

As the Holy One upon the throne slowly turned the leaves of the ledger, and His eyes rested for a moment upon individuals, His glance seemed to burn into their very souls, and at the same moment every word and action of their lives passed before their minds as clearly as though traced before their vision in letters of fire. Trembling seized them, and their faces turned pale. Their first appearance when around the throne was that of careless

---

14   Ezekiel 36:26–29

indifference. But how changed their appearance now! The feeling of security is gone, and in its place is a nameless terror. A dread is upon every soul, lest he shall be found among those who are wanting. Every eye is riveted upon the face of the One upon the throne; and as His solemn, searching eye sweeps over that company, there is a quaking of heart; for they are self-condemned without one word being uttered. In anguish of soul each declares his own guilt and with terrible vividness sees that by sinning he has thrown away the precious boon of eternal life.[15]

Preparation is of utmost importance! This is a solemn warning that ought to be proclaimed to the whole world!

From 1844 to present, Seventh-day Adventists have taught the biblical doctrine of the investigative judgment. Following the Great Disappointment shared by Millerite or Adventist believers, much prayerful study revealed that a review of certain books would take place. This resulted in the writing of many periodicals and books by those who recognized the doctrine's great importance. One of the best I have ever read on the subject is John Nevins Andrews' book *The Judgment: Its Events and Their Order.*

This book carefully outlines chapter by chapter, from the Bible, the doctrine regarding the investigative judgment,[16] just what kind of books are examined,[17] God the Father as judge,[18] the offices of Christ in the judgment,[19] the judgment warnings to the world,[20] the sanctuary in heaven,[21] the coronation of Christ,[22] the executive judgment,[23] and what role the redeemed saints have in judgment before the wicked are at last destroyed.[24]

In this great controversy between God and Satan, no revelation of God's love and justice goes unopposed. It is ever Satan's objective and determined work to prevent truth from rooting in the soil of the heart so that it can bear a fruitful harvest. We are warned exactly how Satan hopes to achieve his goals.

---

15   White, *Testimonies for the Church*, vol. 4, 385. (The complete vision is recording on pages 384–387.)
16   Psalm 9:12 says, "When he maketh inquisition for blood, he remembereth them: he forgetteth not the cry of the humble." Inquisition is an archaic word that means investigation. This same word is used in Deuteronomy 19:18 where God commands that "the judges shall make diligent inquisition." In the NASB we read, "The judges shall investigate thoroughly." We see God investigating prior to execution of judgment at the tower of Babel (Gen. 11:5–8) and the destruction of Sodom (Gen. 18:17, 20–32), at which time Abraham called the LORD "Judge of all the earth" (Gen. 18:25).
17   Genesis 32:32, 33; Psalm 56:8; 69:28; 87:6; Isaiah 4:3; Ezekiel 13:9; Daniel 12:1; Luke 10:20; Philippians 4:3; Hebrews 12:23; Revelation 3:5; 13:8; 17:8; 20:12,15; 21:27; 22:19
18   Daniel 7:9–14
19   Deuteronomy 18:15–18 points out the prophetic office of Christ; Hebrews 7:24, 25 tells us that Christ is our Intercessor and High Priest; Psalm 110:1–7 teaches us that Christ does not execute judgment until He is crowned King of kings; and Daniel 7:9–14 shows us that the judgment commences before Christ receives His kingdom.
20   Revelation 14:6–13; 18:1–10 reveals the warnings of the angel from heaven. These warnings indicate that the judgment is not yet concluded until the censor of intercession is cast down as indicated in Revelation 16:17 and 21:6.
21   Exodus 25:8, 9; 2 Samuel 22:7, 8; Psalm 11:4; 18:6, 7; Hebrews 9:23, 24; Revelation 11:19; 14:17, 18; 15:5; 16:17
22   Psalm 45:1–7; Hebrews 1:8, 9
23   John 5:22–30, specifically verse 27 –"authority to execute judgment"–reveals Jesus' authority. Revelation 19:11–21 tells us when the execution of that judgment takes place.
24   Daniel 7:21, 22; 1 Corinthians 6:1–3; Revelation 20:4–6

The great deceiver has many agents ready to present any and every kind of error to en-snare souls—heresies prepared to suit the varied tastes and capacities of those whom he would ruin. It is his plan to bring into the church insincere, unregenerate elements that will encourage doubt and unbelief, and hinder all who desire to see the work of God advance and to advance with it. Many who have no real faith in God or in His word assent to some principles of truth and pass as Christians, and thus they are enabled to introduce their errors as Scriptural doctrines.

The position that it is of no consequence what men believe is one of Satan's most suc-cessful deceptions. He knows that the truth, received in the love of it, sanctifies the soul of the receiver; therefore he is constantly seeking to substitute false theories, fables, another gospel.[25]

We should especially be vigilant in discerning between the genuine doctrine and the spurious deception as we approach the end of global probation. Satan is striving to prevent us from preparing for our case as our own docket time approaches. He has evolved and refined the sophistries of spiritualism to make it more attrac-tive than ever. The warning is raised by the pen of inspiration against the subtle errors of spiritualism.

Spiritualism asserts that men are unfallen demigods; that "*each mind will judge itself;*" that "true knowledge places men above all law;" that "all sins committed are innocent;" for "whatever is, is right," and "*God doth not condemn.*" The basest of human beings it rep-resents as in heaven, and highly exalted there. Thus it declares to all men, "It matters not what you do; live as you please, heaven is your home." Multitudes are thus led to believe that desire is the highest law, that license is liberty, and that *man is accountable only to himself.*[26]

Again, Ellen White warns us:

Even in [spiritualism's] present form, so far from being more worthy of toleration than formerly, it is really a more dangerous, because a more subtle, deception. While it formerly denounced Christ and the Bible, it now *professes* to accept both. But the Bible is inter-preted in a manner that is pleasing to the unrenewed heart, while its solemn and vital truths are made of no effect. Love is dwelt upon as the chief attribute of God, but it is degraded to a weak sentimentalism, making little distinction between good and evil. God's justice, His denunciations of sin, the requirements of His holy law, are all kept out of sight.[27]

---

25   White, *The Great Controversy*, 520.
26   Ellen G. White, *Education* (Mountain View, CA: Pacific Press Publishing Association, 1903), 227, 228, emphasis added.
27   White, *The Great Controversy*, 558

Is this happening even within the remnant church of the last days? If so, then how?

John the beloved disciple tells us, "And I saw another angel fly in the midst of heaven, having the everlasting gospel to preach unto them that dwell on the earth, and to every nation, and kindred, and tongue, and people, Saying with a loud voice, Fear God, and give glory to him; for the hour of his judgment is come: and worship him that made heaven, and earth, and the sea, and the fountains of waters."[28]

The Adventist pioneers recognized this call to fear God as a time to give worship and reverence to the Sovereign of the Universe because He was about to judge the earth. Initially they taught that He would judge and cleanse the earth/sanctuary by the second coming of Jesus. But as they prayerfully studied, they realized they had it wrong. "Both the prophecy of Daniel 8:14, 'Unto two thousand and three hundred days; then shall the sanctuary be cleansed,' and the first angel's message, 'Fear God, and give glory to Him; for the hour of His judgment is come,' pointed to Christ's ministration in the most holy place, to the investigative judgment, and not to the coming of Christ for the redemption of His people and the destruction of the wicked."[29]

Upon learning this truth they began proclaiming that God was about to judge, and that judgment would commence with the deceased saints and carry through until the living saints here on earth received the seal of God in their foreheads. In order to receive the seal, the character and life of each professor of Christ would be judged against the standard of righteousness—God's moral law.

How does one such as Satan oppose this message of warning? By taking the emphasis of the first angel's warning of judgment off of those who are being judged and causing people to believe that God is the defendant in this courtroom. And this is occurring within the Seventh-day Adventist church and has been for some time. I first heard it when attending Pacific Union College as a theology student in 1980, although I didn't fully grasp the importance of the stormy debate at that time. The church was rife with controversy in those days. My desire was to let nothing come between me and my comfortable spiritual position. I tried to ignore the topic, thinking that eventually the storm would die away. And while it appeared to dissipate over the last twenty-five or thirty years, it has only begun to reorganize and gain strength to the degree that already some churches within our denomination are being shattered by disagreement when the subject is broached. Many of my friends left the ministry decades ago, and I have recently had friends turn against me because I cannot keep silent regarding the biblical truth of the investigative judgment.

Not too long ago, I attended the 2010 Kansas/Nebraska Conference camp meeting where I listened to Dr. Bill Liversidge speak on the sanctuary. After reading Revelation 14:6, 7, he remarked, "We were judged at Calvary in Christ.... God is the only One who's ever been on trial."

I was concerned about what I had heard, so I approached Dr. Liversidge after the meetings and asked for clarification. I wanted to know how he could conclude as he did when Revelation 6:9–11 clearly calls for a judgment that has yet to occur. He simply replied, "The words of Jesus set the context for what John wrote in Revelation."

I knew without asking that he was referring to Christ's words in the modern translations: "Truly, truly, I say to you, he who hears My word, and believes Him who sent Me, has eternal life, and does not come into

---

28   Revelation 14:6, 7
29   White, *The Great Controversy*, 424.

judgment, but has passed out of death into life."[30] He was definitely accepting and preaching that we will not have to concern ourselves with an ongoing investigation into our life records. And by accepting a spurious translation of Christ's words, his response to me makes Christ's words contradict the biblical teaching supported by Scripture elsewhere—even in the illustrative instruction of the earthly sanctuary built by Moses during the exodus, and again by Solomon when David abdicated his throne.

The psalmist penned, "God judgeth the righteous, and God is angry with the wicked every day."[31] "But God *is* the judge: he putteth down one, and setteth up another."[32] "God standeth in the congregation of the mighty; he judgeth among the gods.... Arise, O God, judge the earth: for thou shalt inherit all nations."[33]

Paul wrote to the Romans that "every one of us shall give account of himself to God."[34] Peter stated, "For the time is come that judgment must begin at the house of God: and if it first begin at us, what shall the end be of them that obey not the gospel of God?"[35]

Jesus also implied that a judgment would take place prior to the wedding feast of which we hope to attend as guests: "And when the king came in to see the guests, he saw there a man which had not on a wedding garment: And he saith unto him, Friend, how camest thou in hither not having a wedding garment? And he was speechless."[36] That guest was expelled from the banquet for refusing to wear a wedding robe provided by the king. None should think to judge God, since God posed this question to Job when Job thought God unfair to allow his terrible ordeal, "Wilt thou also disannul my judgment? wilt thou condemn me, that thou mayest be righteous?"[37] In light of these scriptures, are we to agree with Dr. Liversidge's conclusion?

Dr. Liversidge is not alone. Nor is he the first. Probably the most recognizable name to us today would be that of Dr. Desmond Ford who "explicitly cited [E. J.] Waggoner's abandonment of the traditional sanctuary as a precedent for his own rejection of it."[38] He wrote in one church magazine the startling proclamation that "God has placed Himself on trial before the universe."[39] His attacks against the investigative judgment doctrine thrust the denomination into upheaval. His teachings were analyzed and debated. Many determined to join and defend him in his position. Even the United States news magazines sat up and took notice, opining, that Ford, who was teaching at Pacific Union College at the time, "made the case that Ellen G. White's 'sanctuary' explication of 1844 no longer stood up in the light of the Bible, and that 'investigative judgment' undercut the whole basis of Protestantism: belief in salvation by God's grace apart from good works."[40]

What is the basis for Ford's conclusions? He wrote:

---

30   John 5:24, NASB
31   Psalm 7:11
32   Psalm 75:7
33   Psalm 82:1, 8
34   Romans 14:12
35   1 Peter 4:17
36   Matthew 22:11, 12
37   Job 40:8; see also Job 10:2
38   Whidden, *E. J. Waggoner: From the Physician of Good News to Agent of Division*, 355.
39   Desmond Ford, "Do Believers and Their Sins Come to Judgment?" *The Signs of the Times* (Australia), June 24, 1957.
40   Richard N. Ostling, Jim Castelli, and Dick Thompson, "The Church of Liberal Borrowings," *Time*, August 2, 1982.

I assume that the sanctuary of Daniel 8:14 is the *earthly* sanctuary, or Temple, in Jerusalem, but according to the apotelesmatic principle (the dual or multiple fulfillment of prophecy), it also becomes the symbol of the kingdom of God (in earth and heaven) in all ages....

The Bible does not teach an investigative judgment as we proclaim it.... In Daniel, judgment has to do with unbelievers, not believers.... I further affirm that "at every point in His intercession, Christ knows whether professed believers are truly abiding in Him," that "the professed Christian must stand before the judgment bar of God," and that men are being judged *now*....

But, according to the apotelesmatic principle, there is no biblical basis for the year-day principle....

The antitypical day of atonement thus spans the entire Christian era, with its inauguration at the cross and its consummation when Christ appears a second time.[41]

The problem with his conclusion is that he overlooks the concept of an investigative judgment within the King James Version's usage of the word inquisition,[42] or how the principle of inquisition/investigation is demonstrated by the confusion of languages at the Tower of Babel or the destruction of Sodom and other cities of the plain. This problem is compounded by his reliance upon the "apotelesmatic principle," which contradicts the day for a year application according to the Scriptures. Ezekiel 4:6 tells us that for some time prophecies, "I have appointed thee each day for a year." This is consistent with the experience of rebellious Israel when they rejected the report of Joshua and Caleb: "After the number of the days in which ye searched the land, even forty days, each day for a year, shall ye bear your iniquities, even forty years, and ye shall know my breach of promise."[43]

William Miller rightly associated the 2,300 days of Daniel 8:14 as a portion of time in which God would scatter His people for walking contrary to His ways. He wrote:

> Daniel saw the same thing as Moses, only to Daniel the time was divided. He was informed that the little horn would "speak great words against the Most High, and shall wear out the saints of the Most High, and think to change times and laws; and they shall be given into his hand until a time, times, and the dividing of time." This makes Moses' seven times, for twice three and a half are seven, and twice 1260 are 2520 common years. But you may inquire, are not these two things the same in Daniel? I answer, no. For their work is different, and their time of existence is at different periods. The one scatters the holy people; the other wears out the saints. The one means the kingdoms which Daniel and John saw; the

---

41   Desmond Ford, "Daniel 8:14 and the Day of Atonement," *Spectrum Magazine*, vol. 11, no. 2, 1980.

42   "Inquisition: 1) the act of inquiring : examination; 2) a judicial or official inquiry or examination usually before a jury; *also* : the finding of the jury" (Merriam-Webster.com, http://1ref.us/m [accessed December 2, 2013]). An inquisition, when properly carried out, will either exonerate or provide enough evidence to continue a formal trial of the one being examined.

43   Numbers 14:34

other means Papacy, which is called the little horn, which had not come up when the people of God were scattered by Babylon and the Romans. The first means literal Babylon or the kings of the earth, the other means mystical Babylon or Papacy. And both together would scatter the holy people and wear out the saints "seven times," or 2520 years.[44]

Liversidge, Ford, and Adventist ministers and theologians who preach that God is the only One being judged are virtually denying that Adventist pioneers are correct in their understanding of the Scriptures. With the type of error they are presenting on the judgment, what can we expect to happen when a refined spiritualism professing to accept Christ and the Bible reveals its more insidious nature?

Ellen White cautioned, "The great waymarks of truth, showing us our bearing in prophetic history, are to be carefully guarded, lest they be torn down and replaced with theories that would bring confusion rather than genuine light."[45] She also warned, "When each thought, and word, and motive, is revealed as it stands registered in the books of Heaven, when every soul shall be tried by the one perfect standard, the law of God, how will our case stand? When God makes inquisition for the blood of souls, when the undershepherds gather with their flocks around the great white throne, where will those stand with whom we have been associated, whom we have influenced? In that day, may it be seen that we have done well the work committed to our hands."[46] We must be concerned about the validity and the outcome of our work and the influence our words and doctrines have on that outcome!

Paul tells us of his personal concern for his own spiritual welfare when he wrote, "But I keep under my body, and bring it into subjection: lest that by any means, when I have preached to others, I myself should be a castaway."[47] Ellen White comments about his concern, stating, "Paul feared lest, having preached to others, he himself should be a castaway. He realized that if he did not carry out in his life the principles he believed and preached, his labors in behalf of others would avail him nothing. His conversation, his influence, his refusal to yield to self-gratification, must show that his religion was not a profession merely, but a daily, living connection with God."[48]

The time is coming when ministers will preach contrary to what the apostles intended and lying spirits will give strength to the deception. "The apostles, as personated by these lying spirits, are made to contradict what they wrote at the dictation of the Holy Spirit when on earth."[49]

Without the biblical doctrine of the investigative judgment, we are left with alternative conclusions, which are contrary to Scripture:

- Purgatory
- Predestination
- Secret rapture

---

44   William Miller, *Miller's Works. Views of the Prophecies and Prophetic Chronology*, vol. 1 (Boston: Joshua V. Himes, 1842), 44, 45.

45   White, *Manuscript Releases*, vol. 1, 54.

46   Ellen G. White, "At the Southern Camp-Meeting," *The Signs of the Times*, May 25, 1882.

47   1 Corinthians 9:27

48   White, *The Acts of the Apostles*, 314.

49   White, *The Great Controversy*, 1911), 557.

- Multiple chance/probations, karma/reincarnation
- Universalism: everybody is saved because God's love is unconditional
- Once saved, always saved

Scripture presents to us a plan of salvation that has conditions as formulated by a God whose very character is the definitive demonstration of love. In order to formulate a conditional salvation, love itself presents conditions or else love is inconsistent with its own plan. That plan is progressive, as illustrated in the sanctuary rituals and ceremonies by the daily and annual ministries. Scripture reveals multiple atonements associated with the dual compartments and their respective, yet distinctly separate, rituals of ministry. These are described as follows:

- Sinner confesses sins while laying hands upon the lamb (daily).[50]
- Priest sacrifices to atone for himself and his house (daily and annual).[51]
- Atonement for the holy place in the sanctuary (annual).[52]

On a daily basis the sinner was to offer sacrifice and confess his sin as an act of faith in the process of atonement. That sin was transferred from the sinner to the sacrificial beast, the blood of which was then transferred to the holy place and sprinkled before the veil. This represented the transfer of sin from the sinner to the sanctuary. The priests, who represented Christ as His ambassadors of intercession, were also subject to the daily sacrifices when they sinned after the manner of the people.

The annual sacrifice marked the beginning of a new ministry. Here the sins were confessed by the priest on behalf of the people, himself, and his household, and the blood was sprinkled—not before the veil as was done in the daily ministry, but—on the mercy seat of the ark of the covenant. It was at this time that the veil was renewed or replaced.[53] So the sanctuary was cleansed of the people's sins every year.

These ceremonies yielded valuable instruction.

> Important truths concerning the atonement are taught by the typical service. A substitute was accepted in the sinner's stead; but the sin was not canceled by the blood of the victim. A means was thus provided by which it was transferred to the sanctuary. By the offering of blood the sinner acknowledged the authority of the law, confessed his guilt in transgression, and expressed his desire for pardon through faith in a Redeemer to come; but he was not yet entirely released from the condemnation of the law. On the Day of Atonement the high priest, having taken an offering from the congregation, went into the most holy place with the blood of this offering, and sprinkled it upon the mercy seat, directly over the law, to make satisfaction for its claims. Then, in his character of mediator, he took the sins upon himself and bore them from the sanctuary. Placing his hands upon the head of

---

50 Leviticus 1:4
51 Leviticus 4:3; 16:6
52 Leviticus 16:14–16, 20, 21, 33, 34; 23:27, 28; Ezekiel 45:18–20
53 Ellen White refers to this when she mentioned the tearing of the veil at the crucifixion of Christ: "... a strong, rich drapery that had been renewed yearly" (*The Spirit of Prophecy*, vol. 3 [Battle Creek, MI: Seventh-day Adventist Publishing Association, 1878], 166).

the scapegoat, he confessed over him all these sins, thus in figure transferring them from himself to the goat. The goat then bore them away, and they were regarded as forever separated from the people.[54]

This symbolism of the removal of sins from the sanctuary by the scapegoat pointed forward to the promise first grasped firmly by faith at the cross of Calvary and finally realized when Satan will be judged for being the originator of those sins—"As far as the east is from the west, so far hath he removed our transgressions from us."[55]

Let's read the Scripture to better understand the location and timing of this antitypical atonement: "Then I heard one saint speaking, and another saint said unto that certain saint which spake, How long shall be the vision concerning the daily sacrifice, and the transgression of desolation, to give both the sanctuary and the host to be trodden under foot? And he said unto me, Unto two thousand and three hundred days; then shall the sanctuary be cleansed."[56]

Mathematically speaking, 2300 literal days is more than six literal years by a little more than four months. So it is not a reference to the annual cleansing, nor to a jubilee. It is in Daniel 9 that we see the mention of a decree by which we may fix a date to this prophecy:

> Therefore understand the matter, and consider the vision. Seventy weeks are determined upon thy people and upon thy holy city, to finish the transgression, and to make an end of sins, and to make reconciliation for iniquity, and to bring in everlasting righteousness, and to seal up the vision and prophecy, and to anoint the most Holy. Know therefore and understand, that from the going forth of the commandment to restore and to build Jerusalem unto the Messiah the Prince shall be seven weeks, and threescore and two weeks: the street shall be built again, and the wall, even in troublous times. And after threescore and two weeks shall Messiah be cut off, but not for himself: and the people of the prince that shall come shall destroy the city and the sanctuary; and the end thereof shall be with a flood, and unto the end of the war desolations are determined. And he shall confirm the covenant with many for one week: and in the midst of the week he shall cause the sacrifice and the oblation to cease, and for the overspreading of abominations he shall make it desolate, even until the consummation, and that determined shall be poured upon the desolate.[57]

Daniel knew that the end of the seventy years of Babylonian captivity predicted by Jeremiah was approaching. His concern that the captivity might continue must have been influenced by the lack of spirituality demonstrated by the Jews. Only three had remained faithful on the plain of Dura, when Nebuchadnezzar ordered

---

54   White, *The Great Controversy*, 420.
55   Psalm 103:12
56   Daniel 8:13, 14
57   Daniel 9:23–27

the worship of his golden image. For nearly seventy years the temple in Jerusalem had lain in ruins. No annual atonement ceremonies, no cleansing of an earthly temple, had taken place during that time, so what could this vision mean? The angel Gabriel then drew Daniel's attention to the seventy weeks cut out of the 2300 days in the previous vision—the vision of the cleansing of the sanctuary. This period of time would commence with the command "to restore and to build Jerusalem"—to rebuild the city and temple, and to restore a degree of autonomy. Once again, the 2300 days is connected to Moses' "seven times" and the scattering of God's people.

We return to William Miller's calculations:

"Seven times," in Nebuchadnezzar's dream, was fulfilled in seven years. Nebuchadnezzar, for his pride and arrogancy against God, was driven among the beasts of the field, and was made to eat grass as oxen, until seven times passed over him, and until he learned that the Most High ruled in the kingdoms of men, and gave it to whomsoever he would. This being a matter of history, and as an allegory or sample to the people of God for their pride and arrogancy, in refusing to be reformed by God, and claiming the power and will to do these things themselves, —they, too, like Nebuchadnezzar, must be driven among the beasts of the field, (meaning the kingdoms of the world,) until they learn the sovereignty of God, and that he dispenses his favors to whomsoever he will. That, being a matter of history, and a sample only, was fulfilled in seven years; but this, being a prophecy, will only be fulfilled in seven prophetic times, which will be 7 times 360 years, which will make 2520 years; for one half of 7 times, that is, 3 times and a half, is called, in Revelation 12:6, 1260 days, (fulfilled in so many years.) See also Revelation 12:14; 13:5. Forty-two months is the one half of 2520, for twice 1260 is 2520. Therefore the sum and substance of the whole is, that the people of God would be among the beasts, or kings of the earth, seven times, which is 2520 years, one half of which time they would be among be under literal Babylon, which means the ruling kings of the earth, viz. 1260 years; and the other half under mystical Babylon, the mother of harlots, the abomination of the whole earth, 1260 years; making in all 2520 years. Therefore seven times would the people of God be punished for their sins, to fill up the measure of the sufferings of Christ, before they would be delivered from all their enemies, and come into possession of the glorified kingdom which was prepared for them from the foundation of earth. And Ezekiel alludes to the same "seven times," Ezekiel 39:9, 10, "And they that dwell in the cities of Israel shall go forth, Jeremiah 15:1–3, and shall set on fire and burn the weapons, Jeremiah 5:14, both the shields and the bucklers, the bows and the arrows, and the handstaves and the spears, and they shall burn them with fire seven years; so that they shall take no wood out of the field, nor cut down any out of the forests; for they shall burn the weapons with fire; and they shall spoil those that spoiled them, and rob those that robbed them, saith the Lord God." Ezekiel here gives us to understand that, by means of the people of God being driven out of their cities, and by the word of God, they would be enabled to destroy or be destroying their enemies, and to spoil those who had been spoiling them, and rob those who had robbed them; and this, too, would take seven years, or 2520 days; and, Ezekiel being commanded to reckon each day for a year, 4:4–6, then it would be 2520 years.

The proper question would now be, "When did those years begin?" I answer, They must have begun with the first captivity of the tribe of Judah, the inhabitants of Jerusalem, in Babylon; for all the prophets agree in this thing, that Babylon would be the kingdom which would carry the Jews into captivity. See Jeremiah 15:4. "And I will cause them to be removed into all the kingdoms of the earth, because of Manasseh, the son of Hezekiah king of Judah, for that which he did in Jerusalem." Also let those who wish to read more on this subject, read Jeremiah, chapter 21st to the 29th, inclusive; and the prophecy of Ezekiel, from the beginning of the 1st chapter to the end of the 39th chapter; also the chapter in which is our text; —and we cannot for a moment doubt but that Babylon is the nation which was to make desolate Judah and Jerusalem.

Then, if Babylon was the nation which was to scatter the people of God, and this, too, in the days of Manasseh, I ask, When was this captivity? I answer, In the year 677 before Christ; see 2 Chronicles 33:9–13; see also the Bible chronology of that event; this being the first captivity of Judah in Babylon. Then take 677 years, which were before Christ, from 2520 years, which includes the whole "seven times," or "seven years," prophetic, and the remainder will be 1843 after Christ; showing that the people of God will be gathered from among all nations, and the kingdom and greatness of the kingdom will be given to the saints of the Most High; mystical Babylon will be destroyed by the brightness of his coming; and sin, and suffering for sin, will be finished to those who look for his coming. "And this spake he not of himself: but being high priest that year, he prophesied that Jesus should die for that nation; and not for that nation only, but that also he should gather together in one the children of God that were scattered abroad," John 11:51, 52.[58]

One cannot fault Miller's reasoning concerning the calculations except on the points that he misunderstood the event of cleansing the sanctuary as an actual return of Christ to this earth instead of as an investigative judgment commencement and that the starting point was in 677 BC. Experts place the timing of Manasseh's capture by Assyrians at about 678 BC, referring to Manasseh's forced visit to Ninevah as recorded in the Assyrian literature of that date.[59] It could very well be that Manasseh was forced to stay in Ninevah for as long as two years before being imprisoned in Babylon about 676 BC. If one then assumes this as the starting point, the calculation carries to 1844, and not 1843 as Miller supposed. It is a certainty that if one reverses the calculating from 1844 to the time of the rebuilding and restoration of Jerusalem in 457 BC, we have 2300 years. And if that period of time is a portion of the 2520 years according to Moses and Ezekiel, then the starting point

---

58   William Miller, *Evidence from Scripture and History of the Second Coming of Christ about the Year 1843* (Boston: Joshua V. Himes, 1842), 261–263.

59   Merrill F. Unger, *Unger's Bible Dictionary*, 3rd ed. (Chicago, IL: Moody Press, 1966), 690.

of the second application of "seven times" would be 676 BC, which is definitely connected with Manasseh's imprisonment in Babylon.[60]

This review of the scriptural and historical facts supporting the Bible doctrine on judgment, and God being Judge of the earth, can only strengthen us in our understanding of the nature of God's love. Unconditional love teaches that God is not judgmental, or it teaches that God unconditionally pardons and saves all of His creation. But the Bible does not teach this. The Bible and Spirit of Prophecy teach that we have a judgment for which to prepare:

> Great and small, high and low, rich and poor, are to be judged "out of those things which were written in the books, according to their works." Day after day, passing into eternity, bears its burden of records for the books of Heaven. Words once spoken, deeds once done, can never be recalled. Angels of God have registered both the good and the evil. The mightiest conqueror upon the earth cannot call back the record of even a single day. Our acts, our words, even our most secret motives, all have their weight in deciding our destiny for weal or woe. Though they may be forgotten by us, they will bear their testimony to justify or condemn. They go before us to the Judgment.[61]

> The grand judgment is taking place, and has been going on for some time. Now the Lord says, Measure the temple and the worshipers thereof. Remember, when you are walking the streets about your business, God is measuring you; when you are attending your household duties, when you engage in conversation, that God is measuring you. Remember that your words and actions are being daguerreotyped [photographed] in the books of heaven, as the face is reproduced by the artist on the polished plate.[62]

> God's law reaches the feelings and motives, as well as the outward acts. It reveals the secrets of the heart, flashing light upon things before buried in darkness. God knows every thought, every purpose, every plan, every motive. The books of heaven record the sins that would have been committed had there been opportunity. God will bring every work into judgment, with every secret thing. By His law He measures the character of every man. As the artist transfers to the canvas the features of the face, so the features of each individual character are transferred to the books of heaven. God has a perfect photograph of every man's character, and this photograph He compares with His law. He reveals to man the defects that mar his life, and calls upon him to repent and turn from sin.[63]

---

60   Leviticus 26:18, 21, 24, 28 refers to "seven times"; Ezekiel 39:9 refers to "seven years."

61   White, *Spirit of Prophecy*, vol. 4, 311.

62   Ellen G. White, *Sermons and Talks*, vol. 2 (Silver Spring, MD: Ellen G. White Estate, 1994), 53.

63   Ellen G. White, "A Perfect Law," *The Signs of the Times*, July 31, 1901.

What a record is made upon the books of heaven of unkind looks and words that bite and sting like an adder. And this is not the record of one day in the year merely, but of day after day. Oh that these families would consider that angels of God are taking a daguerreotype of the character just as accurately as the artist takes the likeness of the human features; and that it is from this that we are to be judged![64]

Those who are living upon the earth when the intercession of Christ shall cease in the sanctuary above are to stand in the sight of a holy God without a mediator. Their robes must be spotless, their characters must be purified from sin by the blood of sprinkling. Through the grace of God and their own diligent effort they must be conquerors in the battle with evil. While the investigative judgment is going forward in heaven, while the sins of penitent believers are being removed from the sanctuary, there is to be a special work of purification, of putting away of sin, among God's people upon earth.[65]

In Scripture, and in the Spirit of Prophecy, we see judgment as a part of God's nature and work. We see the books in heaven used in the judgment:
- Book of the law of God (Deut. 31:26; Josh. 24:26)
- Book of remembrance (Mal. 3:16)
- Book of life (Phil. 4:3; Rev. 3:5; 20:12)
- "The books are opened, the book of life and the book of death; the book of life contains the good deeds of the saints, and the book of death contains the evil deeds of the wicked."[66]

In addition to the various books used in the judgment, there are different phases of judgment:
- Judge the righteous dead–1844 to ? (Rev. 6:9–11)
- Judge the righteous living until Christ ends His mediatory work (Rev. 7:2–4, 17; 16:17; 21:4)
- Judge the wicked (1 Cor. 6:3; Rev. 3:5; 20:12)

Our understanding of the judgment and need for preparation is sound based on Bible truth and the insight of the Spirit of Prophecy. As Ellen White wrote:

Our faith in reference to the messages of the first, second, and third angels was correct. The great way-marks we have passed are immovable. Although the hosts of hell may try to tear them from their foundation, and triumph in the thought that they have succeeded, yet they do not succeed. These pillars of truth stand firm as the eternal hills, unmoved by all the efforts of men combined with those of Satan and his host. We can learn much, and should be constantly searching the Scriptures to see if these things are so. God's people are now to have their eyes fixed on the heavenly sanctuary, where the final ministration of our great

64   Ellen G. White, "Unwise Marriages," *The Review and Herald*, February 2, 1886.
65   White, *The Great Controversy*, 425.
66   Ellen G. White, *The Review and Herald*, November 1, 1850.

High Priest in the work of the judgment is going forward,–where he is interceding for his people.[67]

Some people struggle with the idea of the investigative judgment, but during my first year as an assistant auditor for the General Conference Auditing Services Department, I began to see the investigative judgment in a new light. As auditors, we open books prepared by our clients. We examine the books to see if their records meet nationally established accounting procedures that govern the accounting process. As auditors we are also governed by nationally established auditing procedures. In other words, our clients aren't supposed to do what is right in their own eyes. They are supposed to follow certain rules (Generally Accepted Accounting Principles) already established by a higher entity. Likewise, auditors are governed by Generally Accepted Auditing Standards; they aren't supposed to do what is right in their own eyes for the same reason. The whole process in both functions is intended to preserve integrity and trust.

Occasionally, auditors find departures from the established standard. These mistakes may be intentional and meant to hide fraudulent acts, but in most cases they are unintentional and are because of laziness or carelessness. When such a discovery occurs, auditors have a teachable moment in which they can educate accountants on how to better manage their books. The error is brought to the client's attention. Discussion occurs as to the proper way to proceed. If the client allows the auditor to make the necessary adjustments, then most likely the audit will conclude with an unqualified letter from the auditor stating that the financial statements of the entity are fairly stated. If not, well, I think you get the picture.

This simple illustration helps us understand the importance of the investigative judgment. We are sinners who are judged by a righteous law–the Ten Commandments of God–and we fall under the condemnation of that law. We are not in a position to overturn that condemnation. But Jesus, who chose to be our Substitute, who also lived a perfectly righteous life of obedience, comes to us as the Chief Auditor to offer the necessary adjustments in the books of our lives. Not only that, but He gives us what we need so our books not only balance, they are in the black! We are no longer morally and spiritually bankrupt!

So, what will you do when offered such a generous gift? Accept it? Scorn it? Jesus calls us to repentance and gives us ample warning to accept God's gift of salvation and obtain eternal life. As the True Witness, He tells us, "I counsel thee to buy of me gold tried in the fire, that thou mayest be rich; and white raiment, that thou mayest be clothed, and that the shame of thy nakedness do not appear; and anoint thine eyes with eyesalve, that thou mayest see."[68] He warns us that time is short and that we should be diligent lest we wait until it is too late. "Behold, I will send my messenger, and he shall prepare the way before me: and the Lord, whom ye seek, shall suddenly come to his

> *Not only that, but He gives us what we need so our books not only balance, they are in the black!*

---

67   Ellen G. White, "Notes of Travel," *The Review and Herald*, November 27, 1883.
68   Revelation 3:18

temple, even the messenger of the covenant, whom ye delight in: behold, he shall come, saith the Lord of hosts."[69] "Behold, I come as a thief. Blessed is he that watcheth, and keepeth his garments, lest he walk naked, and they see his shame."[70]

It is dangerous to reject the call to repentance. It is just as dangerous to postpone repentance. We are warned:

> Beware of procrastination. Do not put off the work of forsaking your sins and seeking purity of heart through Jesus. Here is where thousands upon thousands have erred to their eternal loss. I will not here dwell upon the shortness and uncertainty of life; but there is a terrible danger—a danger not sufficiently understood—in delaying to yield to the pleading voice of God's Holy Spirit, in choosing to live in sin; for such this delay really is. Sin, however small it may be esteemed, can be indulged in only at the peril of infinite loss. What we do not overcome, will overcome us and work out our destruction....
>
> Let us not regard sin as a trivial thing.
>
> Every act of transgression, every neglect or rejection of the grace of Christ, is reacting upon yourself; it is hardening the heart, depraving the will, benumbing the understanding, and not only making you less inclined to yield, but less capable of yielding, to the tender pleading of God's Holy Spirit.[71]

Why not accept God's love for what it is? Why not surrender to the conditions He holds up to us for our own eternal happiness? If we do, we will pass from condemnation and death unto life everlasting when we are judged. The penalty for not heeding His call will be a final and complete separation realized by the destruction of all who refuse to repent. The reward for heeding His call will be realized from here to eternity.

69   Malachi 3:1
70   Revelation 16:15
71   White, *Steps to Christ*, 32, 33.

Chapter 9

Ambassadors of Love

Ambassadors are the representatives of their respective countries. They are not to do anything that would misrepresent the character and authority invested upon them. Historically, ambassadors traveled to other kingdoms to deliver messages between sovereigns, as King David did when he heard that Nahash, king of the Ammonites, had died. Hanun chose to accept his counselors' advice to mistreat David's ambassadors, and war ensued.[1]

Solomon well understood diplomacy as it related to affairs of state, as shown by two of his many sayings: "For by wise counsel thou shalt make thy war: and in multitude of counsellors there is safety"[2]; "A wicked messenger falleth into mischief: but a faithful ambassador is health."[3]

Today, most ambassadors live in their host countries for long periods of time, which makes it far easier for them to establish close ties because they can be better acquainted with the culture and local people. This builds trust, making ambassadors more politically effective at accomplishing goals that are mutually beneficial to both countries.

However, sometimes ambassadors are too caught up in their own personal beliefs and ambitions to be an effective representative of the sovereign or president of their nation. One example of such a case is when President Franklin Delano Roosevelt appointed Joseph Patrick Kennedy Sr. as the United States ambassador to the United Kingdom in 1938. Europe was dissolving into turmoil with the rhetoric of Adolf Hitler.

While ambassador to England, Kennedy attempted repeatedly to meet with Hitler, without the State Department's consent, in order to somehow improve relations between Germany and the United States. Then he argued against Roosevelt's policy of lend/lease military and economic aid to the United Kingdom. The *Boston Sunday Globe* reported on November 10, 1940, Kennedy stating, "Democracy is finished in England." Kennedy showed disdain for England's predicament as he rambled on about Britain's solitary struggle against Germany. "It's all a question of what we do with the next six months. The whole reason for aiding England is to give us time.... As long as she is in there, we have time to prepare. It isn't that she's [Britain] fighting for democracy. That's the bunk. She's fighting for self-preservation, just as we will if it comes to us... I know more about the European situation than anybody else, and it's up to me to see that the country gets it."[4]

---

1   2 Samuel 10
2   Proverbs 24:6
3   Proverbs 13:17
4   Louis M. Lyons, "Kennedy Says Democracy All Done," *Boston Sunday Globe*, November 10, 1940.

This only served to break down trust between the British government and Kennedy. The relationship further deteriorated when Kennedy removed himself and his family from London to protect his family from the German bombings. The growing mistrust of Kennedy is reflected in the remarks of Josiah Wedgwood, a member of parliament, who had himself opposed Prime Minister Chamberlain's earlier appeasement policy: "We have a rich man, untrained in diplomacy, unlearned in history and politics, who is a great publicity seeker and who apparently is ambitious to be the first Catholic president of the United States."[5] Kennedy finally resigned. When he later repented of his political position, Roosevelt refused to reinstate him because of his terrible gaffes.

> *Jesus was an ambassador for God the Father. If we follow in His footsteps, we will also be ambassadors of the King of kings.*

Comparing this story to that of Jesus and Peter, we can learn an interesting lesson about love and forgiveness. Roosevelt refused to forgive Kennedy for his mistakes; however, Jesus gladly forgave Peter after he made the mistake of denying the Savior three times. Jesus encouraged Peter—through the message given by the angel at the empty tomb—to accept the invitation and meet Him at the appointed place in Galilee.[6] This doesn't mean that Roosevelt had conditional love for Kennedy and Jesus had unconditional love for Peter. It means that Jesus chose to forgive Peter. Unconditional love needs no forgiveness because there is no condition by which injury can occur. Without injury there is no need for the option of forgiveness to arise. Jesus knew that the power of unselfish love that chooses to forgive would convert Peter into a marvelous witness and ambassador for the furthering of God's kingdom.

Notice what Ellen White wrote regarding Christ's mission here on earth:

> Jesus came to this earth to accomplish the greatest work ever accomplished among men. He came as God's ambassador, to show us how to live so as to secure life's best results. What were the conditions chosen by the Infinite Father for His Son? A secluded home in the Galilean hills; a household sustained by honest, self-respecting labor; a life of simplicity; daily conflict with difficulty and hardship; self-sacrifice, economy, and patient, gladsome service; the hour of study at His mother's side, with the open scroll of Scripture; the quiet of dawn or twilight in the green valley; the holy ministries of nature; the study of creation and providence; and the soul's communion with God—these were the conditions and opportunities of the early life of Jesus.[7]

These conditions blessed Jesus because they prepared Him for the greater conflict that would arise from

5   John H. Davis, *The Kennedys: Dynasty and Disaster* (New York: S.P.I. Books/Shapolsky Publishers, Inc., 1992), 94.
6   Mark 16:5–7
7   Ellen G. White, *The Adventist Home* (Hagerstown, MD: Review and Herald Publishing Association, 1952), 132, 133.

His later ministry, death, and resurrection. The salvation of humanity and the reclaiming of His rightful ownership of this world rested upon His perfect obedience of the law of God.

Jesus was an ambassador for God the Father. If we follow in His footsteps, we will also be ambassadors of the King of kings. By daily walking under the banner of Christ, we will deepen our relationship with Jesus and mirror His character. This is what the disciples did. Peter learned new lessons every day as he ministered after Christ's ascension. Sure, he made a mistake regarding the Gentile issue, but when Paul rebuked him, Peter repented and strove to restore all that his hypocrisy had stolen. Because Peter learned these lessons, he was able to eloquently sum them up in the simple illustration of the spiritual ladder, which we, as Christ's ambassadors, ought to be climbing:

> Grace and peace be multiplied unto you through the knowledge of God, and of Jesus our Lord, according as his divine power hath given unto us all things that pertain unto life and godliness, through the knowledge of him that hath called us to glory and virtue: Whereby are given unto us exceeding great and precious promises: that by these ye might be partakers of the divine nature, having escaped the corruption that is in the world through lust. And beside this, giving all diligence, add to your *faith* virtue; and to *virtue* knowledge; and to *knowledge* temperance; and to *temperance* patience; and to *patience* godliness; and to *godliness* brotherly kindness; and to *brotherly kindness charity*.
>
> For if these things be in you, and abound, they make you that ye shall neither be barren nor unfruitful in the knowledge of our Lord Jesus Christ. But he that lacketh these things is blind, and cannot see afar off, and hath forgotten that he was purged from his old sins. Wherefore the rather, brethren, give diligence to make your calling and election sure: for *if ye do these things, ye shall never fall*: For so an entrance shall be ministered unto you abundantly into the everlasting kingdom of our Lord and Saviour Jesus Christ.[8]

Did you comprehend the rungs of this ladder? Do you see the orderly progression from faith to love? Do you see the assurance of marvelous success?

The True Witness tells the lukewarm Laodicean church to obtain gold refined and purified in the fire, as well as white raiment and eyesalve.[9] What does this gold symbolize? "The gold that Jesus would have us buy of him is gold tried in the fire; it is the gold of faith and love, that has no defiling substance mingled with it. The white raiment is the righteousness of Christ, the wedding garment which Christ alone can give. The eye-salve is the true spiritual discernment that is so wanting among us, for spiritual things must be spiritually discerned."[10] "The counsel of the True Witness is full of encouragement and comfort. The churches may yet obtain the gold of truth, faith, and love, and be rich in heavenly treasure."[11] When we combine these statements, we see that

---

8   2 Peter 1:2–11, emphasis added
9   Revelation 3:17–19
10   Ellen G. White, "Repentance the Gift of God," *The Review and Herald*, April 1, 1890.
11   Ellen G. White, "How Do We Stand?" *The Review and Herald*, July 24, 1888.

the gold is truth, faith, and love without the defilement of selfishness, worldly pleasure, and indolent, willful neglect.

Interestingly enough, we have a spiritual ladder that begins with the first rung of faith and ends with the desired top rung of love. Peter's spiritual ladder is golden! Better yet, that golden ladder is Christ.[12] "We ascend to heaven by climbing the ladder—the whole height of Christ's work—step by step. There must be a holding fast to Christ, a climbing up by the merits of Christ. To let go is to cease to climb, is to fall, to perish. We are to mount by the Mediator and all the while to keep hold on the Mediator, ascending by successive steps, round above round, stretching the hand from one round to the next above."[13] Clinging and climbing, we grow into the stature of Christ's character—accepted by God the Father as a peculiar people sanctified by Him.

Remember, in the second chapter, we looked at the definitions Dean VanDruff gives for agape love and phileo love: "*agape* = an abstract or spiritual love, a willful love; *phileo* = a heart-felt or spontaneous love, an affectionate love."[14] What we see in Peter's metaphor, at the top of this marvelous ladder, are the two rungs "brotherly kindness" and "charity." The first is translated from the Greek word "philadelphia," which has the same root as "phileo." Only after obtaining brotherly kindness, or brotherly love, can we climb higher to the rung of that willful, deliberate, principled agape love. It is one thing to have brotherly affection toward those already recognized as being a part of the family of God. But we must also obtain from God that purposeful love which is capable of choosing to forgive—even bless—those who persecute us for righteousness sake.[15] Only then can we unite with Christ in His sufferings to such an extent that our prayers—like those of Stephen at his stoning—will unite with Christ's intercessory prayers as recorded at His crucifixion, "Father, forgive them for they know not what they do."[16]

We can only join our prayers with those of Christ for as long as probation is open and there is hope of reconciling sinners to the Savior. In other words, we should not cease in doing what good we can for sinners until Christ Himself has ceased to intercede—when the censor is cast down, and the cry is heard, "It is done.... He that is unjust, let him be unjust still: and he which is filthy, let him be filthy still: and he that is righteous, let him be righteous still: and he that is holy, let him be holy still. And, behold, I come quickly; and my reward is with me, to give every man according as this work shall be."[17]

How can we know what our condition will be when such a proclamation is made at the close of probation? In the spiritual ladder presented by Peter, we have the fantastic assurance that God will perfect us and recreate us into His image—His character—while living here in this world. This was Jesus' prayer for His disiciples:

12   "Christ, who connects earth with heaven, is the ladder" (Ellen G. White, *Testimonies for the Church*, vol. 6 [Mountain View, CA: Pacific Press Publishing Association, 1901], 147).

13   White, *Our High Calling*, 75.

14   "Agapao & Phileo in Peter's Restoration," Acts 17:11 Bible Studies, http://1ref.us/c (accessed January 22, 2014). This direct quote no longer appears on the Web page referenced in this footnote. The original quote was written by Dean and Laura VanDruff; however, they have modified their Web site. The quote now states, "From the document previously mentioned, my definition is: 'an abstract or spiritual love,' as opposed to *phileo*, which seems to be more 'from-the-heart,' more 'of-the-feelings' sort of love.'"

15   Matthew 5:9–12, 43, 44

16   Acts 7:59, 60; Luke 23:34

17   Revelation 16:17; 22:11, 12

While I was with them in the world, I kept them in thy name: those that thou gavest me I have kept, and none of them is lost, but the son of perdition; that the scripture might be fulfilled. And now come I to thee; and these things I speak in the world, that they might have my joy fulfilled in themselves. I have given them thy word; and the world hath hated them, because they are not of the world, even as I am not of the world. I pray not that thou shouldest take them out of the world, but that thou shouldest keep them from the evil. *They are not of the world, even as I am not of the world. Sanctify them through thy truth: thy word is truth. As thou hast sent me into the world, even so have I also sent them into the world. And for their sakes I sanctify myself, that they also might be sanctified through the truth.*

Neither pray I for these alone, but for them also which shall believe on me through their word; that they all may be one; as thou, Father, art in me, and I in thee, that they also may be one in us: that the world may believe that thou hast sent me. And the glory which thou gavest me I have given them; that they may be one, even as we are one: I in them, and thou in me, *that they may be made perfect in one*; and that the world may know that thou hast sent me, and hast loved them, as thou hast loved me. Father, I will that they also, whom thou hast given me, be with me where I am; that they may behold my glory, which thou hast given me: for thou lovedst me before the foundation of the world. O righteous Father, the world hath not known thee: but I have known thee, and these have known that thou hast sent me. And I have declared unto them thy name, and will declare it: *that the love wherewith thou hast loved me may be in them, and I in them.*[18]

When has God the Father ever refused a request by Christ, other than the one to remove the cup of suffering in the Garden of Gethsemane? There was no other way than for Christ to drain all that cup. And because Jesus drank that cup for us, we have the absolute assurance that we will be sanctified and perfected while living in this world of sin! Read just how this prayer is answered, as Ellen White describes the process and its results:

The sinner who comes to Christ in faith, is joined soul to soul with his Redeemer, united in holy bonds with Jesus. Then he has love and benevolence through his constant union with Christ. And through faith and experience he has confidence that Jesus not only will but does save him to the uttermost. This confidence brings to his soul an abiding trust, a peace, a joy, that passeth understanding. Christ is to him an all-sufficient Saviour; he clings to Christ, receiving of his Spirit, until he works as Christ worked, is compassionate as Christ was compassionate, having an unselfish love, giving disinterested service, not to a few who are most congenial, but to those who most need the help he can give.[19]

Just as Jesus perfected His character in His sphere, we are encouraged to do the same in our individual

---

18   John 17:12–26, emphasis added
19   Ellen G. White, "Genuine Religion," *The Signs of the Times*, August 3, 1891.

spheres. It doesn't have to be an unsuccessful undertaking. In fact, we are given the following assurance:

> None need fail of attaining, in his sphere, to perfection of Christian character. By the sacrifice of Christ, provision has been made for the believer to receive all things that pertain to life and godliness. God calls upon us to reach the standard of perfection and places before us the example of Christ's character. In His humanity, perfected by a life of constant resistance of evil, the Saviour showed that through co-operation with Divinity, human beings may in this life attain to perfection of character. This is God's assurance to us that we, too, may obtain complete victory.[20]

So, not only are we conditionally guaranteed absolute success in perfecting our characters here and now—for we must submit to God's conditions just as Jesus did—but we have the assurance that we can be perfectly united as one—with God, and with each other. God's work is to reconcile sinners to Himself through faith in Christ. Paul proclaimed, "Now then we are ambassadors for Christ, as though God did beseech you by us: we pray you in Christ's stead, be ye reconciled to God."[21] All who are reconciled to God are called to be gospel laborers with Christ.

> *God calls upon every true worker to be an ambassador of love.* The Lord is at the door, and all the manhood and womanhood of our spiritual being is to be called into activity. We are to be justified by faith and judged by works. God's law claims obedience from all, and condemns disobedience. All are tested and proved, to see if they will keep the law of the heavenly courts. At this time, when universal contempt is shown by the professed Christian world to the royal law of Jehovah, God's witnesses are to arise and show their loyalty by keeping his law. Their prayer will be, "It is time for thee, Lord, to work: for they have made void thy law."[22]

Success or failure in our ambassadorial role depends upon our connection with Christ, for He serves as High Priest and Intercessor on our behalf.

> In order to be a truly successful minister, one must wholly consecrate himself to the work of saving souls. It is highly essential that he should be closely united with Christ, seeking continual counsel from him, and depending upon his aid. Some fail of success because they trust to the strength of argument alone, and do not cry earnestly to God for his wisdom to direct them and his grace to sanctify their efforts....
>
> The true ambassador of Christ is in perfect union with Him whom he represents, and his engrossing object is the salvation of souls. The wealth of earth dwindles into insignificance

---

20   White, *The Acts of the Apostles*, 531.
21   2 Corinthians 5:20
22   Ellen G. White, "Waiting and Working for Christ," *The Review and Herald*, April 12, 1898, emphasis added.

when compared with the worth of a single soul for whom our Lord and Master died. He who weigheth the mountains in scales and the hills in a balance, regards a human soul as of infinite value.[23]

Failure to properly represent Christ in doctrine and deportment will surely bring evil results. We are warned how every professor of truth and light must live consistently with that profession because others will conform to it by imitating it. In writing this testimony to one such brother engaged in the gospel work, Ellen White addresses a challenge—a danger—many of us face today:

> You may intelligently believe the truth, but the work is still before you to bring every action of your life and every emotion of your heart into harmony with your faith. The prayer of Christ for His disciples just prior to His crucifixion was: "Sanctify them through Thy truth: Thy word is truth." The influence of the truth should affect not merely the understanding, but the heart and life. Genuine, practical religion will lead its possessor to control his affections. His external conduct should be sanctified through the truth. I assure you before God that you are seriously deficient in practical piety. Ministers should not assume the responsibility of teachers of the people, in imitation of Christ, the great Exemplar, unless they are sanctified to the great work, that they may be ensamples to the flock of God. An unsanctified minister can do incalculable harm. While professing to be the ambassador of Christ, his example will be copied by others; and if he lacks the true characteristics of a Christian, his faults and deficiencies will be reproduced in them.
>
> Men may be able to repeat with fluency the great truths brought out with such thoroughness and perfection in our publications; they may talk fervently and intelligently of the decline of religion in the churches; they may present the gospel standard before the people in a very able manner, while the everyday duties of the Christian life, which require action as well as feeling, are regarded by them as not among the weightier matters. This is your danger. Practical religion asserts its claims alike over the heart, the mind, and the daily life. Our sacred faith does not consist either in feeling or in action merely, but the two must be combined in the Christian life. Practical religion does not exist independent of the operation of the Holy Spirit.[24]

It is the acts of faith and love in the so-called little things of life, the spirit of Christ manifested at home, in the field, in the workshop, as well as in the church, that make us living epistles known and read of all. Men may combat and defy our logic, they may resist our appeals; but a life of holy purpose, of disinterested love, is an argument in favor of the truth which they can not gainsay. Far more can be accomplished by humble, devoted, virtuous lives, than can be gained by preaching when a godly example is lacking.[25]

---

23   White, *Gospel Workers*, 71.
24   White, *Testimonies for the Church*, vol. 4, 371, 372.
25   Ellen G. White, "Missionary Work in the Neighborhood," *The Review and Herald*, April 30, 1901.

Another serious matter of consideration is the temptation to flatter those ministers we admire the most. Again, we are warned of a danger that exists today: "Ministers of Christ should ever feel that a sacred work engages all their souls; their efforts should be for the edification of the body of Christ, and not to exalt themselves before the people. And while Christians should esteem the faithful minister as Christ's ambassador, they should avoid all praise of the man."[26] Yet how many times have we heard an introduction of a prominent speaker filled with praise or flattery of accomplishments that leads to pride and its subsequent fall?

> *Ambassadors of love must be willing to fulfill every duty that God calls us to do—even the unpleasant ones.*

Ambassadors of love must be willing to fulfill every duty that God calls us to do—even the unpleasant ones. Some may ask, if we are to be ambassadors of love, should we refrain from preaching unpopular truths? Jesus didn't. He told the people that they must eat His flesh and drink His blood in order to obtain eternal life, and many of His disciples left Him—never again to rejoin His ranks.[27] Eleven of the twelve closest disciples determined to remain with Jesus even as they witnessed the departure of so many professed disciples. We ought to be like the disciples and not like Korah!

The faithful ambassador of Christ is not ashamed of the banner of truth. He does not cease from proclaiming the truth, however unpopular it may be. In all places, in season, out of season, he heralds the glad tidings of salvation. Missionaries for God are called to face dangers, endure privations, and suffer reproach for the truth's sake, yet amid dangers, hardships, and reproach they are still to hold the banner aloft....

They are not easily moved away from the faith once delivered to the saints. These will be strengthened by their leader to cope with difficulties. They are messengers of righteousness, representatives of Christ, revealing the triumphs of grace.[28]

If you seek to turn aside the counsel of God to suit yourselves, if you lessen the confidence of God's people in the testimonies He has sent them, you are rebelling against God as certainly as were Korah, Dathan, and Abiram. You have their history. You know how stubborn they were in their own opinions. They decided that their judgment was better than that of Moses and that Moses was doing great injury to Israel. Those who united with them were so set in their opinions that, notwithstanding the judgments of God in a marked manner destroyed the leaders and the princes, the next morning the survivors came to Moses and said: "Ye have killed the people of the Lord." We see what fearful deception will come upon the human mind. How hard it is to convince souls that have become imbued with a

---

26   White, *Testimonies for the Church,* vol. 5, 173.
27   John 6:51–57, 66
28   Ellen G. White, *Reflecting Christ* (Hagerstown, MD: Review and Herald Publishing Association, 1985), 347.

spirit which is not of God. As Christ's ambassador, I would say to you: Be careful what positions you take. This is God's work, and you must render to Him an account for the manner in which you treat His message.[29]

Paul writes to Timothy: "Be thou an example of the believers in word, in conversation, in charity, in spirit, in faith, in purity." "Take heed unto thyself, and unto the doctrine; continue in them, for in so doing thou shalt both save thyself and them that hear thee." The ambassador must be obedient and faithful in the performance of his work as an instrument of God in the salvation of others. He cannot be saved himself if he is an unfaithful servant. He must be the light of the world. He must erect the standard of Christ in families, in villages, and cities, and in the hearts of men.[30]

Some may prefer speaking in churches, auditoriums, and camp meeting tents rather than visit with individuals in their homes, apartments, or businesses. Yet, as ambassadors for Christ, the work of visitation is not to be neglected.

> The minister should not merely present the truth from the desk, but as the shepherd of the flock he should care for the sheep and the lambs, searching out the lost and straying, and bringing them back to the fold. He should visit every family, not merely as a guest to enjoy their hospitality, but to inquire into the spiritual condition of every member of the household. His own soul must be imbued with the love of God; then by kindly courtesy he may win his way to the hearts of all, and labor successfully for parents and children, entreating, warning, encouraging, as the case demands. Let him seek to keep the church alive, and laboring with him for the conversion of sinners. This is good generalship; and the results will be found far better than if the minister performed all the work alone.[31]

Unfortunately, some grow weary of the constant conflict between obeying God or following worldly standards. They think that the unpopular truths can be edited, altered, or changed into something that will make it popular among sinners who will not be converted by the clear Word of God. Many get caught up in side issues or methods of presentation—anything that will ease the discomfort of presenting unpopular but necessary truth. Are there not similarities between some ministers today and the one whom Ellen White simply referred to as Brother D?

> That which Brother D calls light is apparently harmless; it does not look as though anyone could be injured by it. But, brethren, it is Satan's device, his entering wedge. This has been tried again and again. One accepts some new and original idea which does not seem to conflict with the truth. He talks of it and dwells upon it until it seems to him to be clothed

29 White, *Testimonies for the Church*, vol. 5, 66, 67.
30 Ellen G. White, "Christ's Followers the Light of the World," *The Signs of the Times*, January 8, 1880.
31 Ellen G. White, " 'Preach the Word,' " *The Signs of the Times*, January 28, 1886.

with beauty and importance, for Satan has power to give this false appearance. At last it becomes the all-absorbing theme, the one great point around which everything centers; and the truth is uprooted from the heart....

Brethren, as an ambassador of Christ I warn you to beware of these side issues, whose tendency is to divert the mind from the truth. Error is never harmless. It never sanctifies, but always brings confusion and dissension. It is always dangerous. The enemy has great power over minds that are not thoroughly fortified by prayer and established in Bible truth.[32]

There are a thousand temptations in disguise prepared for those who have the light of truth; and the only safety for any of us is in receiving no new doctrine, no new interpretation of the Scriptures, without first submitting it to brethren of experience. Lay it before them in a humble, teachable spirit, with earnest prayer; and if they see no light in it, yield to their judgment; for "in the multitude of counselors there is safety."[33]

Others grow forgetful of the depths of sin from which they were plucked. They think themselves still ambassadors of Christ, but they are not clinging and climbing the golden spiritual ladder of Christ's merits and character. They have lost sight of His love while preaching His law. Ellen White writes poignantly about this condition and its remedy:

In presenting the binding claims of the law, many have failed to portray the infinite love of Christ. Those who have so great truths, so weighty reforms to present to the people, have not had a realization of the value of the atoning Sacrifice as an expression of God's great love to man. Love for Jesus, and Jesus' love for sinners, have been dropped out of the religious experience of those who have been commissioned to preach the gospel, and self has been exalted instead of the Redeemer of mankind. The law is to be presented to its transgressors, not as something apart from God, but rather as an exponent of His mind and character. As the sunlight cannot be separated from the sun, so God's law cannot be rightly presented to man apart from the divine Author. The messenger should be able to say, "In the law is God's will; come, see for yourselves that the law is what Paul declared it to be—'holy, and just, and good.' "It reproves sin, it condemns the sinner, but it shows him his need of Christ, with whom is plenteous mercy and goodness and truth. Though the law cannot remit the penalty for sin, but charges the sinner with all his debt, Christ has promised abundant pardon to all who repent, and believe in His mercy. The love of God is extended in abundance to the repenting, believing soul. The brand of sin upon the soul can be effaced only through the blood of the atoning Sacrifice. No less an offering was required than the sacrifice of Him who was equal

---

32   Ellen G. White, *Counsels to Writers and Editors* (Nashville, TN: Southern Publishing Association, 1946), 46, 47.
33   White, *Testimonies for the Church*, vol. 5, 293.

with the Father. The work of Christ—His life, humiliation, death, and intercession for lost man—magnifies the law, and makes it honorable.

Many sermons preached upon the claims of the law have been without Christ, and this lack has made the truth inefficient in converting souls. Without the grace of Christ it is impossible to take one step in obedience to the law of God. Then how necessary that the sinner hear of the love and power of his Redeemer and Friend! While the ambassador for Christ should plainly declare the claims of the law, he should make it understood that none can be justified without the atoning sacrifice of Christ. Without Christ there can be only condemnation and a fearful looking for a fiery indignation, and final separation from the presence of God. But he whose eyes have been opened to see the love of Christ, will behold the character of God as full of love and compassion. God will not appear as a tyrannical, relentless being, but as a father longing to embrace his repenting son. The sinner will cry with the psalmist, "Like as a father pitieth his children, so the Lord pitieth them that fear him" (Psalm 103:13). All despair is swept from the soul when Christ is seen in His true character.[34]

I wish that one young man had comprehended the love of God and allowed Him to erase the hopelessness he found in life. This young man felt caged up by his parents' strict rules. They were rules for his own good, but he thought they were too restrictive to his freedom. As thoughts of freedom poured through his head, he began to demonstrate hatred for God and disrespect for his family. So his parents decided to send him to a boarding academy—a place where he could gain a work ethic, learn a set of skills, and experience the challenges of the workplace. He worked hard and earned good grades—except in Bible class. He saved up money to run away. After running away and being caught, his parents begged the school administration to accept him back, which they did. But some teachers believed this young man hadn't experienced justice to the proper extent. So, when a respected student falsely accused this known delinquent of a believably, dastardly act, these teachers jumped at the chance to treat him as he "justly deserved."

If only these teachers had read the counsel of Ellen White so many years ago! If they had, they might have had the wisdom to reveal to that young man how God works in the lives of youth just like him! Ellen White reveals how ambassadors of love are to work on behalf of souls such as these:

> Many teachers permit their minds to take too narrow and low a range. They do not keep the divine plan ever in view, but are fixing their eyes upon worldly models. Look up, "where Christ sitteth on the right hand of God," and then labor that your pupils may be conformed to His perfect character. Point the youth to Peter's ladder of eight rounds, and place their feet, not on the highest round, but on the lowest, and with earnest solicitation urge them to climb to the very top.[35]

34   White, *Selected Messages*, book 1, 371.
35   White, *Testimonies for the Church*, vol. 6, 147

Many a youth has been flattered that he has ability as a natural gift; when the ability he thinks he has, can be attained only through diligent training and culture, learning the meekness and lowliness of Christ. Believing he is naturally gifted, he thinks there is no necessity of putting his mind to the task of mastering his lessons; and before he is aware, he is fast in the snare of Satan. God permits him to be attacked by the enemy, in order that he may understand his own weakness. He is permitted to make some decided blunder, and is plunged into painful humiliation. But when he is writhing under a sense of his own weakness, he is not to be judged harshly.

This is the time above all others when he needs a judicious counselor, a true friend, who has discernment of character. This is the time when he needs a friend who is led by the Spirit of God, and who will deal patiently and faithfully with the erring, and lift up the soul that is bowed down. He is not to be lifted up by the aid of flattery. No one is authorized to deal out to the soul this delusive intoxicant of Satan. Rather he is to be pointed to the first rounds of the ladder, and his stumbling feet are to be placed on the lowest round of the ladder of progress. Peter says, "Add to your faith virtue; and to virtue knowledge; and to knowledge temperance; and to temperance patience; and to patience godliness; and to godliness brotherly kindness; and to brotherly kindness charity. For if these things be in you, and abound, they make you that ye shall neither be barren nor unfruitful in the knowledge of our Lord Jesus Christ."

Let the erring one be encouraged to climb step by step, round by round. The effort may be painful to him, but it will be by far the best lesson he has ever learned; for by so doing he will become acquainted with his own weakness, and thus be enabled to avoid in the future the errors of the past. Through the aid of wise counselors, his defeat will be turned into victory. But let no one attempt to begin at the top of the ladder. Let everyone start at the lowest round, and mount step by step, climbing up by Christ, clinging to Christ, ascending to the height of Christ. This is the only way to advance heavenward. Let nothing turn the attention away from the great work that is to be done. Let the thoughts, the aptitude, the keen exercise of the brain power, be put to the highest uses in studying the word and will of God. The Lord has a place for the very best ability He has intrusted to men. In the work of building up His kingdom, we may employ every capacity given of God, as faithfully and earnestly as did Daniel in Babylon, when he was found faithful to every duty to man, and loyal to his God.

God calls for far more tact, more wise generalship, than has yet been given Him by His human agents. There is need of sharp, sanctified thinking, and keen work to counteract the ingenious plans of Satan. There is a call for a higher standard to be met, a holier, more determined, self-sacrificing effort to be put forth in the Lord's work. Our youth must be educated to meet a higher standard, to understand that they are now deciding their own eternal destiny. There is no safeguard for any one, save in having in the heart the truth as it is in Jesus. This must be planted in the heart by the Holy Spirit. Much that is now called religion will sink out of sight when it is assailed by the hosts of Satan. Nothing will stand but the truth,—the wisdom that is from above, which will sanctify the soul.[36]

Instead of following this counsel, undoubtedly because they were ignorant of it (as was I before beginning this pursuit of a better understanding of the truth regarding the nature of God's love), these teachers were instrumental in getting this young man expelled from school.

Fortunately, his parents never gave up on him. They never flattered him when he got in trouble with the law. In fact, his father firmly, but lovingly, told him that if he ever got arrested he would not bail him out. When he was arrested, his father kept to his word, even when his friends' parents bailed them out of jail. Both his mother and father visited him every day they were allowed to do so. When he was mistreated by other prisoners, his parents prayed with him and for him, that he would be a model prisoner. Their prayers were answered, as God gave that young man, who still distrusted Him, the power of self-control to keep his temper in check.

I marvel as I observe how God is working in this and other similar situations to overrule where professed ambassadors—teachers, ministers, parents, siblings, whoever they might be—failed to rightly represent Him.

God is a forbearing, loving God who chooses to forgive those who will acknowledge their transgressions, confess their sins, and ask for forgiveness. Truly we are living in an age of grace and hope—for as long as probation remains open. We are to extend this hope to those around us because "the whole purpose in giving His Son for the sins of the world is that man may be saved, not in transgression and unrighteousness, but in forsaking sin, washing his robes of character, and making them white in the blood of the Lamb. He [God] proposes to remove from man the offensive thing that He hates, but man must co-operate with God in the work. Sin must be given up, hated, and the righteousness of Christ must be accepted by faith. Thus will the divine co-operate with the human."[37]

I cannot express our need any better than this:

> We need a more intimate knowledge of Christ. We should sit at his feet, and learn of him the precious lessons of meekness and lowliness of heart. The more we know of him, the more we shall want to know. As we behold and dwell upon his love, we shall see matchless charms in his character. He was perfect in all things, in soul, in spirit, in word, and in deed. He was all that the law required; but what the law demanded of Christ, it demands of all humanity. We must be Christ-like, and give an example to the world that is worthy of imitation. In this way we shall honor God. And the Lord says, "Them that honor me, I will honor."[38]

May we be found clinging to and climbing up the golden ladder that represents our walk with Jesus Christ, our Savior. May we accept the duties and responsibilities of becoming ambassadors of love for God. May we be found sitting at Jesus' feet to learn about the nature of His love. May we take up His yoke and be bound to

---

36 White, *Fundamentals of Christian Education*, 304–306.
37 White, *Testimonies for the Church*, vol. 5, 631.
38 Ellen G. White, "The Necessity of Connection With Christ," *The Review and Herald*, May 7, 1889.

Him with cords of lovingkindness. May others know we are Christians by His love shining from our hearts and lives. May we be authentic Christians because we possess for our riches the gold of truth, faith, and love—the gold purified in the fire. May we be found clothed in the white raiment of Christ's righteousness. And most importantly, may others find grace and repentance with God because they have seen us reconciled to God.

When we follow this pattern, we will demonstrate to the world the true nature of God's love, a love that is infinite yet desires willing, cheerful obedience. May we live each day as Jesus lived, fully surrendered to God and following His will for our lives while basking in His love and acceptance.

Bibliography

Andrews, John Nevin. *A Review of the Remarks of O.R.L. Crozier on the Institution, Design and Abolition of the Sabbath.* Rochester, NY: James White, 1853.

"Agapao & Phileo in Peter's Restoration." Acts 17:11 Bible Studies. http://1ref.us/d.

"Author Profile: Q & A with Sarah Young." The Christian Broadcasting Network. http://1ref.us/k.

Barker, Ralph, ed. *Sermons on Several Subjects and Occasions, by the Most Reverend Dr. John Tillotson, Late Archbishop of Canterbury, Volume the Eleventh.* London, 1757.

Baum, William Wakefield Card. "Decree of the Sacred Penitentiary on the Conditions for Gaining the Jubilee Indulgence." Eternal Word Television Network, Inc. http://1ref.us/j.

Beach, B. B. "I Believe… in the Principle of Stewardship." *Review and Herald,* March 2, 1972.

Blavatsky, Helena. *Isis Unveiled.* Vol. 2. 6th ed. New York: J. W. Bouton, 1891.

Borg, Marcus. *The God We Never Knew.* New York: HarperCollins Publishers Inc., 1998.

——. *The Heart of Christianity: Rediscovering a Life of Faith.* New York: HarperCollins Publishers, Inc., 2003.

Boteach, Shmuley. *Hating Women: America's Hostile Campaign Against the Fairer Sex.* New York: HarperCollins, 2005.

Brooke, Stopford Augustus. *The Gospel of Joy.* New York: Dodd Mead & Company, 1898.

Bujalski, Edmund. "Relationship Boxes." *The National Spiritualist Summit,* June 2001.

Carroll, Michael P. *The Cult of the Virgin Mary: Psychological Origins.* Princeton, NJ: Princeton University Press, 1992.

Clark, Matthew. *Two Sermons, One On 2 Timothy ii. 15. Preach'd at the Rev. Mr. Nesbitt's, The Other On 1 Cor. iii. 6. At Girdlers Hall, At the setting apart the Reverend Mr. Hurrion, to the Office and Work of a Pastor in Mr. Nesbitt's Church; and the Reverend Mr. Wright, in the late Mr. Foxon's.* London: Bible and Crown, 1725.

Clifford, John H. *The Works of Abraham Lincoln.* Vol. 3. Edited by Marion M. Miller. New York: Newton & Cartwright, 1908.

Cloutier, David. *Love, Reason, and God's Story.* Winona, MN: Saint Mary's Press, Christian Brothers Publications, 2008.

Corliss, John Orr. "The Message and Its Friends—No. 7: J. H. Waggoner, Theologian and Editor." *The Advent*

Review and Sabbath Herald, vol. 100, no. 39, September 27, 1923.

———. "The Mystery of Divine Fellowship." *The Signs of the Times*, vol. 48, no. 36, September 13, 1921.

Cornwell, John. *Hitler's Pope: The Secret History of Pius XII*. London: Viking Penguin, 1999.

Davis, John H. *The Kennedys: Dynasty and Disaster*. New York: S.P.I. Books/Shapolsky Publishers, Inc., 1992.

Day, Samuel Phillips. *Life and Society in America*. London: Newman and Co., 1880.

Dobson, James C. *Love Must Be Tough: New Hope For Families In Crisis*. Waco, TX: Word Books, 1983.

Douglass, Herbert E. *Messenger of the Lord: The Prophetic Ministry of Ellen G. White*. Nampa, ID: Pacific Press Publishing Association, 1998.

———. *Truth Matters: An Analysis of the* Purpose Driven Life *Movement*. Nampa, ID: Pacific Press Publishing Association, 2006.

Erskine, Thomas. *The Unconditional Freeness of the Gospel*. Edinburgh: Edmonston and Douglas, 1870.

Finley, Mark. *Solid Ground*. Hagerstown, MD: Review and Herald Publishing Association, 2003.

Folkenberg, Robert S. *We Still Believe*. Nampa, ID: Pacific Press Publishing Association, 1994.

Ford, Desmond. "Daniel 8:14 and the Day of Atonement." *Spectrum Magazine*, vol. 11, no. 2, 1980.

———. "Do Believers and Their Sins Come to Judgment?" *The Signs of the Times* (Australia), June 24, 1957.

Friesen, Brenda. "Love One Another." *Review and Herald*, March 30, 1978.

Fromm, Erich. *The Art of Loving, Fiftieth Anniversary Edition, P.S.* New York: Harper Perennial Modern Classics, 2006.

Froom, LeRoy Edwin. *The Conditionalist Faith of Our Fathers*. Vol. 2. Washington, D.C.: Review and Herald Publishing Association, 1965.

Geen, C. C. In *Revivalism and Separatism In New England, 1740-1800*. New Haven, 1962.

Gessen, Keith. "Introduction." In *All Art Is Propaganda: Critical Essays*. First Mariner Books, 2008.

Gibson, Ty. *See with New Eyes: The True Beauty of God's Character*. Nampa, ID: Pacific Press Publishing Association, 2000.

———. *Shades of Grace*. Nampa, ID: Pacific Press Publishing Association, 2001.

Gillilan, Hugh. "In Appreciation: Erich Fromm." Humanists of Utah. http://1ref.us/e.

Gosselin, Bradley E. "Love and Light: Trance messages from One Feather." *The National Spiritualist Summit*, August 2001.

———. "Source of Love: An inspired trance message, from a Spirit Helper." *The National Spiritualist Summit*, February 2002.

Graebner, Theodore. *Spiritism: A Study of Its Phenomena and Religious Teachings*. St. Louis, MO: Concordia Publishing, 1919.

Grant, Ulysses S. *Personal Memoirs of U. S. Grant*. New York: Charles L. Webster & Company, 1894.

Henry, Ray. "Rhode Island Slavery Legacy Prompting Name Change." *Huffington Post*. http://1ref.us/b.

Himes, Joshua V. "Behold! The Bridegroom Cometh!! Go Ye Out To Meet Him!!!" *The Advent Herald and the Signs of the Times Reporter*, July 24, 1844.

Hohnberger, Jim. *It's About People: How to Treat Others, Especially Those We Disagree With, The Way Jesus Treats Us.* Nampa, ID: Pacific Press Publishing Association, 2003.

Horney, Karen. *The Neurotic Personality of Our Time.* London: Kegan Paul, Trench, Trubner & Co., Ltd., 1937.

Hull, Moses. *Woodhull & Claflin's Weekly*, August 23, 1873.

"Inquisition." Merriam-Webster.com. http://1ref.us/m.

Johnson, Lyman H. "Spiritualism, Or Devil Worship." *The Stumblingstone*, vol. 2, no. 12, January 1872.

Jones, Alan. *Reimagining Christianity.* Hoboken, NJ: John Wiley & Sons, Inc., 2005.

Josephus. *Jewish Antiquities.* Book six. Ware, Hertfordshire: Wordsworth Editions Limited, 2006.

Kiley, John Cantwell. *The Final Restoration.* Lincoln, NE: iUniverse, Inc., 2004.

Knight, George R. *Angry Saints: Tensions and Possibilities in the Adventist Struggle Over Righteousness by Faith.* Hagerstown, MD: Review and Herald Publishing Association, 1989.

Lewis, C. S. *The Four Loves.* New York, NY: Harcourt, Brace, 1960.

Lucka, Emil. *The Evolution of Love.* London: George Allen & Unwin Ltd., 1922.

Lyons, Louis M. "Kennedy Says Democracy All Done." *Boston Sunday Globe*, November 10, 1940.

Manning, Brennan. *Above All.* Brentwood, TN: Integrity Publishers, 2003.

Marin, Andrew. *Love Is an Orientation: Elevating the Conversation with the Gay Community.* Downers Grover, IL: InterVaristy Press, 2009.

Maxwell, A. Graham. "God's Law and My Freedom." *Signs of the Times*, April 1971.

——. "God's Respect for Us Sinners." *Signs of the Times*, August 1978.

——. "The Sacrifice of Christ, Our Victory." *Review and Herald*, September 30, 1965.

——. "What the Father Means to Me." *Adventist Review*, September 18, 1986.

——. "Why Did Jesus Have to Die?" *Signs of the Times*, July 1978.

McLoughlin, William G. "Free Love, Immortalism, and Perfectionism in Cumberland, Rhode Island, 1748–1768." In *Rhode Island History*. Vol. 33. Providence, RI: The Rhode Island Historical Society, August and November 1974.

Miller, William. *Evidence from Scripture and History of the Second Coming of Christ about the Year 1843.* Boston: Joshua V. Himes, 1842.

——. *Miller's Works. Views of the Prophecies and Prophetic Chronology.* Vol. 1. Boston: Joshua V. Himes, 1842.

Montgomery, Sharon (a pseudonym). "Alone!" *Review and Herald*, June 12, 1975.

Mosier, John. *Grant.* New York: Palgrave Macmillan, 2006.

Mullahy, Patrick. *Oedipus Myth and Complex: A Review of Psychoanalytic Theory.* New York: Grove Press, 1955.

Museum on Radio History and Visual Arts, Gliwice Radio Station. http://1ref.us/l

Neander, Augustus. *The Scriptural Expositions of Dr. Augustus Neander: III. The First Epistle of John Practically Explained.* New York: Lewis Colby and Co., 1853.

Nelson, Dwight K. *What "Left Behind" Left Behind: What the Bible Really Says About the End of Time*. Fallbrook, CA: Hart Research Center, 2001.

Nix, James R. "The Tragic Story of Moses Hull." *Adventist Review*, August 27, 1987.

Oakland, Roger. *Faith Undone*. Silverton, OR: Lighthouse Trails Publishing, 2008.

O'Ffill, Richard. "Broken Cisterns." RevivalSermons.org. http://1ref.us/9.

Ogden, Lewis R. "My Uncle Moses." *Review and Herald*, July 5, 1973.

Ostling, Richard N., Jim Castelli, and Dick Thompson. "The Church of Liberal Borrowings." *Time*, August 2, 1982.

Paul, Pope John, II. *Address of His Holiness John Paul II*. Libreria Editrice Vaticana. http://1ref.us/i.

Paulien, Jon. *Everlasting Gospel Ever-Changing World: Introducing Jesus to a Skeptical Generation*. Nampa, ID: Pacific Press Publishing Association, 2008.

——. *John: The Beloved Gospel*. Nampa, ID: Pacific Press Publishing Association, 2003.

Peace and War, United States Foreign Policy 1931–1941. Washington, D.C.: U.S. Government Printing Office, 1943.

Penniman, Alford Brown. *The Fruit of the Spirit and Other Sermons from a Greylock Pulpit*. Adams, MA: Freeman Book and Job Print, 1898.

Pfortmiller, Rev. Sandra, NST. "Body=Mind=Health!" *The National Spiritualist Summit*, April 1998.

——. "Thanksgiving–Gratitude Day!" *The National Spiritualist Summit*, November 1995.

Philipps, James. *Turning Points: Unlocking the Treasures of the Church*. New London, CT: Twenty-Third Publications, 2006.

"Plantation." Merriam-Webster.com. http://1ref.us/a.

Potter, Alicia. "Free Love Grows Up." The Phoenix Media/Communications Group. http://1ref.us/h.

Pryor, Elizabeth Brown. *Reading the Man: A Portrait of Robert E. Lee Through His Private Letters*. New York: Penguin Group, 2007.

Richo, David. *Mary Within Us: A Jungian Contemplation of Her Titles and Powers*. Berkeley, CA: Human Development Books, 2007.

Robinson, John A. T. *Honest to God*. Louisville, KY: Westminster John Knox Press, 2002.

Roche, John. *Moravian Heresy*. Dublin, Ireland, 1751.

Sequeira, Jack. *Beyond Belief*. Nampa, ID: Pacific Press Publishing Association, 1993.

Sigurdsson, Rev. Rupert, NST. "Spiritualism! What It Is! What It Is Not!" *The National Spiritualist Summit*, November 2002.

Smith, Uriah. "What Is the Penalty of the Law?" *Advent Review and Sabbath Herald*, April 9, 1857.

Spicer, W. A. *How the Spirit of Prophecy Met a Crisis: Memories and Notes of the "Living Temple" Controversy*. 1938.

TIME staff. "Brian McLaren: Paradigm Shifter." *Time*, February 7, 2005.

Tozer, A. W. *Tozer: Fellowship of the Burning Heart*. Alachua, FL: Bridge-Logos, 2006.

"Unconditional Love: Ursula journal." Power to Share: The Practical Spirituality of Unconditional Love. http://1ref.us/g.

Unger, Merrill F. *Unger's Bible Dictionary*. 3rd ed. Chicago, IL: Moody Press, 1966.

VanDruff, Dean and Laura. "UnConditional Love? A Critical Review of a Pop Religious Truism." Dean and Laura VanDruff's Dialogs & Commentary. http://1ref.us/c

Vaughan-Lee, Llewellyn. *Catching the Thread: Sufism, Dreamwork, and Jungian Psychology*. Inverness, CA: The Golden Sufi Center, 1998.

Venden, Morris L. *95 Theses on Righteousness by Faith: Apologies to Martin Luther*. Pacific Press Publishing Association, 2003.

——. *Faith That Works*. Hagerstown, MD: Review and Herald Publishing Association, 1980 and 1999.

Waggoner, E. J. "The Epistle to the Galatians. Love, the Fulfilling of the Law." *The Present Truth*, April 28, 1898.

——. *Fathers of the Catholic Church*. Oakland, CA: Pacific Press Publishing Company, 1888.

——. *The Glad Tidings*. Oakland, CA: Pacific Press Publishing Company, 1900.

Waggoner, J. H. *The Atonement*. Mountain View, CA: Pacific Press Publishing Association, 1884.

——. *The Nature and Tendency of Modern Spiritualism*. 4th ed. Battle Creek, MI: Steam Press of the Seventh-day Adventist Publishing Association, 1872.

Wai, Maurice Nyunt. *Pañcasila And Catholic Moral Teaching: Moral Principles As Expression Of Spiritual Experience in Theravada Buddhism And Christianity*. Roma: Editrice Pontificia Università Gregoriana, 2002.

Walton, Lewis R. *Omega*. Hagerstown, MD: Review and Herald Publishing Association, 1981.

——. *Omega II – God's Church on the Brink*. Glennville, CA: Orion Publishing, 1995.

Webster, Eric C. *Crosscurrents in Adventist Christology*. New York: Peter Lang, 1984, republished by Andrews University Press, 1992.

Whidden II, Woodrow W. *E. J. Waggoner: From the Physician of Good News to Agent of Division*. Hagerstown, MD: Review and Herald Publishing Association, 2008.

White, Arthur L. *Ellen G. White: The Early Years: 1827–1862*. Vol. 1. Washington, D.C.: Review and Herald Publishing Association, 1985.

White, Ellen G. *The Acts of the Apostles*. Mountain View, CA: Pacific Press Publishing Association, 1911.

——. *The Adventist Home*. Hagerstown, MD: Review and Herald Publishing Association, 1952.

——. "An Address in Regard to the Sunday Movement." *Review and Herald*, December 24, 1889.

——. "An Appeal for the Canvassing Work." *Review and Herald*, January 22, 1901.

——. *An Appeal to the Youth*. Battle Creek, MI: Seventh-day Adventist Publishing Association, 1864.

——. "At the Southern Camp-Meeting." *The Signs of the Times*, May 25, 1882.

——. "Beware of Fanciful Doctrines." *The Review and Herald*, January 21, 1904.

——. "The Bible to be Understood by All." *The Signs of the Times*, August 20, 1894.

——. "Bible Religion." *The Signs of the Times*, February 24, 1890.

——. "Business Principles in the Religious Life." *The Bible Echo*, December 9, 1895.

——. *Child Guidance.* Washington, D.C.: Review and Herald Publishing Association, 1954.

——. "Christ or Barabbas?" *The Review and Herald*, January 30, 1900.

——. "Christ Our Complete Salvation." *The Signs of the Times*, May 30, 1895.

——. "Christ Our Sacrifice." *The Review and Herald*, September 21, 1886.

——. "Christ's Followers the Light of the World." *The Signs of the Times*, January 8, 1880.

——. *Christ's Object Lessons.* Washington, D.C.: Review and Herald Publishing Association, 1900.

——. *Christian Education.* Battle Creek, MI: International Tract Society, 1894.

——. "The Christian Light-Bearer." *The Signs of the Times*, March 25, 1886.

——. "Christianity." *Bible Training School*, October 1, 1916.

——. "Communications to Elder M. Hull." *The Review and Herald*, January 19, 1864.

——. "The Conference in Sweden." *The Review and Herald*, October 5, 1886.

——. *Confrontation.* Washington, D.C.: Review and Herald Publishing Association, 1971.

——. *Counsels to Writers and Editors.* Nashville, TN: Southern Publishing Association, 1946.

——. "A Crucified and Risen Saviour." *The Signs of the Times*, July 12, 1899.

——. "Danger in Rejecting Light." *The Review and Herald*, October 21, 1890.

——. *The Desire of Ages.* Mountain View, CA: Pacific Press Publishing Association, 1898.

——. "Divinity in Humanity." *The Signs of the Times*, March 5, 1896.

——. "A Doomed People." *The Signs of the Times*, August 24, 1882.

——. "The Duty of Confession." *Review and Herald*, December 16, 1890.

——. "Duty of Parents to Their Children." *The Review and Herald*, September 19, 1854.

——. *Education.* Mountain View, CA: Pacific Press Publishing Association, 1903.

——. *The Ellen G. White 1888 Materials.* Washington, D.C.: Ellen G. White Estate, 1987.

——. *Evangelism.* Washington, D.C.: Review and Herald Publishing Association, 1946.

——. " 'Even at the Door.' " *Southern Watchman*, December 1, 1909.

——. "Exercise Compassion." *The Signs of the Times*, September 19, 1895.

——. "An Extract from a Letter Written to a Distance Female Friend." *The Review and Herald*, September 16, 1862.

——. "Faith and Works." *The Signs of the Times*, March 30, 1888.

——. *The Faith I Live By.* Washington, D.C.: Review and Herald Publishing Association, 1958.

——. *Fundamentals of Christian Education.* Nashville, TN: Southern Publishing Association, 1923.

——. "Genuine Religion." *The Signs of the Times*, August 3, 1891.

——. "God's Claims Equally Binding on All." *Bible Echo*, September 19, 1898.

——. *Gospel Workers.* Battle Creek, MI: Review and Herald Publishing Co., 1892.

——. "The Government of God." *The Review and Herald*, March 9, 1886.

——. *The Great Controversy.* Mountain View, CA: Pacific Press Publishing Association, 1911.

——. "Heaven's Unspeakable Gift." *The Review and Herald*, February 25, 1915.

——. "How Do We Stand?" *The Review and Herald*, July 24, 1888.

——. "The Influence of the Truth." *The Review and Herald*, February 26, 1901.

——. "Is Not This a Brand Plucked Out of the Fire?" *The Signs of the Times*, June 2, 1890.

——. "Journeyings of the Israelites." *The Signs of the Times*, April 15, 1880.

——. "Justification by Faith." *The Signs of the Times*, November 3, 1890.

——. *The Kress Collection*. Payson, AZ: Leaves-Of-Autumn Books, 1985.

——. "The Law in the Christian Age." *The Signs of the Times*, August 5, 1886.

——. "The Law Revealed in Christ." *The Signs of the Times*, November 15, 1899.

——. "Lessons from the Christ-Life." *The Review and Herald*, March 12, 1901.

——. "Let the Trumpet Give a Certain Sound." *The Review and Herald*, December 13, 1892.

——. *Life Sketches of James White and Ellen G. White 1880*. Battle Creek, MI: Seventh-day Adventist Publishing Association, 1880.

——. *Loma Linda Messages*. Payson, AZ: Leaves-Of-Autumn Books, 1981.

——. "Love Among Brethren." *The Review and Herald*, June 3, 1884.

——. "Love Toward God and Man." *Review and Herald*, September 13, 1906.

——. *Manuscript Releases*. Vol. 1. Silver Spring, MD: Ellen G. White Estate, 1981.

——. *Manuscript Releases*. Vol. 5. Silver Spring, MD: Ellen G. White Estate, 1990.

——. *Manuscript Releases*. Vol. 6. Silver Spring, MD: Ellen G. White Estate, 1990.

——. *Manuscript Releases*. Vol. 7. Silver Spring, MD: Ellen G. White Estate, 1990.

——. *Manuscript Releases*. Vol. 11. Silver Spring, MD: Ellen G. White Estate, 1990.

——. *Manuscript Releases*. Vol. 12. Silver Spring, MD: Ellen G. White Estate, 1990.

——. *Manuscript Releases*. Vol. 18. Silver Spring, MD: Ellen G. White Estate, 1990.

——. *Manuscript Releases*. Vol. 21. Silver Spring, MD: Ellen G. White Estate, 1993.

——. "The Marriage in Galilee." *The Bible Echo*, August 28, 1899.

——. *Medical Ministry*. Mountain View, CA: Pacific Press Publishing Association, 1932.

——. "Mercy." *The Signs of the Times*, May 21, 1902.

——. "Ministering Spirits." *Bible Echo*, December 10, 1900.

——. *The Ministry of Healing*. Mountain View, CA: Pacific Press Publishing Association, 1905.

——. "Missionary Work in the Neighborhood." *The Review and Herald*, April 30, 1901.

——. "The Necessity of Connection With Christ." *The Review and Herald*, May 7, 1889.

——. "No Union Between the Church and the World." *The Review and Herald*, February 26, 1895.

——. "Notes of Travel." *The Review and Herald*, November 27, 1883.

——. "Notes of Travel." *The Review and Herald*, December 11, 1883.

——. *Our High Calling*. Washington, D.C.: Review and Herald Publishing Association, 1961.

——. *Patriarchs and Prophets*. Washington, DC: Review and Herald Publishing Association, 1890.

——. *The Paulson Collection of Ellen G. White Letters*. Payson, AZ: Leaves-Of-Autumn Books, 1985.

——. "A Peculiar People." *The Review and Herald*, November 18, 1890.

——. "A Perfect Law." *The Signs of the Times*, July 31, 1901.

——. "Preach the Word." *Review and Herald*, April 24, 1888.

——. "'Preach the Word,'" *The Signs of the Times*, January 28, 1886.

——. "The Privilege of God's People." *The Review and Herald*, October 23, 1888.

——. "The Privileges and Duties of the Followers of Christ." *Review and Herald*, December 3, 1908.

——. "Redemption—No. 1." *Second Advent Review and Sabbath Herald*, February 24, 1874.

——. *Reflecting Christ*. Hagerstown, MD: Review and Herald Publishing Association, 1985.

——. "Repentance the Gift of God." *The Review and Herald*, April 1, 1890.

——. *SDA Bible Commentary*. Vol. 1. Washington, D.C.: Review and Herald Publishing Association, 1953.

——. "The Sabbath of the Lord—No. 2." *The Signs of the Times*, April 7, 1898.

——. "Science and Revelation." *The Signs of the Times*, March 13, 1884.

——. "Sealed by Christ's Atonement." In *God's Amazing Grace*. Washington, D.C.: Review and Herald Publishing Association, 1973.

——. *Selected Messages*. Book 1. Washington, DC: Review and Herald Publishing Association, 1958.

——. *Sermons and Talks*. Vol. 1. Silver Spring, MD: Ellen G. White Estate, 1990.

——. *Sermons and Talks*. Vol. 2. Silver Spring, MD: Ellen G. White Estate, 1994.

——. "Shall We Awake?" *Bible Training School*, November 1, 1911.

——. "Sin Condemned in the Flesh." *The Signs of the Times*, January 16, 1896.

——. "The Spirit of Christ." *The Review and Herald*, June 22, 1886.

——. *The Spirit of Prophecy*. Vol. 3. Battle Creek, MI: Seventh-day Adventist Publishing Association, 1878.

——. *The Spirit of Prophecy*. Vol. 4. Battle Creek, MI: Seventh-day Adventist Publishing Association, 1884.

——. *Spiritual Gifts*. Vol. 1. Battle Creek, MI: Seventh-day Adventist Publishing Association, 1858.

——. *Spiritual Gifts*. Vol. 2. Battle Creek, MI: Seventh-day Adventist Publishing Association, 1860.

——. *Steps to Christ*. Mountain View, CA: Pacific Press Publishing Association, 1892.

——. *The Story of Redemption*. Hagerstown, MD: Review and Herald Publishing Association, 1947.

——. *Testimonies for the Church*. Vol. 1. Mountain View, CA: Pacific Press Publishing Association, 1868.

——. *Testimonies for the Church*. Vol. 2. Mountain View, CA: Pacific Press Publishing Association, 1871.

——. *Testimonies for the Church*. Vol. 3. Mountain View, CA: Pacific Press Publishing Association, 1875.

——. *Testimonies for the Church*. Vol. 5. Mountain View, CA: Pacific Press Publishing Association, 1889.

——. *Testimonies for the Church*. Vol. 6. Mountain View, CA: Pacific Press Publishing Association, 1901.

——. *Testimonies for the Church*. Vol. 8. Mountain View, CA: Pacific Press Publishing Association, 1904.

——. *Testimonies to Ministers and Gospel Workers*. Mountain View, CA: Pacific Press Publishing Association, 1923.

——. *That I May Know Him*. Washington, D.C.: Review and Herald Publishing Association, 1964.

——. "This Do and Thou Shalt Live." *The Signs of the Times*, November 24, 1887.

——. *Thoughts from the Mount of Blessing*. Mountain View, CA: Pacific Press Publishing Association, 1896.

——. "The Trial of Your Faith." *The Review and Herald*, June 20, 1907.

——. "The Truth as It Is in Jesus." *The Review and Herald*, June 17, 1890.

——. "The Truth Revealed in Jesus." *The Review and Herald*, February 8, 1898.

——. "Unwise Marriages." *The Review and Herald*, February 2, 1886.

——. *Upward Look*. Washington, D.C.: Review and Herald Publishing Association, 1982.

——. "Waiting and Working for Christ." *The Review and Herald*, April 12, 1898.

——. "The Word Made Flesh." *The Review and Herald*, April 5, 1906.

——. "The Words and Works of Satan Repeated in the World." *The Signs of the Times*, April 28, 1890.

——. "Words to Ministers." *The Review and Herald*, April 20, 1897.

——. "Words to the Young." *The Youth's Instructor*, August 17, 1893.

——. "Ye Are Complete in Him." *The Signs of the Times*, February 22, 1892.

White, James. "A Universalist Sermon." *Advent Review and Sabbath Herald*, January 7, 1862.

Wieland, Robert J. *Is Beyond Belief Beyond Belief?* Paris, OH: The Committee, 1993.

Wilcox, Francis McLellan. "Why Our Educational Symposium? The Alpha and the Omega of Deadly Error. (Part 2)." *Review and Herald*, vol. 107, no. 54, October 23, 1930.

Yancy, Philip. *What's So Amazing About Grace?* Grand Rapids, MI: Zondervan, 1997.

Young, Sarah. *Jesus Calling: Enjoy Peace in His Presence.* Nashville, TN: Thomas Nelson, Inc., 2012.

We invite you to view the complete
selection of titles we publish at:

www.TEACHServices.com

Scan with your mobile
device to go directly
to our website.

Please write or email us your praises, reactions, or
thoughts about this or any other book we publish at:

TEACH Services, Inc.
P U B L I S H I N G
www.TEACHServices.com • (800) 367-1844

P.O. Box 954
Ringgold, GA 30736

info@TEACHServices.com

TEACH Services, Inc., titles may be purchased in bulk for
educational, business, fund-raising, or sales promotional use.
For information, please e-mail:

BulkSales@TEACHServices.com

Finally, if you are interested in seeing
your own book in print, please contact us at

publishing@TEACHServices.com

We would be happy to review your manuscript for free.

CPSIA information can be obtained
at www.ICGtesting.com
Printed in the USA
FFOW05n0208210814

9 781479 602698